The Brain Book

By the same author
The TM Technique

The Brain Book

Peter Russell

ROUTLEDGE

First published 1979
by Routledge & Kegan Paul
Reprinted and first printed as a paperback 1980
Reprinted 1982, 1984, 1985 (twice) and 1986

Reprinted 1989, 1990, 1992, 1994, 1997
by Routledge
11 New Fetter Lane, London EC4P 4EE

Printed and bound in Great Britain by
St Edmundsbury Press Ltd, Bury St Edmunds, Suffolk

British Library Cataloguing in Publication Data
A catalogue record for this book is available from the British Library

ISBN 0–415–03455–8

Contents

Preface

Within our own heads lies one of the most complex systems in the known universe. Its power and versatility far surpass that of any man-made computer, and, as the late Professor Anokhin of Russia remarked, no human being has ever come anywhere near to using its full potential. There are two principal reasons for this underuse. First, most people's brains are to some degree hampered by fatigue and stress. We cannot get as much from a brain that is tired and dull as we can from a fully alert, stress-free nervous system. The growing realization of the need to free ourselves from deep-rooted stresses and negative conditioning is reflected in the continually expanding interest in meditation, relaxation, stress reduction, psychotherapy, Gestalt, bioenergetics, biofeedback, counseling, rolfing, massage, yoga, etc.

Yet freeing ourselves from accumulated tensions is not in itself enough. We also need to know how to use the enormous potential that is thereby being made available to us. Unfortunately no handbook came with the brain and no one told us how to get the most out of it: Instead we have learned to use it very much through "trial and error." Over the last two decades research into the function of the human brain has given us a much clearer idea of how it works. By applying these findings to everyday tasks all of us can begin to benefit from the brain's natural way of functioning and so begin to use our incredible potential that much more fully.

It is toward this second aspect of self-improvement that the present book is directed, and as such is complementary to my earlier book on meditation and the reduction of stress. My own interest in this particular aspect of mental development owes much to Tony Buzan, who has already done considerable work in this area. I first met Tony through one of those synchronistic chains of events in which everything seems to fit into place. (More and more nothing appears to happen by chance.) The day that I finished the final typescript for my book *The TM Technique* I sat back in an armchair, and deciding to switch off for a while, switched on the television—a rare indulgence. On came a program called "The Enchanted Loom," about the brain's vast untapped potential and the many ways in which people were now beginning to use it more fully, particularly through a deeper understanding of the roles of the left and right sides of the brain. I immediately recognized that the approaches being discussed complemented my studies and interest in meditation—they were the relative, or particular, side of mental development, as opposed to the absolute approach of meditation. The two were obviously not in conflict but very complementary; each approach had a lot to offer to the other. I resolved somehow to get in touch with the originator, and one of the key figures in the program, Tony Buzan.

Three days later a Mr. Mark Brown visited me with an interest in meditation. During our conversation it came out that he was involved with a certain Mr. Buzan! He duly gave me Tony's telephone number, and being in London a week later I took the opportunity to get in touch. Meanwhile Tony had already heard through Mark of my own work, and on the evening that I telephoned had been discussing with an American colleague, who also wanted to meet with me regarding meditation, how they should get in touch. So when I introduced myself saying "You don't know me but. . . ." I was greeted with "Oh yes, but I do. I was just talking about you. Come on over." We talked into the night and into most of the next week; both of us sharing with each other as much as possible of our respective work and skills.

Since that meeting in 1974 many creative sparks have flown between us and we have worked together on a number of projects, including the writing of this book. One of the aims of the book is to present and supplement the theoretical background used by Buzan to support the practical methods suggested in his book *Use Your Head* (based on the BBC TV series of the same name, published in America under the title *Use Both Sides of Your Brain*), and to relate many findings from experimental psychology to the everyday use of the brain.

APPROACHING THE BOOK

The book has been divided into two sections. The first part gives some basic information about the human brain, its development and structure. It is impossible to deal adequately with such a large and expanding field in less than a hundred pages—one could hardly do it justice in a thousand pages. The purpose of this section is to provide a general background to the second part in which specific brain functions and ways of improving them will be discussed. Aspects of brain research not relevant to this have had to be omitted.

Any book that selects some avenues of research and ignores others is going to be biased, and this book is no exception. By far the greater part of brain research to date has been hell-bent on trying to measure present levels of ability—to see how well or how badly the brain performs in the suboptimum conditions in which we all live and the grossly suboptimum conditions of the experimental laboratory. Very little research has been directed toward how we can maximize our abilities.

In this book I have argued for a much greater optimism with regard to brain potential. I am more interested in the amazing things the human brain *can* accomplish and the ways in which we can help it do so than I am in the ways at which we are at present using it. So I have been selective. But the fact that a book can be filled with optimistic news about the brain is for me a source of optimism in itself.

As with many books, you do not necessarily have to start with the first chapter and plod through in sequence. You might like to turn first to the short section that deals with this very point (pp. 202–07), or to the last chapter, which gives an overview of the whole book, or anything else that takes your fancy or seems relevant. Flipping through also gives a good overview of what to expect and helps comprehension when it comes to looking at the book in depth. In the second part of the book much of the advice on using your brain is given at the end of each chapter; you might like to take this in first and come back to the theoretical side later. Whatever your approach, make sure you enjoy the reading.

The summaries at the end of each chapter are in the form of mind maps. (The development and use of these is explained in chapter 13.)

The main points are better organized if one starts with a general concept at the center of the page and branches out using lines, arrows, boxes, and colors to represent the more detailed points and the ways in which they are related to each other. Such maps can take a variety of forms, but they all share the attribute of breaking away from the restrictions imposed by ordinary linear prose.

Going over the map provided will serve as a good review of the chapter and has been shown to improve memory of the material significantly. Even better is to make your own maps. Guidelines on this are given on pages 176–82.

Regular courses are run on most of the topics covered here. For details of courses offered in North America, Europe, and elsewhere, please contact:

The Learning Methods Group
BM Noetics,
London,
WC1N 3XX,
England.

In addition I welcome feedback and discussion and can always be contacted through the publisher.

Acknowledgments

Special thanks to Tony Buzan for the many discussions that led to this book and for his valuable criticism during its writing. Thanks to Mark Brown and Brian Helweg-Larsen for comments and feedback and for several ideas which have innocently percolated the text. Thanks also to Fru Segal and Ruth Walmsley for their flexibility when it came to typing large chunks of the book in "no time" and to Brian Weller for designing the Mind Maps.

Part One

DEVELOPMENT AND STRUCTURE

1.
The Spearhead of Evolution

What are the brain's limits?
Is the brain like a computer?
Why don't we use our brains fully?
What makes a genius?
Does early environment affect a child?

There are brains that can detect the minutest changes in light, sound, smell, and touch; delicately and accurately integrate the actions of many muscles; regulate the functioning of the body's many organs so as to preserve the optimum conditions for life. Such brains learn from experience, and they have found ways to communicate with each other through simple "languages" and so share their knowledge. They are also sensitive to magnetic and electric fields and ultraviolet light. They can analyze the polarization of sunlight and use it to tell directions. They keep a constant track of time, even through the night. These brains function as accurate guidance systems; compensating for wind direction, they correlate the rapid beating of four tiny wings, landing their little bodies delicately at the center of a waving flower. Such brains are the size of a grain of salt, contain a mere nine

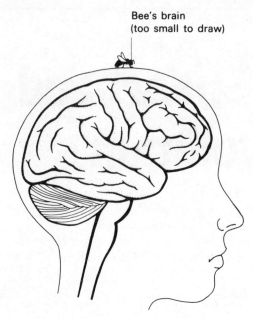

Figure 1 The bee and the human brain.

hundred neurons, and can be found inside a bee's head. What then can we expect from our own brains, ten million times the size, and many billion times as complex?

Clearly the human brain has to control a much larger body. This, however, is only part of the answer; a much smaller brain could carry out all the necessary functions quite satisfactorily. A shark, for example, has a large body and very accurate senses, but its brain is very much smaller than ours.

Where we differ most radically from bees and sharks—and from virtually every other creature—is in our highly developed use of language, our capacity to learn not only from our own experience but from that of others, and our ability to adapt the environment to our own needs.

A human being has the faculty of self-consciousness, in the sense of being aware of his own experiences and of himself as a conscious being.* With this awareness of his own conscious processes comes free-

*Because I find the alternatives unwieldy, I use "he" throughout in its everyday androgynous sense of "he or she" except where "he" is obviously intended.

dom of choice and the ability to make deliberate actions. He is also an intelligent being. Intelligence, in its broadest sense, may be defined as the ability to modify instinctive behavior in the light of previous experience; to abstract common elements from situations that may appear to have nothing in common and to apply these insights to future activities. Intelligence and self-consciousness together give human beings the unique capacity to progress and evolve within their own lifetimes.

The smallest development in physical evolution takes thousands of generations. Mental evolution is many times faster. An individual's nervous system is continually changing and adapting to the environment throughout his life. Our knowledge of ourselves and the world around us is growing at a fantastic rate. The number of new books and scientific papers, for example, is doubling every eight years.[1] The more we apply this knowledge to our own betterment, the faster we will progress and evolve, both as individuals and as a race.

The culmination of millions of years of evolution has been the development of the human brain. Not only is the human brain aware of its own existence, but through it the universe has begun to know itself. Our minds have become the spearhead of evolution, and the degree to which we progress depends upon the degree to which we make use of this most incredible product of nature—the degree to which we use our intelligence and our consciousness to the full.

UNLIMITED POTENTIAL

The intricate web of nerves that constitutes the human nervous system weighs only three and a half pounds yet is probably the most complex system known in the universe. And, by the awe and wonderment it produces, it is for some the most beautiful.

The more that is learned about the human brain, the more its capacities and potentials are found to go far beyond earlier speculations. The storage capacity of the brain, for example, is sufficient to record a thousand new bits of information every second from birth to old age, and still have room to spare. Recent experiments suggest we may in fact remember everything that happens to us.

As a processor of information the brain is extraordinarily fast. It can, for instance, receive the visual image of a person's face in a few hundredths of a second; analyze its many details in a quarter of a second; and synthesize all the information into a single whole, create a conscious three-dimensional full-color experience of the face, recognize this face out of thousands of others recorded in memory—even though the face may never before have been seen in this position, this light, these surroundings, or with this expression on it—and recall from memory details about the person and numerous ideas, associations, and images connected with the person, all in less than a second. At the same time it will be interpreting the expression on the face, generating emotional feelings toward the person, deciding on courses of action, possibly starting intricate combinations of muscle processes throughout the body, resulting in an outstretched hand, a smile, and complex vibrations of the vocal cords (full of subtle intonations), saying "Hi, Sam." While all the foregoing transpires, the brain will be analyzing and digesting other visual data and data from the other senses, using some of them, such as sounds and smells, to help identify the face. It will also be monitoring and adjusting the body's position, keeping it in balance or moving smoothly; and it will continually be checking on several hundred internal physiological parameters, such as the temperature and chemical constituents of the blood, and compensating for any deviations from normal so as to maintain the body in its optimum state of functioning. The brain continues in this way, perceiving, remembering, monitoring, and integrating a myriad different functions every second of every day of our lives.

Human perception is extremely acute. The nose, for example, can detect one molecule of gas, while a cell in the retina of the eye is sensitive to a single photon of light, and if the ear were any more sensitive, it would pick up the sound of the random vibrations of its own molecules. The brain is sensitive to magnetic and electric fields, to the phases of the moon, and possibly to the positions of the planets as well.[2] There is now increasing evidence that we are also sensitive to the mental activities of other people, being directly affected by their moods and thoughts.[3]

In order to cope with the problems of day-to-day survival the normal brain appears to limit its awareness, filtering out a large part of its sensory input. However, the brain's full sensitivity is sometimes revealed in pathological cases. Physicist Leonid Vasiliev reported on a man who could suddenly make out tiny objects from great distances. He died within twenty-four hours, and a blood clot was found on the right side of his optic prominence. Schizophrenics show abnormal sensory acuity. Addison's disease (a shortage of adrenal cortical hormones) enhances taste *150 times* and sharpens smell and hearing.[4]

It is frequently stated that we use only 10 percent of our full mental potential. This, it now appears, is rather an overestimate. We probably do not use even 1 percent—more likely 0.1 percent or less. The apparent limits of the human brain are only the limits of the uses to which we put it, and the limits of what we believe is possible.

In terms of its complexity and versatility, the human brain far surpasses any computer on earth. Computers, it is true, are very fast at mathematical calculations and step-by-step logical processes, but these represent only a small part of the brain's many abilities.

The most important difference between the brain and a computer is that the brain not only works in a linear step-by-step fashion, but also performs parallel processing, integrating and synthesizing information, and abstracting from it generalities. Whereas the human brain can recognize a face in less than a second, there is no computer in the world that could do the same. Computers have been developed which can recognize a simple object such as a cup from a collection of ten or so other objects, but they will take several minutes to do this. Moreover, they cannot recognize individual objects—only general classes of objects.

A transistorized computer capable of all the human brain can do would not fit inside Carnegie Hall. Recent advances in electronic miniaturization allow the circuitry for a sophisticated pocket calculator to be put on a small chip only a few millimeters square. Yet even using such tiny circuits, a computer containing the same potential as your brain would weigh more than ten tons. Conversely, the whole of the world's telephone system is equivalent to only about one gram of your brain—a piece the size of a pea!

Despite the vast amount being discovered about the brain's fantastic capacity and the ways in which it works, few people know how to make the best use of their brains. A major reason for this is that as children few of us were taught about mental functions themselves. We were probably told to remember various facts but not taught about how memory works and how best to remember, told to study and digest books but not taught how to approach a book in order to get the most out of it, told to read but not taught how the eye and brain work during reading, told to observe but not taught about the processes of attention, told to make notes but not taught in what form information is most easily assimilated by the brain. It is little wonder then that people continually complain of poor memory, slow reading, and lack of concentration.

There are numerous handbooks on gardening, building, television repair, travel, car maintenance, solar generators, and windmills; and many handbooks on the body, health, diet, and sex. But there is almost nothing on how the brain works and how to get the most out of it. In this book recent research on the brain and its potential will be brought together to show how your brain can be used more efficiently and how to take the best care of it.

A BORN GENIUS?

Until recently, it was thought that a chimpanzee could not learn language. Studies in the United States, however, have now shown this to be false. The chimp's deficiency lies not in its brain but in its larynx. It has no proper voice box. So researchers have concentrated on using various forms of sign language rather than speech to investigate the chimp's linguistic abilities.

In the late 1960s Allen and Beatrice Gardner, at the University of Nevada, taught a female chimp the sign language used by deaf-mutes, and within three years she had a vocabulary of over eighty words and was making up combinations of words on her own.[5] Following this, David Premack, at the University of Los Angeles at Santa Barbara, taught a chimp a language using simple plastic shapes of various colors. In this case, the chimp not only readily mastered a vocabulary of 120 words but began to make abstractions and form concepts from them.[6] Even more impressive work has been done at the Stanford Research Institute, where a gorilla has learned a vocabulary of over one thousand words.[7] And a thousand words is the working vocabulary of the average American. If a "dumb" gorilla can do this, what can a human brain do given a real chance?

Numerous studies on geniuses and gifted children suggest that our mental abilities are not genetically inherited in the same way as are red hair, blue eyes, or ear lobes. Our mental aptitudes seem to be determined more by the quality of our early environment, especially the periods immediately before and after birth. A common feature of nearly all gifted children is that they were brought up in a rich and varied environment with plenty of opportunities to learn.

In 1800 a German doctor called Witte decided to give his child Karl as rich an environment as possible. Although slow initially, Karl

Witte quickly caught up. By the age of six he was described as a "precocious lad"; at nine he entered the University of Leipzig; at fourteen he gained his Ph.D., and at sixteen his Doctor of Law.[8]

Dr. Witte's program became the model for many aspiring parents in the nineteenth century. Professor Berle, at Tufts University near Boston, gave all four of his children a rich and varied environment during their early years, and all four developed the most remarkable minds. The odds against all four being so-called "natural" geniuses are many millions to one.

In England a Mr. Thompson applied the principle to his two sons, and both grew up to lead most successful lives. The second entered Glasgow University when only ten years old and went on to become one of the greatest physicists of the nineteenth century, Lord Kelvin. He continued to lead a full and healthy life right up to the age of eighty-three, contradicting the popular notion that such people burn themselves out early in life.

John Stuart Mill, probably one of the greatest nineteenth-century philosophers, had a similar early education and by the age of three was learning Greek. Mozart, born into a family of musicians, heard his father's music and had instruments around him from a very early age. By five he was playing and composing for the violin and at eight had written his first symphony. Many centuries before him, Julius Caesar first started acquiring his tactical skills when he rode into battle at the age of three, seated behind his uncle. Similarly with Alexander the Great. Time and again we find that the great names of history had benefited from a full and stimulating environment during the earliest years of life.

Georges Gurdgieff, the mystical teacher, once wrote that a person needs three forms of nourishment: air, food, and experience. Deprive him of any of these and he will die. That air and food are essential has long been obvious, but only recently have we recognized the value of experience. Deprived of sight, hearing, touch, taste, and smell, a person starts hallucinating, may lose touch with normal reality, and become extremely frightened. Few people have withstood such conditions of total deprivation of experience for more than a few hours.[9]

The newborn child is in a particularly sensitive state and even a slight restriction of nourishment can have lasting effects on its development. We now recognize the need to ensure that a child has plenty of air and the most suitable foods, but as far as experience goes, most babies are half-starved. Little wonder then that geniuses are such a rarity.

THE EARLY ENVIRONMENT

At birth most babies, when held up with their feet on the floor, will begin to behave as if they were trying to walk. We in the West have tended to belittle this, believing that a child should not start walking until the age of fourteen months or so. In Uganda, however, where mothers encourage this walking reflex, babies are found walking at seven to ten months. This is not a special characteristic of the race, for if a Ugandan baby is brought up in England, he generally does not walk until fourteen months.

At six weeks the Ugandan child is sitting up on his own with no support and participates actively with the world around him. And at one year he is talking as well, with a large vocabulary. The mother follows the infant in helping him with whatever he tries to do: Playing, grasping, and talking are all positively encouraged.[10] Unfortunately, though, the Ugandan child is virtually abandoned by his mother at the age of four, and this rapid early development is largely wasted.

A child is born with a natural insatiable curiosity to explore and find out more about the world he is inhabiting. He is born thirsting for experience and knowledge. Yet too often in trying to help children we hinder them. We don't give them problems to solve so much as answers to remember, and if this intense curiosity is not exploited, it may be wasted forever.

Babies who are spoken to as human beings rather than just cooed at have a much greater opportunity to pick up the basics of human language. They start speaking earlier and generally stay ahead in their development. It is found, for example, that children in professional families, who have a rich verbal environment, develop speech faster than those in families of blue-collar workers.

Generally, though, we still impose severe handicaps on the young child trying to learn language. At the time when his brain is soaking up language, we teach him that a certain four-legged creature is called a "woof-woof." A little later he has to relearn that it is a "doggie," and later still that it is really a "dog." By the time the second or third relearning is taking place a lot of time, energy, and potential learning capacity have been wasted. Treat a baby as a simpleton, and he will behave like one. Treat him as a conscious, learning, evolving center of creative intelligence, and he will show that he is just that.

Winifred Stoner tried putting these theories into practice, treating her daughter as an adult and encouraging her natural inquisitiveness from birth onward. By the age of three she could use a typewriter and was composing poetry, and by five she could speak eight languages fluently, including Esperanto.[11]

In New York, in 1952, Aaron Stern, a survivor from a Nazi concentration camp, decided to start giving his newborn daughter, Edith, a rich environment from the moment she was born. The radio was tuned to classical music all day. He talked to her as much as possible, though baby talk was forbidden, and showed her flash cards with numbers and animals on them. At one year she spoke simple sentences; at two she knew the alphabet; and by the age of four and a half she had read volume one of the *Encyclopaedia Britannica* from beginning to end. At six she read two books and the *New York Times* every day. She skipped alternate years in elementary school, skipped secondary school entirely, and enrolled in college at the age of twelve. At fifteen she was teaching higher mathematics at Michigan State University and working on her Ph.D. Her IQ score is a consistent 200, on a scale where 150 represents "genius."[12] Edith's education was not an all-around education but was very biased toward intellectual learning and was also very dry and not the sort that we would necessarily wish upon our children. Nevertheless, it does bring out the sort of remarkable development that can take place when a child is given intensive stimulation and encouragement from an early age.

What is interesting about such children is that generally they are not just gifted in one particular field; they are not just brilliant mathematicians with no ability in literature or art; they are natural all-rounders, showing equal abilities in a diversity of studies, in sports, in art, in leadership, or in whatever else they turn their attention to. Nor are they social misfits; providing the training is not forced, they are very much the opposite.

This should be the normal pattern of mental development.

A rich early environment explains why the eldest child of a family is often found to be the brighter and more successful one. A survey of top scientists reveals that 70 percent of them were the first child in a family.[13] Parents generally tend to devote more of their attention to the first child; by the time the second and third come along, their attention is divided and the novelty has begun to wear a little.

Interestingly, this trend is sometimes reversed in very large families—the later children showing increased intellectual growth. The theory is that a large number of elder brothers and sisters enriches the later child's early environment, compensating for the lack of parental attention—what is called the big-brother effect.[14]

EARLY EDUCATIONAL PROGRAMS

Maria Montessori established a broad network of schools based on the idea of encouraging the child's own natural learning ability—his insatiable curiosity and unending questioning. Believing there to be no practical limits to the child's ability to assimilate his environment, she provided a rich diversity of experience for the child. Most children in her schools were reading effortlessly by the age of three or four. Over the years she looked after six mongoloid children, who would ordinarily have grown up mentally retarded. Montessori treated them just like other children at her school. By the time they had finished, they were equal in intellectual abilities to "normal" children in conventional schools.

In 1965 the United States set up Head Start, a diverse program designed to increase the development of socially deprived children. It was not as intensive as some of the individual programs just described. In a typical program children would be given just two hours a week of increased attention, and facilities not available at home. Yet even this small enrichment had positive and lasting effects. Ninety-six studies have now been completed and all show some beneficial changes. Far fewer Head Start children need to attend special schools. In one study only 1 percent needed special education, compared with 30 percent of similar children not participating. IQ scores rose significantly from an average of 92 to 100, and remained at this higher level. Mathematical and linguistic abilities increased, and Head Start children also showed greater confidence and social competence than control groups.[15]

In another study forty babies, all of whom had mothers with an IQ of 70 or less, were divided into two groups. One group received personal, highly intensive enrichment treatment on a daily basis. By the time they were four years old, they showed an IQ of 130—which is gifted by normal criteria. The other group, who had no special attention, had an IQ of 80 on the same tests (there is usually a tendency to shift toward the mean of 100 from parent to child).[16] Similar enrichment programs in England and Europe have been equally revealing.

Another remarkable innovation in early education has been the television series "Sesame Street." Much of theory has here been applied to millions of children at a time and with profound results. Their later performance at school in reading, writing, spelling, mathematics, and general education has startled many of their teachers.

Education in many other countries has likewise begun to recognize the value of early learning. Public education in Russia, for example, begins at the age of three rather than at five, and it is claimed that as a result Russian children are, on average, up to two years ahead of those in the West.

A rich early environment can, though, be wasted if not properly followed through. Our present educational system is not well equipped to deal with prodigious rates of mental development, and it is an unfortunate fact that the gifted child is sometimes held back by traditional ideas of what should be normal.

A typical case is the girl whose mother gave her a rich and varied environment from the very beginning and always treated her and spoke to her as another adult. The little girl began to show the rapid development characteristic of such children. By the age of three she had mastered the basis of arithmetic, doing the mental calculations of a nine-year-old; she could hold a fluent, coherent conversation with adults; and she was continually questioning everything that happened, soaking up her environment and learning at an accelerated rate.

At the age of five she went to the local school along with other children of her age. But the educational system was simply not geared to deal with such a bright child. Becoming embarrassed, the poor child began to pretend she did not know as much as she did. Within a few months she had begun to become "normal," and began to lose her abilities. She found it much easier to get on at school if she did not know the meanings of long words, if she could not do her sums, and if she could only count as far as ten, like all the other children. The worrisome thing is that when prodigious children begin to perform this way, they are very clever at it; they can hide their abilities so well that often the teachers themselves are completely deceived by it and have no idea of their real abilities.

A recent study by the Social Sciences Research Council in England has measured just how much such children can be held back by the educational system. It was found that, on the average, gifted children were two and a half years behind their mental age. Though only around eight and a half years old, the children studied had a mental age of fourteen, as measured by their IQ. But they were found to be performing only as well as children of eleven and a half.[17] Compared with others of their age, they were still gifted, but in terms of their true capacity they were backward.

Yet even were he not held back, the most gifted child would probably still be functioning at only a fraction of his full potential. The possibilities that await us once we fully understand how to educate our brains are truly fantastic.

Figure 2

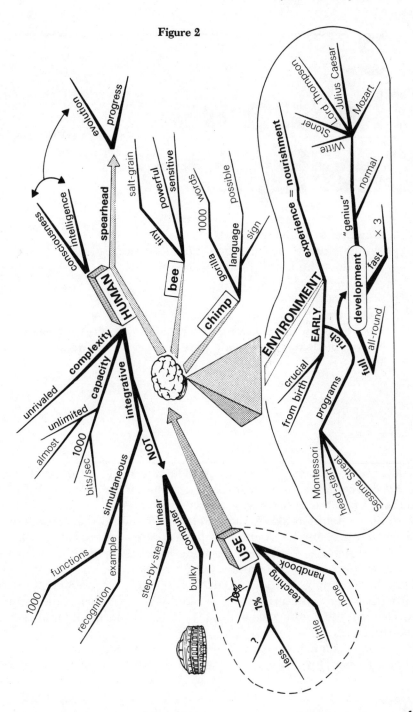

2.
The Brain's Development

What did the ancients know of the brain?
How has the brain evolved?
Are dolphins more intelligent than humans?
How does the baby's brain develop
  before birth?
  after birth?
Can learning take place in the womb?
How do environment and nutrition affect the growing brain?
Why is birth such a delicate time for the young brain?

The ancient Indians, Egyptians, and Chinese made little connection between mental faculties and the brain. One of the first recognitions that the brain was in some way involved with mental functioning came with the ancient Greeks. Aristotle felt that the mind was in some way associated with the heart and that the brain served to cool the blood. Plato had suggested that the reasoning faculties lay within the head, and saw the brain as a mental wax, recording experiences as impressions. Interestingly, Herophilus, in the next century, thought that many of man's higher abilities were associated with the folds in the brain's surface, but the significance of this conclusion lay dormant for over two thousand years.

The next advances came from Galen, who lived in the latter days of the Roman Empire. Galen was the grandfather of anatomy and performed some of the first dissections of the brain. He too felt that the seat of the soul was in the brain and believed that the ventricles, the open spaces in the brain usually filled with cerebrospinal fluid, were very important. This emphasis on the ventricles continued through the Middle Ages, both Saint Augustine and many of the Arab anatomists of the time believing them to be involved in man's higher faculties. There were still many, though, who associated the mind with the heart. And in India it was thought that the mind could not be localized anywhere in the body, but was a function of the whole organism—a theory still held by some Indian teachings.

For fifteen hundred years little progress was made, practical research often being hampered by the feeling that to examine the brain was to violate the seat of the soul. It was not until the eighteenth century that it became clearer that the whole of the brain was involved in mental functioning. By this time many of the major nerves were being traced and the general electrical activity of the brain had been discovered.

By the early nineteenth century it had become apparent that if certain areas of the brain were damaged, this could result in the loss of specific functions. By studying different types of damage, researchers such as Franz Gall, the German anatomist and physiologist, built up careful maps of the brain's surface allocating specific functions to each area of the brain. From this grew the science of phrenology, which held that by studying the shape of a person's skull, in particular the bumps upon the skull, it was possible to assess his or her mental aptitudes.

By the beginning of the twentieth century, however, it had become apparent that mental functions could not be so neatly localized. Hughlings Jackson, the famous English neurologist, had suggested that complex mental processes involved the whole of the brain's activity, and Sir Charles Sherrington, a pioneer in neurophysiology, made the now famous remark that the brain resembles "an enchanted loom, where millions of flashing shuttles weave a dissolving pattern, always a meaningful pattern though never an abiding one, a shifting harmony of sub patterns. It is as if the Milky Way had entered upon some cosmic dance."

Over the last fifty years our knowledge of the human brain has grown at a prodigious rate. Psychology itself has become one of the most rapidly expanding fields of knowledge. It now draws on subjects as diverse as biochemistry, microtechnology, and cybernetics and has itself specialized into disciplines such as neuropsychology, physiological

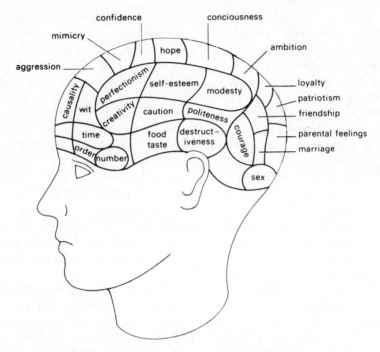

Figure 3 Phrenologists' map of the brain.

psychology, developmental psychology, and clinical psychology.

The human brain has become the most challenging frontier of science, and brain research now generates more than half a million scientific papers each year. Psychologists and neurophysiologists are no longer the only people seeking to understand the brain and its potentials. Chemists are looking at the 100,000 different chemical reactions occurring each second in the brain; molecular biologists are marveling at the highly sophisticated transformations taking place in each nerve cell; cyberneticists are applying information theory in an attempt to understand the brain and its almost limitless potential for memory; mathematicians are having to use computers to investigate their own relatively simple models of brain processes; and quantum physicists are investigating the possibility that brain activity may even involve superconductivity and "electron tunneling."

Yet still we seem hardly to have begun. The old saying that "the more you know of a subject, the more you discover what you do not know" seems particularly true as far as the brain is concerned. We know that functions are not well localized, and we know that the brain does not work like a simple telephone exchange, passing on messages from one call to another, nor does it behave like an electronic computer responding in fixed ways to the stimuli it encounters. As to how it does work we are still very much in ignorance. We know far more about what happens in the rest of the world around us than we do about what happens within that intricate web of nerves within our own heads.

THE EVOLUTION OF THE BRAIN

The first nervous systems grew out of simple sensory receptors located at the surface of primitive multicellular organisms. The receptors passed information about heat, light, acidity, etc., to the interior of the organism. Over the eons other cells developed that passed messages back from the interior to the surface, and on this basis simple nervous systems evolved. In the first jellyfish-like creatures the elementary nervous system had become a loose network of nerve cells extending throughout the organism, and with the evolution of simple molluscs the nerve cells began to clump together into a number of small groups called ganglia. Segmented worms were the first creatures to develop specific front and back ends, and in them the sense organs and associated ganglia are found gathering together toward the front, that is, the head. Over the ensuing millennia the ganglia grew more intricate and interwoven until, in the early fishes, the first simple brains appeared. From that time all vertebrates—that is, all animals with a backbone—have possessed a well-developed brain and spinal cord, with nerves radiating to all parts of the body.

In many respects the lower parts of our brain and spinal cord have not changed significantly since the time of the early fishes, 100 million years ago. The major changes that have taken place have entailed the massive extension and enlargement of the top end of the primitive brain. In reptiles came the first signs of a cerebral cortex, though it was still very tiny and only one cell layer thick. By the time the first mammals had appeared, some 50 million years ago, this simple cortex had expanded to take up half of the brain volume and was largely concerned with the sense of smell. On top of this a new layer of cells, the neocortex, began to grow. In man the neocortex consists of six cellular layers covering the whole surface of the brain. In fact it is several times larger than the surface of the brain and has become folded in upon itself many

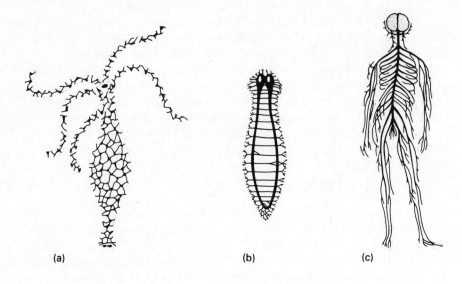

Figure 4 Evolution of the nervous system. (a) Simple net, (b) worm, (c) man.

times—if spread out flat it would cover an area of four hundred square inches. Although only three millimeters thick, our highly developed neocortex is responsible for many of our higher capacities, such as language, the development of skills, a virtually unlimited storage capacity, and our higher thought processes.

There are several animals with larger brains than ours—elephants (and elephants, it is said, never forget), whales, and dolphins. Whales and dolphins also have larger and more convoluted cortices, it being generally thought that the degree of convolution is significant as far as overall intelligence is concerned. Few experiments have been conducted on whales, but a large number have been performed with dolphins, and it appears that in several respects the mind of a dolphin is superior to that of man. The left and right halves of the brain appear to be even more specialized than our own. They can speak in stereo, by controlling the left and right air passages separately, and hold two or possibly three conversations at once using different frequency bands. In one experiment that set out to study dolphin language, the dolphins had begun to put their noses out of the water and make humanlike noises in the air—a very strange behavior for dolphins in the wild—as if they were attempting to communicate with the experimenters. This started happening long before the experimenters had succeeded in gaining the slightest inkling about dolphin languages.[1] In another experiment dolphins were found teaching other dolphins to count to ten in English and teaching them far more effectively than the human experimenters could. It is also of interest that a dolphin's life is based upon love more than competition—they seem to have learned to live in harmony, both with one another and with their environment. When John Lilly, one of the pioneers in dolphin research, realized that he was probably dealing with very advanced beings, he closed down his laboratories, feeling that his research could not be ethically justified.

THE GROWING BRAIN

The brain is by far the most complex organ in the human body. It takes longer than any other organ to reach its full development, and its pattern of growth is markedly different. In most other organs the basic structural development is completed during a relatively short period while in the womb. Any further growth in size is through cellular division as the organism grows. With the brain the opposite occurs. The brain has its full complement of cells long before birth—that is why the heads of babies seem out of proportion to the rest of their bodies. But its structural development continues throughout life, as the nerve cells become more and more intricately interconnected.

The human child is born into the world in a relatively helpless

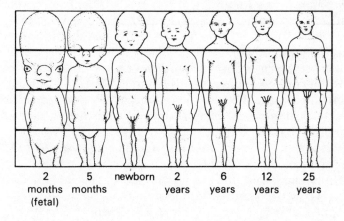

| 2 months (fetal) | 5 months | newborn | 2 years | 6 years | 12 years | 25 years |

Figure 5 Relative sizes of the brain and body at different ages.

state. Unlike many other animals that can fend for themselves within minutes or hours of birth, the human infant needs the care of its parents for many years. This gives it a major advantage over other animals. It is no longer reliant upon instinct for its survival: Instead it is flexible and can learn from experience, adapt to its environment, develop skills, and learn language.

The growing fetus passes through very similar stages in its development from single cell to human being, as did the species over its four billion years of evolution. As with the first primitive organisms, the brain of the early embryo starts from the surface. A small plate appears on the top side and then curls up to form a groove. The sides of the groove meet, forming a tube that then becomes sealed at one end. This is a rudimentary spinal column, and from the sealed end of this tube the rest of the brain grows—one second of development in the fetus corresponding to a thousand years of evolution. Five weeks after conception the top part of the tube has become enlarged and bent over in the shape of a question mark. And at eight weeks the first of the two brain spurts begins.

The term *brain spurt* is given to those periods in which there is a very rapid development of the brain. The first such growth occurs from eight to thirteen weeks after conception and entails the proliferation of billions of cells called neuroblasts. It is from these neuroblasts that the neurons themselves develop, each neuroblast developing into one neuron. Thus the number of neuroblasts formed at this stage determines the total complement of nerve cells.

Nutrition is very important at this stage. It has been found that if the mother is undernourished, particularly if she lacks certain amino acids, the total number of neuroblasts, and hence the total number of neurons, is significantly reduced. Studies of children in the Third World whose mothers were undernourished, have shown that many are born with only 40 percent of the neurons found in Western children.[2] It has also been suggested that one of the reasons why Western children born in January, February, and March show a higher incidence of mental retardation is that the crucial period in brain growth would have occurred during the summer months of June, July, and August, when mother; were more likely to be eating salads than steaks.

Though significant, the number of neurons in the brain is not the most important factor in determining mental abilities. Of far greater consequence is their degree of interconnectedness. The wiring up of the neurons occurs during the second brain spurt, starting some ten weeks before birth and continuing for about two years after birth. It is during this period that much of our basic learning takes place.

During the second brain spurt each neuron starts sending out numerous fine feathery fibers in all directions, making connections with thousands of other neurons, sometimes as far away as the other side of the brain. The cell bodies themselves grow larger and the cortex becomes much thicker. Also at this stage many of the longer fibers traversing the brain are coated with an insulating material called myelin, which speeds the conduction of neural impulses.

This prolific increase in connectivity results in a rapid growth of the brain. At birth the brain weighs 350 grams, 25 percent of its adult weight, but it is growing at the rate of 1 milligram a minute. At six months it is 50 percent of its adult weight; at two and a half years 75 percent; and at five years 90 percent. At this stage the major part of the child's intellectual development has already been completed.

It is during the second brain spurt, when the neurons are making their trillions of interconnections, that much of our basic learning and

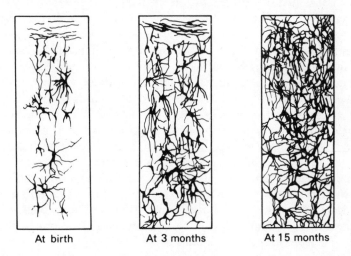

| At birth | At 3 months | At 15 months |

Figure 6 Sections from the cerebral cortex of children at birth, at 3 months, and at 15 months old, showing increased number of fibers and a thickening of fibers. Pictures such as these are produced by first staining the tissue with a dye that is taken up by only about 1 percent of the cells. There are therefore about one hundred times as many cells in each picture as those shown here. (From R. H. Lindsay and D. A. Norman, *Human Information Processing*, New York; Academic Press, 1972. Reprinted with permission.)

mental development takes place. But even before this, the growing fetus is responding to and learning from its environment in the womb. Simple reflex conditioning has been shown to take place in the spinal cord after only eight weeks, long before the cortex has begun to develop. Doctors have inserted a thin optical fiber into the womb and observed the embyro at ten weeks reacting to changes in its environment. At five months the electroencephalogram (EEG) shows that the fetal brain responds to light in much the same way that an adult brain does. And later it responds to specific sounds coming in from the outside through the mother's abdomen.

PRENATAL PSYCHOLOGY

There has in this century been a growing awareness that the first years of life are crucial to a person's development. We realize that what happens to a child when it is one or two years old can affect the rest of its life. More recently it has become apparent that the time could be pushed back further and further, to the first few months and the first few days after birth even. Now psychologists are realizing that what happens before birth is also crucially important. Education begins not at five, not at three, two, or one, nor even at birth, but at conception —a point which the Chinese have always recognized, their children being considered nine months old at birth. Indeed the habit of dating our age from birth rather than from conception may well have encouraged us to neglect the crucial first nine months of life. Only in the 1970s has prenatal psychology become a recognized branch of psychology.

It has now been shown that the senses are already well developed at birth, that young babies can discern patterns clearly. Previously it had been thought that the newborn child simply saw areas of light and dark. But, by simply measuring the amount of time that babies looked at various patterns, it has been shown that newborn babies have a well-developed visual acuity in that they can distinguish lines one eighth of an inch apart ten inches away.[3]

Tom Bower, who has done considerable research on infant perception at the University of Edinburgh, took this work further and showed that right from birth the child experiences a three-dimensional world. Using polarizing goggles so that the left and right eye see different images, he created the visual illusion that there was a solid object in front of the baby. He found that even newborn babies stretched out their hands to touch the apparent object, but as soon as their hand closed upon empty air instead of a solid object the baby started crying. This showed that at birth the child expects visual objects to be tangible and indicates a simple unity of the visual and tactile senses.[4]

Other experiments at Edinburgh have shown that sound and sight are similarly integrated, the newborn baby turning its head in the direction of a sound to see what is there. They have shown that a baby is also born with the ability to recognize smells as pleasant or unpleas-

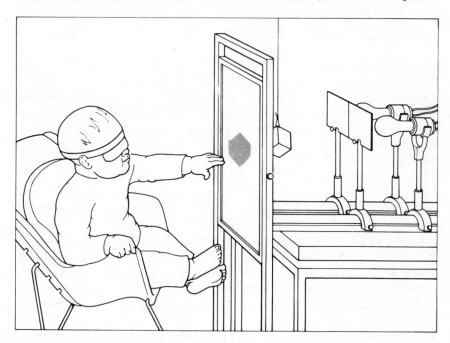

Figure 7 Intangible object is produced by a shadow caster, in which two oppositely polarized beams of light cast a double shadow of an object on a rear-projection screen. An infant views the double shadows through polarizing goggles that make a different shadow visible to each eye. The innate processes of stereopsis fuse the two images to make the infant think he is seeing a solid object in front of the screen. When the infant tries to grasp the virtual image, he is startled when his hand closes on empty air; within a fraction of a second he cries and his face expresses surprise. When a real object is placed in front of the screen, none of the infants shows any sign of surprise when he touches it. These results indicate that the infants expect a seen object to be solid and tangible. © 1971 by *Scientific American*, Inc. All rights reserved. Reproduced with permission of *Scientific American*.

ant, turning its head away from unpleasant smells.[5] Thus at birth the sensory system is already sufficiently developed to localize objects by sight, touch, sound, and smell.

The newborn child can also recognize a human face. Robert Fantz, a researcher at Western Reserve University in Cleveland, presented day-old children with the choice of looking at a picture of a face, a bull's-eye, newsprint, and circles of various colors. He found a distinct preference for the human face, most of the babies looking at it far more than the other objects.[6] During the next two weeks of life the child learns to recognize those particular faces that it sees the most.

Much of this complex perceptual organization takes place during the last two months in the womb. Then after birth the basic perceptual frameworks are refined and developed according to the types of experience that the infant encounters. Studies with newborn kittens have demonstrated the crucial role of early experience in the development of perception. A kitten brought up in an environment containing only horizontal lines, was, as an adult, found not to have the ability to see vertical lines clearly, stumbling into chair legs as though they were not there, though happily jumping onto the horizontal seat of the chair.[7] An analysis of the visual cortex of the brain showed that the corresponding cells for vertical lines were far less well developed than those for horizontal-line recognition. Whether this is because the relevant systems never developed or because they were there but atrophied through disuse is still a matter of debate, but either way, it is clear that the newborn brain modifies itself after birth in a way that best suits the environment in which it finds itself.

To assess the effect of a rich environment on brain growth, Mark Rosenzweig and colleagues, at the University of California at Berkeley, allowed a group of baby rats to grow up in a cage full of ramps, ladders, wheels, tunnels, trapezes, and other stimuli, while a second group was left in ordinary barren cages. They were actually looking for changes in enzyme levels, but when, after 105 days, the brains of the rats were examined, it was found that the cortices of those rats raised in the rich environment were larger than the "impoverished" rats. There were 15 percent more glia cells (see chapter 3), and although the number of neurons had not increased, the neuron bodies were 15 percent larger, the fibers were more prolific, and most importantly, they were making more interconnections with other neurons.[8]

CAN LEARNING OCCUR IN THE WOMB?

A field in which there has been a lot of interest recently is the acquisition of language. "Normal" children—that is, those who have not had a particularly rich early environment—usually begin talking after the first year of their life. By eighteen months they have a vocabulary of about half a dozen words and at two years a vocabulary of more than a hundred words. The traditional view has been that during the first year of life, babies are not mature enough to learn languages. Talking, however, is only the outer manifestation of the development of language; long before he first utters a meaningful word a baby can be observed responding to the language of others.

Studies have shown that *even at birth* the child responds positively and specifically to the tones of the human voice. A high-speed film of a newborn baby when slowed down many times and examined frame by frame shows that tiny gestures on the part of the child are synchronized with specific tones and syllables from the parents. Sounds other than the human voice, however, produce no such response.[9] The fact that this is happening at birth implies that some simple linguistic skills are learned while in the womb, presumably by the fetus hearing speech from the outside world and using it to acquire the basic sounds and rhythms of language.

While he's in the womb, a child learns the sound of his mother's heartbeat, and after birth the sound of a human heart will have a very soothing effect on the baby. It has been suggested that this also accounts for the universal appeal of rhythmic music to adults. The pace of the rhythm is usually within the range of the human heart, and the faster the rhythm the more "exciting" the music. An unusual example of learning in the womb comes from a mother who used to sing in a Bach choir while pregnant. With the birth of her child, she gave up the singing yet found that whenever there was a Bach choir on the radio, her baby daughter would become totally absorbed in the music, losing interest in everything else, even food.

THE VULNERABILITY OF THE YOUNG BRAIN

Although the second brain spurt is from ten weeks before birth until two years after birth, it is greatest during the first few months after birth. It is at this stage that the brain is said to be most plastic—plastic in the sense of being most easily modified by its environment. The recent research on the newborn child suggests the height of plasticity occurs around the time of birth itself. But not only is the brain's learning ability greatest at this stage, the brain is also at its most vulnerable.

There is now accumulating physiological evidence for the psychoanalysts' common claim that many problems in later life can be traced back to traumas in early childhood, particularly birth traumas. Sigmund Freud showed how early childhood experiences could affect our attitudes and behavior for the rest of our lives. Melanie Klein, the distinguished child psychologist, took the idea further showing how much the first months of life were important. Arthur Janov, the originator of primal therapy suggested that our experiences of birth itself can have profound psychological effects. Now R. D. Laing has argued that we are conditioned by our fetal life and even by conception itself, reenacting these periods throughout our adult life.[10]

Similar ideas are at the basis of several modern approaches to birth. Frederick Leboyer, for example, recommends that the newborn child not be greeted with harsh light, a slap on the back, and separation from his mother, but be given a gentle, loving transition from life in the womb to life in the outside world. Such babies seldom start howling immediately after birth, and their mortality is reduced by half. A follow-up study on 120 "Leboyer babies" found that, on average, the babies began to walk two months earlier and generally developed faster. In addition, the babies were happier, with few sleeping problems, and none of their mothers reported difficulties with toilet training.[11]

There has recently been a lot of concern about the effects of smoking during pregnancy. Smoking reduces the oxygen supply to the fetus, and it has been found that the reading scores of children whose mothers smoked during pregnancy were significantly lower than those of children whose mothers did not. There are many other factors that have been found to have equally damaging repercussions on the growing fetus. Alcohol, lead in the air and water supplies, certain food dyes, the emotional stability of the mother, the father's behavior, fatigue, noise, and the mother's social habits all have measurable effects.

At birth the child is particularly vulnerable, and yet this is very often the time at which the mother is most heavily drugged. Babies born to mothers who have been given drugs to reduce labor pains are often measurably "stoned" when they are born—and even one month later.

There is evidence that the amino acid taurine is important for brain development. The young child has only a limited ability to synthesize taurine but has a high uptake of the amino acid during the most active growth phase, deriving his main supply from milk. Human milk has twice as much taurine as cow's milk, which suggests that breast feeding may have important benefits for the brain's physiological development as well as for the child's psychological development.[12]

Malnutrition is a factor to which the growing brain is particularly susceptible. Normally the brain is protected from any undernourishment by what is called brain sparing. If there is any lack of essential vitamins, proteins, amino acids, oxygen, etc., then it is the other organs of the body that suffer first—the organism makes sure that the brain receives its essential supplies as long as possible. Far more of the individual's energy, time, and resources have been put into the development of the brain than have gone into any other organ. It is our most valuable organ and one that should be protected above all else. During the first two years, however, undernourishment can have severe effects on the developing brain, despite natural brain sparing.

When undernourishment occurs over the first two years of life, brain development is severely impaired. The brain is smaller, the number of glia cells (see pages 40–41) is reduced, there is less myelination of fibers (see page 23), and enzyme levels are lowered.[13] It is also found that the cerebellum suffers more than the rest of the brain in size reduction (probably because the cerebellum is the last part of the brain to form, beginning to develop only three months before birth and finishing about one year after birth). Among other things, the cerebellum is responsible for the integration of limb movements, which explains why early undernourishment has often been found to result in poor body coordination.

The most significant effect of poor nutrition is the reduction of the number of connections made between nerve cells. To study this effect researchers fostered a group of baby rats onto a mother who already had nine pups of her own, thus reducing the amount of food available for each rat in the litter. After weaning, they were fed on a similarly restrictive diet. When the brain cortex was later examined under an electron microscope, it was found that the total brain mass had been reduced by 23 percent and, even more significantly, the number of connections between neurons had been reduced by an average of 41 percent. It is the number of interconnections between neurons that is important, and it is likely that all aspects of nervous and mental development had been severely damaged by the poor nutrition.[14]

The situation is further compounded by the damaging effects of a poor environment. Two studies, one of children in Mexico City and the other of Jamaican infants, have shown that children who were not only undernourished but also came from homes that provided a poor environmental background, suffered far more than those who were simply undernourished.[15] Conversely, severely undernourished children who, at about the age of eighteen months, were adopted into middle-class American homes showed remarkable recoveries, both in physical and in intellectual terms. Many factors are important in the overall development of the brain. In this case the richer environment was sufficient to compensate for the earlier poor nutrition.[16]

NATURE OR NURTURE?

So far the emphasis has been on the crucial effects of early environment, including those vitally important first nine months. There is also the question of the extent to which mental skills are genetically inherited, and which is the more important—*environment* or *inheritance.* The widespread debate over this question is often called the "nature-nurture" controversy.

The "nature" camp would say that Mozart's musical talent, for example, was largely inherited from his parents, being encoded in the genes. The "nurture" lobby on the other hand, would claim that being born into a musical family, he had a rich musical environment very early on—even in the womb—and it was this that led to his great musical talent.

A third factor in individual differences could come from small variations in chemicals within cells. If a chemical was only present in minute quantities and was not being constantly synthesized, then it could become unevenly distributed between the daughter cells at the time of cell division, and so possibly lead to different behaviors at a later date. Such an effect would be neither genetic nor environmental. Supporting evidence for this third factor comes from the finding that genetically identical bacteria reared under identical conditions can show individual variations in behavior.[17] It is quite possible that similar factors play a part in the development of the growing human embryo, all the body's cells having descended originally from one cell.

The principal debate, though, is still one of nature or nurture. Much of the research in this field has centered on studies of twins. Monozygotic twins—that is, twins that have split from the same egg—

have the same genetic makeup, whereas dizygotic twins—coming from separate eggs—have different sets of genes. The extent to which inheritance plays a part can be evaluated by the extent to which monozygotic twins are more alike than dizygotic twins.

The early studies suggested that inheritance played a significant part in mental faculties. More recent work, however, suggests that the environment is far more important than hitherto supposed.

The issue is, however, still far from settled, and it is one that is guaranteed to bring out the emotional side of objective psychologists. Perhaps the most interesting study in this field is the one that showed a significant correlation between the attitudes and backgrounds of the researchers and the results of their research.[18] Researchers who had been brought up in a rural environment, for example, tended to find that differences were innate, as did also the younger researchers.

It is only since the late 1960s that psychologists have begun to realize the extent to which the very young brain can absorb and adapt to its environment. Many factors that were previously thought to have little or no effect on the young child are now being shown to play a considerable part in his development. With these findings has come a general shift toward nurture as playing a very large role in individual differences, and is the principal factor behind genius.

Figure 8

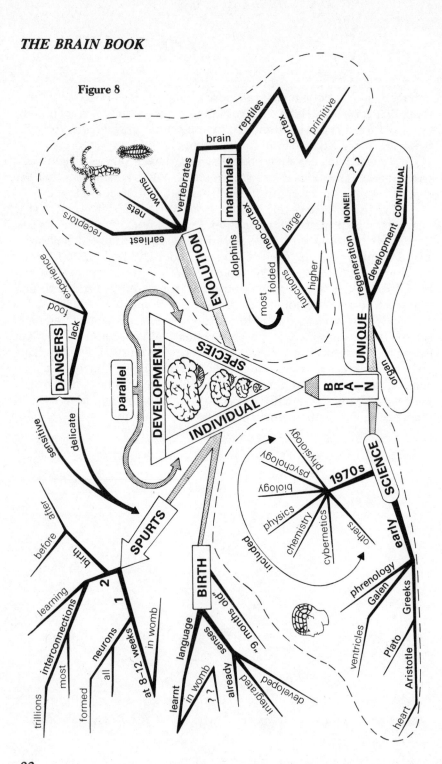

3.
Ten Billion Neurons

What is a neuron?
Do neurons die?
How do they work?
What are dendrites and axons?
What do they do?
What is a synapse?
Why is it so important?
What do the glia cells do?
How is the brain structured?
What is the brainstem? the midbrain? the cortex?

The most well known of the brain's cells are the neurons. The human brain contains something on the order of ten billion neurons—that's about three times as many neurons as there are people inhabiting this planet, or about as many neurons as there are stars in the Milky Way. This vast number immediately suggests that the cells themselves are minute, and also that the brain is immensely complex. A typical neuron in the cortex of the brain may make over ten thousand connections with other cells, and the total number of synapses in the brain is probably on the order of ten trillion at least—10,000,000,000,000. The mind boggles at its own complexity.

There is little hope that we can analyze all the interconnections in a single brain. Research workers at Cambridge University have spent three years analyzing the nervous system of a very simple worm. This creature has only twenty-three neurons, yet it took a team of scientists and a computing system three years just to analyze the interconnections of these few neurons. To try to analyze the interconnections of the neurons in a human brain by this method would take longer than the projected life of the universe.

DO NEURONS DIE?

Neurons are unlike nearly every other type of cell found in the human body in that they do not usually reproduce themselves. In every other organ of the body there is a continual turnover of cells, some being replaced every few hours, some every few weeks, and some every few years. But the neurons you are born with, or rather the neurons you have three months after conception, are the same neurons you will have when you are eighty.

It is often said that although neurons do not usually regenerate, they are nevertheless constantly dying, at the rate of about a thousand a day. There is, however, very little evidence to support this claim. In the last hundred years there have been only twenty studies on the decrease of neurons with age; ten of these studies were with humans, and ten with animals. Generally the results are far from conclusive: Half the human studies show there is a decrease in the number of neurons with age, half show there is not. Even the studies that show there is a decrease are highly contestable. Two of the principal ones were done in 1919 and 1928 and the brain tissue examined came from just a few museum specimens.[1] Nor was this a representative sample—two of the patients had in fact died in hospitals for the insane. From this very limited study extrapolations were made applying to the whole human race. With regard to the animal studies, in those cases that showed a loss of neurons with age the animals were left alone in isolation. When the animals lived together and had a normal level of stimulation, no loss was found.[2]

Even if neurons were to die at the rate of, say, several thousand a day, by the time you were eighty, you would have lost $1,000 \times 365 \times 80$ neurons, in other words, a mere 29.2 million or so neurons. I say "mere" because the total number of neurons is approximately ten billion, so you would have lost less than 1 percent of the total. Since there is an enormous redundancy in the nervous system, even this minute loss would be very unlikely to have any effect whatsoever on mental functioning. Indeed, since the number of connections between neurons is increasing throughout life, we should expect to see a continual growth in mental abilities, rather than any deterioration and, as we shall see in chapter 5, there is mounting evidence that this is the case.

AXONS AND DENDRITES

The typical neuron consists of a central cell body a few thousandths of an inch across. Its principal fiber, called the axon, usually one

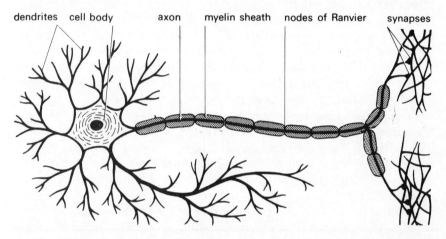

dendrites   cell body   axon   myelin sheath   nodes of Ranvier   synapses

Figure 9 Simplified diagram of typical neuron. Electrical changes are received from other cells by the dendrites. Their overall effect on the cell body governs the rate at which impulses are sent out via the axon and transmitted to the dendrites of other cells at the synapses.

Figure 10 Photograph of a neuron from the cortex of the brain (magnified 1,000 times). The thin line running downward from the cell body in the center is the axon. The thousands of small knobbly projections on the dendrites are the dendritic spines, where connections are made.

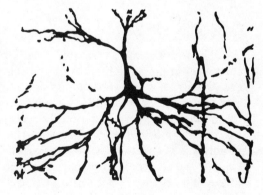

of the longest, carries outgoing information from the cell body to other neurons. There is normally only one axon per neuron, though it may divide along its length into many collaterals going off in different directions. For most of its length the axon is covered in a thin fatty coating of myelin, which both serves as an insulator and speeds conduction of electrical impulses. Toward its end the axon becomes thinner, branching out into fine fibers that terminate on other neurons. They may terminate directly on the cell body of another neuron, or they may make connections with a second type of fiber called dendrites. (The Greek word *dendron* means "tree," and the dendrites of a neuron are so named because of their treelike qualities—hundreds may radiate from a single cell, each one branching off into many fine feathery fibers.)

Whereas the axons transmit pulses from the cell body, the dendrites are generally the receptive part of the neuron, though, as with all brain structures, the distinction is not always so clear-cut. Most dendrites are covered with thousands or even millions of tiny bumps called ·dendritic spines, and it is at these points that they make connections with the axon, or sometimes the dendrites, of other cells. Altogether there are some 100,000 miles of dendrites in a human brain.

Neurons vary widely from one part of the brain to another. Some have hundreds of dendrites on them, some have only few. In some the fibers are only a millimeter or less in length; in others they may be up to two feet in length, stretching from the brain to the base of the spinal cord. Some make tens of thousands of connections with other neurons; some one or two. Yet despite such wide variations, their basic structure is generally the same.

THE SYNAPSE

The point at which two nerve cells meet is called the *synapse.* The word was originally coined by Sir Charles Sherrington, who derived it from the Greek word *synapto* "to clasp tightly." Strictly speaking, however, it is incorrect to talk of two nerve cells meeting, let alone clasping tightly, because there is generally a very small gap of about one five-thousandth of a millimeter between the two sides of the junction. Although this is a minute gap—many times thinner than the ink on this page—it is nevertheless one of the most important points in the nervous system. The synapses determine whether or not a pulse is transmitted from one cell to another; they are therefore the essential modulators of

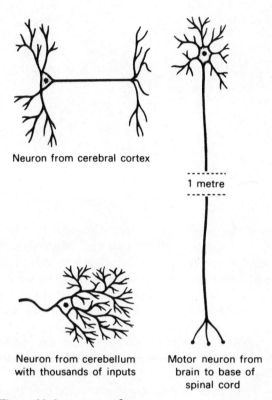

Neuron from cerebral cortex

1 metre

Neuron from cerebellum
with thousands of inputs

Motor neuron from
brain to base of
spinal cord

Figure 11 Some types of neurons.

brain activity and are currently thought to be closely involved in the encoding of memory.

Synapses usually occur at the junctions of axons and dendrites, but several other types of synapses are found in the brain. Axons may synapse directly with other axons, or with the cell body itself. Or dendrites may synapse directly with other dendrites. Synapses have also been discovered in which there is no gap between the two cells. In this case, there appears to be direct electrical transmission between neurons. There are also junctions that do not involve synapses at all. These are called ephatic junctions and occur where very fine unmyelinated dendrites interconnect with each other like the fibers in matted felt, and in this case the transmission is again direct.

Figure 12 Drawing of a cell body with a large number of axons from other cells terminating upon it. Note the small size of the synaptic knob compared with the cell body — the cell itself being only a few thousandths of an inch across.

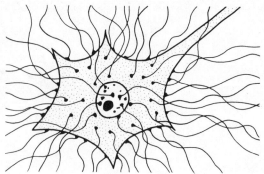

The ends of the axons tend to become much smaller in diameter as they branch out toward other cells, and consequently the nerve impulses are slowed down and considerably reduced in amplitude toward the synapse. This means that the electrical activity in one cell is insufficient to set off electrical activity in the next cell. Instead it causes various chemicals to be released into the synaptic gap, and these cross over to affect the next cell.

Before the pulse arrives, these chemicals are contained in tiny vesicles in the synaptic terminal of the first cell, and there may be several hundred such vesicles waiting to be released. When the pulse arrives, a few of the vesicles near the surface are ruptured and distribute their contents into the gap. One of the chemicals released, called the transmitter substance, flows across the gap and produces a depolarization of the membrane of the second cell. If this membrane is sufficiently depolarized, a new impulse is triggered and starts flowing down the second fiber. One interesting point about this transmission is that it is a one-way process; the vesicles containing the transmitter substance are only on the axon side of the synapse and electrical changes in the dendritic spine cannot set off changes in the axon.

The pulses in the axons and dendrites obey what is called the all-or-none law—each pulse is of the same intensity; there are no half-measures. The electrical changes across the synapse, however, are variable, being proportional to the amount of chemical released into the gap. Thus the greater the frequency of the incoming pulses, the greater the number of vesicles released and the greater the amplitude of the potential change on the other side. Whether or not this potential change results in an impulse being transmitted down the second fiber

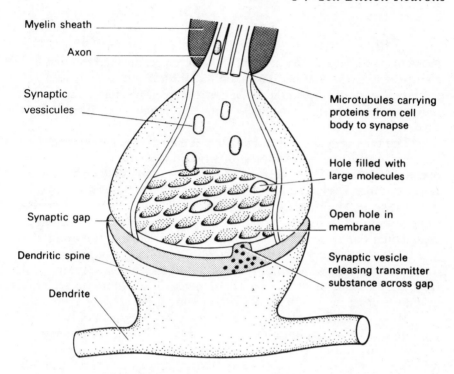

Myelin sheath

Axon

Synaptic vessicules

Synaptic gap

Dendritic spine

Dendrite

Microtubules carrying proteins from cell body to synapse

Hole filled with large molecules

Open hole in membrane

Synaptic vesicle releasing transmitter substance across gap

Figure 13 Simplified diagram of fine structure of synapse. The vesicles fit into a vacant hole at the synaptic membrane and on the arrival of a pulse down the axon release their contents into the synaptic gap. The net amount of transmitter substance received by the second membrane determines whether or not the pulse is propagated in the dendrite of the second neuron.

depends on whether the induced potential change is high enough.

Recent explorations of the synapse under the electron microscope have revealed that the surface is not a simple membrane; rather it is a regular latticework. The points of intersection of the framework form little bumps, and in between are hollows about one-twentieth of a micron across (a micron is one-thousandth of a millimeter).[3] This is just the size of the vesicles containing the transmitter substance, and it is thought that a vesicle can only release its contents into the gap once it is resting snugly inside one of these hollows. A typical synapse contains about 150 hollows, but many may already be filled with large molecules and so not be accessible to the vesicles. Thus the number of vesicles available when an impulse arrives, and hence the likelihood of the impulse being transmitted across the gap, depends on the very fine molecular structure of this grid, which is in turn controlled by chemical changes within the neuron. It is thought that some such minute changes in chemicals at the synaptic surface are responsible for learning and memory—something we will be looking at in much more detail in Part Two.

The type of synapse just described is called an excitatory synapse because the nerve impulse in the first neuron excites a nerve impulse in the second one. There is a second kind of synapse called an inhibitory synapse, which works in the opposite manner. It decreases the excitability of the second membrane making it more difficult for a nerve impulse to be generated in the dendrite. Whether or not a pulse is created at a particular dendritic spine depends on the net effect of the excitatory and inhibitory synapses made there. The inhibitory synapses play an important part in moderating the activity of the nervous system. If it were not for them, an excitation would spread like wildfire through the brain, resulting in a continuous state of convulsive activity.

Most, if not all, neurons are spontaneously active all of the time, sending out about ten impulses every second. The collective effect of the incoming pulses from thousands, or in some cases a quarter of a million, synapses does not therefore determine whether or not the cell fires but modulates the pattern of its incessant activity. Thus in any one second there are hundreds of billions of impulses flashing through the brain producing unbelievably intricate waves of shimmering activity, always changing and far beyond our imagination, "as if the Milky Way had entered upon some cosmic dance."

GLIA CELLS

From what has been said, it might be expected that the brain was packed full, with 10 billion neurons and all their fibers. As well as the neurons, however, there are billions of other cells called glia cells. In fact it is estimated that there are some 100 billion glia cells in the human brain—that is, about ten times as many glia cells as there are neurons. Unlike neurons, the glia cells do not have axons or dendrites; they are rounder in shape. The glia are packed between the neurons and cover all their bodies, axons, and dendrites. The only part of a neuron that is not so covered is the gap at the synapse. Indeed, *glia* is the Greek word for "glue"; they glue the brain together.

Glia cells appear to be involved in nearly every aspect of neuronal activity. They look after the nourishment of neurons and are an interface between the blood vessels and the neurons themselves. They act as scavengers, consuming waste products, especially the transmitters and other chemicals released into the synaptic gap between neurons. They insulate neurons from one another, both chemically and electrically, and are the source of the myelin coating that covers the longer fibers. Unlike neurons themselves, the glia can divide and reproduce. This is important not only for maintaining the population of glia, but because where they divide there is an opportunity for an axon to push through and make connections to other cells. Thus the dividing of glia cells may be part of the learning process.

Glia are also electrically sensitive, and it has been suggested that they may act as liquid crystals in resonance with the surrounding electrical fields. That is to say they may have the characteristics of semiconductors. If so, they could pick up very faint electrical changes in the nervous system and amplify them several thousand times in much the same way transistors amplify faint signals in electronic circuits.[4] Just imagine 100 billion transistors inside your head!

AXONAL TRANSPORT

It is also becoming apparent that the neurons themselves perform many other functions than just the simple transmission of electrical impulses. In 1963 it was observed that where an axon had been constricted for some reason, there was a swelling on the axon on the side near the cell body, rather as if matter passing down the axon was being dammed up by the constriction. Six years and 100,000 fibers later this hypothesis was confirmed.[5] Using techniques of cinematography, it was observed that the entire contents of the axon appeared to be moving down toward the tip. Among the particles moving down the axon were mitochondria, commonly described as the powerhouses of the living cell, and the vesicles containing proteins, enzymes, and the transmitter substances released at the synaptic gap. It would seem that much of the material used at the synapse is manufactured in the body of the cell and is then moved down the axon to the synapse itself.

Other experiments, involving the injection of minute amounts of a special amino acid containing silver molecules that show up under the microscope after staining, have allowed neurologists to measure the rate of transport more accurately. Most of the materials seem to be traveling at the rate of a few millimeters a day. This may not seem very fast at first, but when we remember the minute size of the cell, it is a relatively rapid motion. In terms of the mitochondria it represents about one thousand per day passing down the axon, and when we take all the other particles and vesicles into account, we find that the total amount of material transported per day is three times the volume of the cell itself. Each neuron is therefore having to produce three times its own weight each day! Moreover, since the axon does not grow any longer, all the material passing along its length must be consumed in one way or another at the synapses.

This main flow is rapid enough, but it has also been found that some proteins are moved down the axon very much more rapidly still, at the rate of some 2.8 meters per day. This means that proteins generated in the cell body can be at the synapses within an hour or two, or, if the axon is very short, within minutes. This has important implications on memory, for it provides a mechanism by which the cell body can modify the synapses at the end of its axons.[6] Proteins, which on their arrival filled vacant holes in the synaptic grid, would directly affect the amount of transmitter substance that could be released across the gap, and hence the transmission characteristics of the junction.

THE REGIONS OF THE BRAIN

We have looked briefly at the fine structure of the brain, at the neurons and at some of the incredible processes taking place within them, now let us get an overall picture of how the brain is organized. Neuroanatomy is the most complex of the biological sciences, there being thousands upon thousands of different groups of nerve cells performing various specific functions. For our purposes, however, we can consider the brain in terms of just a few basic regions.

Spinal Cord. The oldest part of the brain is the spinal cord, stretching from the neck down the center of the vertebrae to the bottom of the back. As was seen earlier, the spinal cord first forms as a tube, and this is still apparent in the adult spinal cord, there being a thin hollow down its length that is filled with cerebrospinal fluid. There are two principal functions associated with the spinal cord: It performs very simple reflexes, such as the knee jerk reflex, and it acts as the principal communication channel between the head and the rest of the body. The control of the body is conveyed via the spinal cord, and all bodily sensations reach the brain through the spinal cord. All, that is, except those relating to the head itself, which enter and leave through the brain stem.

The Brain Stem. This is situated on top of the spinal cord. It still possesses the tubular structure of the spinal cord, and in some respects can be thought of as an extension of it. In the brain stem is a very intricate network of nerves about the size of your little finger called the reticular formation. It receives nerves from all areas of the brain and likewise sends out nerves in every direction. The reticular formation plays an important role in maintaining wakefulness, and if it is isolated from the rest of the brain, the organism goes into permanent sleep. It also monitors and filters the information coming in through the senses. If, for example, you are in a room with a clock that is ticking quietly, you will quickly habituate to the sound so that after a short while you will no longer hear it. But the sound is still being continually monitored by the brain, and if the clock were suddenly to stop, or to change speed or volume, you would immediately notice it. The reticular formation would have alerted you.

Cerebellum. Connected to the brain stem is the cerebellum, which somewhat resembles the cortex in terms of its neuronal structure,

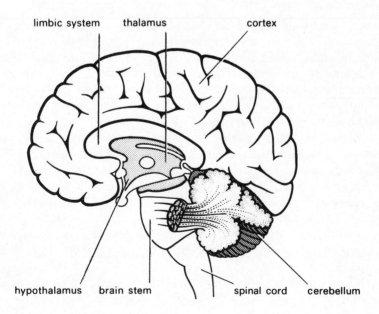

Figure 14 The main regions of the brain.

though it is very much older than the cortex. Although it is undoubtedly involved in a variety of functions, it is primarily concerned with coordination of movements. It seems to integrate the information coming from all the senses with all the muscles so as to produce smooth, finely tuned movements, rather than jerky uncoordinated movements.

Midbrain. On top of the brain stem is the thalamus, a large region containing many nuclei, some relaying information from the sensory organs to the cortex, others relaying information from one area of the cortex to another and interacting with the reticular formation and the limbic system. The limbic system is a group of structures in the middle of the brain that play an important role in emotion and motivation.

Just below the thalamus is the hypothalamus, a tiny structure about the size of a pea, yet a crucial part of the brain. This little organ is largely responsible for the maintenance of homeostasis, ensuring that all the various parameters of bodily function are in balance and function at their optimum. The hypothalamus continually monitors the blood. If there is too little or too much carbon dioxide, it reduces or increases breathing; if blood sugar is low, it makes you feel hungry; if your temperature is too low or too high, it initiates shivering or sweating; if the blood is too salty, it makes you feel thirsty. It also plays a major role in the control of sleep, sexual behavior, and the emotions.

Cortex. Covering the whole of the midbrain is the neocortex, or the cortex, as it is more commonly referred to. Though only one quarter of the brain's total volume, it contains 75 percent of its ten billion neurons. The cortex is also referred to as the gray matter, since the greater density of blood vessels gives it a grayish color. The rest of the brain contains many more myelinated fibers passing from one area to another and so has a more whitish color.

Some areas of the cortex play particular roles in sensory activity. The rear of the cortex, for example, is associated with the processing of visual information, a small area on the side with auditory information, and a strip extending from the top center of the cortex down each side is concerned with the sense of touch and also with the control of the muscles. Large parts of the cortex, though, do not appear to be so specific in their function, rather they seem to be concerned with the integration of information from several different senses, in other words, with building up a total worldview. These areas are called the association areas.

As an example of how the different areas interact, let us consider briefly how a visual signal is analyzed. Information from the eye is

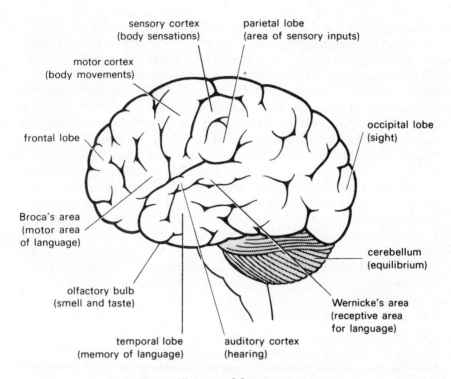

sensory cortex
(body sensations)

parietal lobe
(area of sensory inputs)

motor cortex
(body movements)

occipital lobe
(sight)

frontal lobe

Broca's area
(motor area
of language)

cerebellum
(equilibrium)

olfactory bulb
(smell and taste)

Wernicke's area
(receptive area
for language)

temporal lobe
(memory of language)

auditory cortex
(hearing)

Figure 15 Areas of the cortex.

passed first to the lateral geniculate body, a small group of cells in the thalamus, and from there is relayed to the visual cortex of the brain, though some of it is sent down to the reticular formation. The visual cortex proceeds to analyze the signal: first by picking out lines and boundaries in the information; then picking out lines of specific orientation; then picking out lines not only of a specific orientation but those moving with particular speed, each cell responding to a different combination of line length, angle, and speed; and the next level puts these units together to produce angles and corners moving at specific speeds. This information is then sent forward to what are called the visual association areas, where further analysis seems to take place, and it is probably at this stage that we recognize a handshape as a hand—indeed experiments on monkeys have found cells that do respond to just this shape in the visual field. This information is then sent forward to association areas where it is integrated with other information coming from hearing, touch, smell, taste, and memory.

One of the most striking facts about the human cortex is the large size of the regions commonly referred to as the frontal lobes. Attempts have been made to attribute just about every conceivable function to the frontal cortex—particularly the higher functions, such as emotions, intelligence, memory, and even the will itself. Yet despite the attention paid to these areas, we still have very little idea of their function.

In the 1940s and 1950s, frontal lobotomy (the severing of the fibers to the frontal lobe of the brain) was used in an effort to restore the mental health of psychiatric patients, and with no obvious deterioration in intellectual ability, creativity, problem solving, etc. The only consistent effect was a lack of responsiveness to chronic pain. Patients reported that they still felt the pain but that it no longer bothered them. For this reason the operation is still sometimes used for the relief of incurable pain in terminal cancer.

That the frontal lobes still remain something of an enigma does not mean we should in any way underestimate their value. Remember that it was only a few hundred years ago that the whole of the brain was considered to be of little importance as far as thought processes were concerned.

Meninges. Covering the whole of the brain are a series of membranes called meninges. The outer ones serve a protective function, while the inner ones contain a profusion of arteries and veins carrying blood to the brain. The brain has one of the largest turnovers of chemicals in the whole body. The neurons are continually synthesizing protein, and the more mentally active a person is, the faster is the synthesis. This all requires energy, and the brain has one of the richest blood supplies of any organ in the body. There are literally millions of tiny blood vessels in the brain supplying the cells with nourishment and oxygen. And the brain, though only 3 percent of the body's total weight, consumes 20 percent of its oxygen intake.

The human brain is a highly complex, intricately interconnected web of billions of neurons. Millions of fibers connect each of the different regions with other regions, and in the final analysis the simplified view portrayed here cannot do justice to its true complexity. Most of the different areas are probably involved in almost everything that happens in the brain, the whole forming a dynamic neurological balance, of which science has at present had only the faintest glimpse.

Figure 16

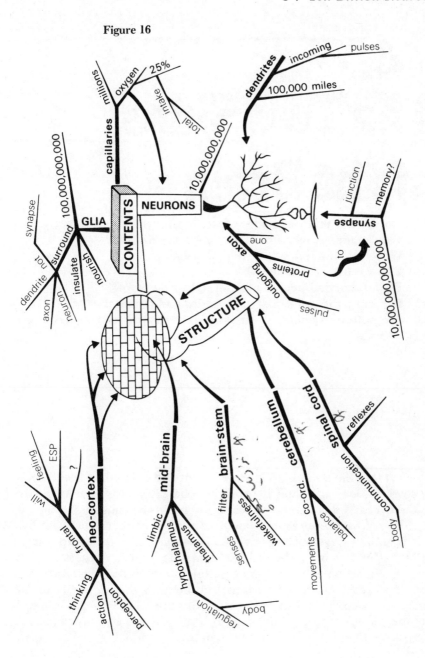

4.
The Two Sides
of the Brain

Do the left and right sides of the brain function differently?
What happens when the two halves are divided?
Why does the left side appear dominant?
Can we use both equally?
Do left-handed people use the right side more?
Is there a difference between males and females?
Are cultural symbols of left and right related to the sides of the
    brain?

The fact that the brain is divided into a left and a right half is not a new discovery. Once the skull is removed, the division is obvious to the naked eye, and it is a common feature of brains throughout the animal kingdom. What is interesting about this division in man is that each half seems to have developed specialized functions, the left side appearing to be better at some tasks and the right side better at others.

The most obvious difference in functioning is that the left side of the brain receives sensations from and controls the right side of the body, and vice versa. The reasons for this are still unclear. Despite a number of interesting theories, there is no obvious advantage in such a crossover. Yet it is found in most mammals and in many other vertebrates.

This crossover effect was one of the first discoveries to be made about the brain, the ancient Egyptians having noticed that injuries to one side of the brain caused a corresponding paralysis to the opposite side of the body. By the beginning of this century it was known that damage to certain areas of the left hemisphere results in the loss of speech, poor reading, and a general deterioration in logical thinking, whereas damage to the corresponding regions of the right hemisphere produces a deterioration in visual and spatial functions, such as the recognition of faces and the ability to dress oneself.

The fact that damage to the left hemisphere produces far more serious defects gave rise to the widespread view that the left hemisphere was dominant. Often the left was referred to as the major hemisphere and the right as the minor one. Recent research, however, has forced psychologists to modify this view on two accounts. First, the right hemisphere has been found to be just as active and just as important as the left hemisphere. And second, each hemisphere partakes to some extent in the functions associated with the other hemisphere, making it more difficult to draw a rigid functional distinction.

THE SPLIT-BRAIN EXPERIMENTS

The left and right halves of the cortex, though separate structures, are connected by a massive bundle of nerves, called the corpus callosum, containing some 200 million fibers. In 1940 two doctors decided to try cutting the corpus callosum in patients with severe epilepsy. They reasoned that if they could confine the seizure to one half of the brain, then the other half could carry on functioning normally, enabling the person to take some medicine or summon assistance. As far as treating the epilepsy was concerned, it seemed to work, and at first there were no observable side effects or disturbances in behavior.[1] This led some psychologists to the view that the corpus callosum played no greater role than physically supporting the two halves of the brain!

Further work on animals, however, suggested that there may be some functional disorders resulting from the operation after all, and this led to a renewed examination of its effects in humans. In the 1960s Roger Sperry, at the California Institute of Technology, began extensive studies on a number of epileptic patients whose corpus callosum had been severed and began uncovering some interesting anomalies. If a patient was given something to hold in his right hand, he could say what he was holding, since the information was going to the left side of the brain. But if the object was in his left hand, he could not describe it, he could only make a guess—though he could later point to the object again with his left hand, showing that the right half had both recognized and remembered the object.[2]

The crossover in the visual system is slightly more complex than in the rest of the body. The eyes themselves are not directly crossed, but the left side of the retina of each eye connects to the left side of the brain, and the right side of the retina of each eye connects to the right side of the brain. Thus, since the retinal image is inverted, the left side of the visual field connects to the right side of the brain and the right side of the visual field connects to the left side. This gave rise to some interesting phenomena in the split-brain patients. If the word *Herman* were flashed to a patient in such a way that his focus lay between the *r* and the *m,* the first three letters would go to the right hemisphere and the last three letters to the left hemisphere. When asked to *say* what he had seen, he would reply "man"; but when asked to point with his left hand to what he had seen, he would point to the word *her.*[3]

The reason that such differences had not been found in the earlier studies was that the two halves of the brain had been able to communicate in other ways. In one of Sperry's experiments a light was flashed in the left visual field so that it arrived in the right hemisphere, and the patient had to say whether the light was red or green. At first the replies were purely guesswork, the left hemisphere having no idea what the right side was seeing, but after a few trials the patient began correcting his mistakes. The left hemisphere might wrongly guess "red" for a green light, but the right hemisphere, on hearing the wrong answer, would start shaking the head and making frowns. The left hemisphere, responding to this information, would immediately say, "Oh no, I meant green."[4] Once such additional sources of information were controlled, the different functions of the two hemispheres began to become more apparent.

One interesting finding was that although the right hand still maintained the ability to write—as we would expect if linguistic abilities are located in the left hemisphere—it lost the ability to draw pictures. With the left hand, however, the opposite was the case. It could not write at all, but it could still draw cubes and simple shapes. The left hand was also better than the right at arranging colored blocks to form a pattern, though it may never have attempted this before.[5]

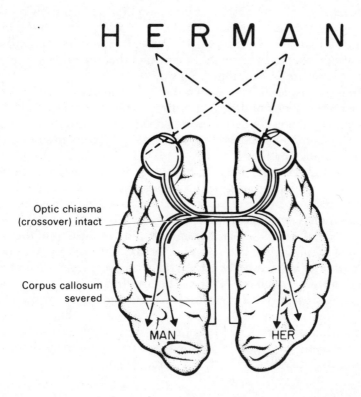

Figure 17 Crossover of visual fields in the brain. The left side of the retina of each eye goes to the left side of the brain, and vice versa. Thus the right visual field goes to the left side of the brain, and vice versa, no matter which eye is being used.

SPECIALIZATION OF FUNCTION

The different functions of the two hemispheres have been confirmed by comparing the electrical activity from the left and right sides of the brain. When the brain is in a fairly relaxed state, it tends to show alpha rhythms—that is, waves of about eight to ten cycles per second. Robert Ornstein in San Francisco compared the relative levels of alpha from the left and right sides of the brain for different mental activities. He found that when he gave his subject a mathematical problem to solve, the alpha increased in the right hemisphere, suggesting that this side was relaxing, and decreased in the left, showing that awareness was focused more in this side. Conversely, when the subject was asked to match colored patterns, the alpha intensity increased in the left and decreased in the right, suggesting that the subject was now making greater use of the right hemisphere.[6]

Other experiments have shown the right hemisphere to be better in the perception of depth,[7] in the appreciation of music (although professional musicians tend to be more analytical and use the left hemisphere more in their appreciation),[8] and also in the recognition of faces and other familiar patterns.[9]

The picture that is beginning to emerge is that the left half of the brain is more specialized in serial processes, that is to say, analysis that involves processing information one bit after another; while the right half of the brain is more specialized in parallel processing, that is, taking several bits of information together and forming a synthesis of them. In writing, for example, one takes an idea, breaks it down into sentences, then into phrases and words. One then takes the words and breaks them down into letters, which are written one after another. This is a serial or analytical process. With regard to recognizing a face, on the other hand, a person does not analyze the image feature by feature starting with the jawline and slowly working his way up, step by step, to the hair. Instead he takes a large number of elements and synthesizes them into a whole. This is parallel, or synthetic, processing.

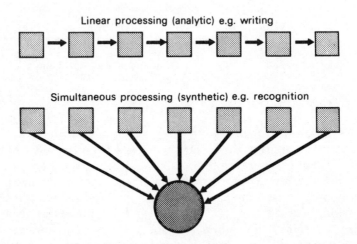

Figure 18 Distinction between linear and simultaneous processing.

Further evidence on this distinction comes from studies of perceptual discrimination. A person generally takes longer to judge whether ten letters are all the same than he does to judge whether two are. This implies that the letters are being evaluated one after another, that is, serially. Conversely, when the items to be matched are shapes, the time taken by the subject is independent of the number of comparisons, suggesting that with nonverbal material the processing is in parallel. When, however, the letters are processed by just one hemisphere (by presenting them in the opposite visual field), the time taken to judge whether or not they are identical increases with the number of letters when they are presented to the left hemisphere, yet stays the same when they are presented to the right. This supports the contention that the left is processing in a serial mode while the right is processing in parallel. But this only occurs for verbal material. When the items are shapes, both hemispheres appear to work in a parallel mode.[10] Presumably the left is now forced to work in a parallel mode, since its verbal abilities are no longer of any use in distinguishing abstract shapes.

While supporting the hypothesis that the left prefers to function in a serial mode and the right a parallel mode, this experiment also shows that this distinction is not absolute—it is only a preference, and, when obliged to, either hemisphere can function in either mode.

The value of specialization of function is that it effectively increases our mental capacity. Each hemisphere tends to analyze its own input first, only swapping information with the other side once a considerable degree of processing has already taken place. Thus we can process two streams of information at once and then compare and integrate them in order to obtain a broader and more sophisticated impression.[11] Specialization of function also divides the load of each hemisphere. It is a very natural course of action to take. We can see it in any organic system—different cells and organs specializing in different tasks—and in any social organization—different groups of people taking on different responsibilities in order to share the load and increase the overall efficiency of the system.

THE QUESTION OF DOMINANCE

Although speech and linguistic abilities in general have for long been associated with a specific area in the left hemisphere (Broca's area in the temporal cortex behind the ear), recent experiments suggest that the right side of the brain also has some well-developed verbal abilities.

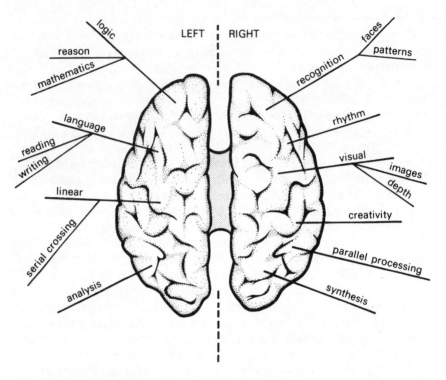

Figure 19 Specializations of the left and right hemispheres.

Damage to the right hemisphere does not usually produce a complete block in linguistic abilities, although it can impede them. A number of patients with right-side-of-brain damage have experienced difficulties in copying and writing, and many have shown difficulties in grammar as well; but they did not show a complete loss of language.[12]

By injecting sodium amytal into the arteries in the left side of the neck, it is possible to anesthetize completely the left hemisphere but leave the right functioning normally. When this is done, it is found that the subject can still understand language, being able to pick out objects that have been described and to follow simple instructions.[13] Other experiments on the right hemisphere have shown that it does seem to possess a moderate degree of syntax, about that of a five-year-old, and the vocabulary of a fourteen-year-old.

The left hemisphere may not be dominant in the sense that it is any more important than the right, but in Western culture at least, the faculties associated with the left do take a more dominant position in our lives. We tend to lay greater emphasis on rational thinking, the ability to express oneself verbally, read well, and generally excel in analytic thinking. We place less emphasis on spatial ability, artistic appreciation, creative processes, and intuitive thought—the faculties more often associated with the right hemisphere.

It is generally much easier for an accountant or a lawyer, say, to be successful than it is for the artist. The highest material rewards go to the logical, rational thinkers, and for them the paths to success are well laid out. For the artist, musician, and the poet the path is much harder. For most it is a question of survival rather than success. Our society, it is true, does support a number of artists, but this is generally regarded as something of a luxury. Providing all the necessities (as judged by our logical minds) have been taken care of, we can afford ourselves a little artistic indulgence. Yet it may well be that art and creativity are as necessary to the survival of our society as science and logic are.

The emphasis on left-hemisphere processes goes back to early school days. When most of us went to school, education was still based largely around the three R's—reading, 'riting, and 'rithmetic—all essentially left-hemisphere functions. There were, of course, art classes, music lessons, and the occasional dance or drama class, but in most cases these were seen as an extra. They were a special treat for Friday afternoons—providing, that is, you had got all your sums right and had corrected all your spelling mistakes.

This type of education, combined with society's emphasis on analytic rather than synthetic thinking, has led to the left hemisphere's becoming dominant in usage. It also has had the unfortunate side effect that children who are better at using their right hemisphere may have been wrongly classed as subnormal or retarded. Indeed, a study at the University of Houston showed that a number of children classified as "mentally retarded" actually showed normal or superior development in artistic ability.[14]

Some schools have tried increasing the proportion of the curriculum devoted to the arts, and with encouraging results. At the Mead School, in Bryam, Connecticut, children spend half their time in art classes of one form or another and the other half in "regular" subjects. As a result their performance in mathematics, science, and a variety of other subjects actually increased. Indeed, the school's performance was above average in nearly every subject.[15] Other schools in both Europe and America that have tried similar projects have found the same: The extra time spent on developing the faculties of the right brain also helps those associated with the left brain. This is because the two do not work in isolation—each supports and complements the activity of the other.

A complete education should give equal emphasis to both verbal-analytic thinking and to aesthetic-synthetic thinking. If only the verbal-analytic side is being educated, the student is effectively being cut off from many ways in which he could directly experience the world around him. And without direct experience education can become dry, meaningless, and boring. As one worker in this field put it, "His brain is being systematically damaged. In many ways he is being de-educated."[16]

Yet, tragically, whenever there is any cutback in the public funding of education, it is the arts program that is hit first. This may seem a good short-term saving, but in the long run it is a grave loss to society.

If we look at the great minds throughout history, we find that time and again they were people who used the faculties of both the left and the right sides. Albert Einstein is a classic example. As soon as you see his name, you probably think of a great scientist, the supreme rational thinker, the great mathematician surrounded by figures and equations, a logical left-hemisphere thinker. Yet Einstein's ideas initially came to him as pictures and images, and only subsequently did he put them into words and mathematical symbols. When Einstein hit upon the theory of relativity, it was not through rational analysis. He did not sit down with pen and paper and step by step work out the theory, eventually arriving at the logical conclusion. The theory was born when Einstein was lying on a grassy hillside one summer's afternoon. He was gazing up at the sun through half-closed eyelids, playing with the light that came through his eyelashes, when he began to wonder what it would be like to travel down a light beam. He lay there in a dream state letting his mind wander freely, imagining himself traveling down a light beam, when suddenly he realized (one almost has to say in a flash) just what it would be like. This realization was the essence of the theory of relativity, and it had come to him not as a logical deduction, but as a creative, intuitive insight, the result of synthetic rather than analytic thinking.

There must have been thousands of people who have had similar deep insights as to the nature of reality but had no ability to express their realizations, and were simply ignored as babbling idiots. What made Einstein so great was the fact that he was also a good rational thinker. He could take his insight and, using a mathematical framework, give it a logical symbolic formulation, and so communicate it to others.

This combined use of both the right and left hemispheres is a common characteristic of the creative process, whether in science or in art. Leonardo da Vinci was as much scientist as artist, an engineer and architect as well as sculptor and painter. His science notebooks contain exquisite drawings of nature and of the human anatomy that were artistically superior to any others of that time, whereas his art notebooks were full of precise analyses of visual perception that were not fully appreciated for several centuries. The notebooks of many other artists similarly reveal concise analytic thinking linked with deep insight and aesthetic appreciation.

LEFT- AND RIGHT-HANDEDNESS

Since the right hand is connected to the left side of the brain, could there be a connection between right-handedness and a greater use of the left hemisphere? The answer is, probably not. Left-handed people are generally left-hemisphere thinkers as much as are right-handed people. And conversely in people who show a much higher use of right-hemisphere faculties there is no strong correlation with left-handedness.[17]

Alternatively, could left-handedness reflect a reversal of the functions of the left and right hemispheres? In a few people the functions of the left and right hemispheres are reversed, linguistic abilities residing more in the right hemisphere, but such people are still mainly right-handed. Conversely the majority of left-handers still have their speech areas in the left hemisphere, and the same is true with ambidextrous people.[18] Just why some people find it easier and better to use their left hand is not yet clear, but it certainly does not usually imply a shift in dominance or a reversal of the functions of the left and right hemispheres.

MALE–FEMALE DIFFERENCES

The specialized functions of the two hemispheres are a little different in males and females. At school boys are generally better at spatial tasks, whereas girls are better at linguistic ones. Newborn girls utter sounds more often than newborn boys, and during the first few years they utter a larger variety of sounds than do boys. On average they say their first words and first sentences earlier, and at the age of two they have larger vocabularies. There also seems to be less specialization in visual-spatial skills in females, there being a much broader overlap between the two hemispheres. This is apparent up to the age of thirteen and possibly continues later. Boys, on the other hand, have visual-spatial skills localized in the right hemisphere by the age of six.[19] Whether or not this is an inborn difference is not clear; it could be a cultural effect stemming from slight differences in approach to baby boys and baby girls.

The female brain appears to retain its plasticity longer. Being more versatile, it is better able to compensate for damage to other areas. This probably explains why girls have only one-sixth of the reading problems that boys do. These differences continue throughout life. It has been observed that in men, damage to the left hemisphere results in more serious deterioration in language function than it does in women, and damage to the right hemisphere results in a more serious deterioration to visual-spatial functions. In women, on the other hand, the relationship between the functions lost and the areas damaged is less specific.[20]

The electrical activity of the brain reveals that men tend to have lower evoked potentials—a measure of the brain's electrical response to stimuli such as light and sound. Men also have better daylight vision than women.

They are, in general, less sensitive to extreme heat and more sensitive to extreme cold. Men have faster reaction times from mid-childhood on; even as infants, they tend to be more interested in objects than in people, and are more skilled at gross motor movements. Boys engage in rough-and-tumble play more than girls [helping the eye and brain learn to adjust to sudden major shifts in the visual environment]; as infants, they spend more time playing with objects other than toys, and invent novel uses for them. Men excel in a wide range of skills involving the perception of depth in space, an ability that gives them an edge in mechanical tasks. Boys' greater ability in math could also be a spatial skill, since it shows strongest when geometry and trigonometry are included. Finally, the fact that boys are more easily distracted by novel objects, combined with their greater exploratory behavior, suggests a kind of curiosity that leads to success in problem-solving tasks that require manipulation.

Women, by contrast, have more sensitive taste, are more sensitive to touch in all parts of the body, have better hearing (particularly in the higher ranges), are less tolerant of loud volumes (at 85 decibels and above, any sound seems twice as loud to them as it does to males), are less tolerant of repetitive sounds, and have better night vision. From infancy on, women excel in many verbal skills, are better in manual dexterity and fine coordination, and process information faster, particularly in tasks (like neurosurgery) that require rapid choices. Women are more interested in people, as infants are more attentive to sounds and their emotional meaning, and are more socially responsive and empathic. They are less distracted by sights while listening, more accurately perceive "subliminal" messages, and are better at remembering the names and faces of old high-school classmates. Women's greater interest in people also shows up in better empathy.[21]

WHAT UNDERLIES THE SPECIALIZATION?

The distinction between left and right functions may well be more fundamental than "verbal" versus "nonverbal" and may exist even at birth. Studies of the electrical activity of the brains of newborn babies have shown that they process the sound of a click in the left hemisphere and a flash of light in the right.[22] This has led to the hypothesis that the left deals with the "recognition of relationship" or "association with previous experience." A click is highly structured auditory information and can be related to past experiences and hence labeled; a visual flash, on the other hand, is unstructured information and is not so easily labeled. If so, then it is the labeling, or referential tendency of the left, that would lead to the processing of language by the left hemisphere. The left brain would not therefore be just analytic and sequential, but also comparative, relational, and referential. And the right brain not only synthetic, but also nonreferential and integrative.

It has also been suggested that the functions associated with the left and right hemispheres parallel what have been called the "active mode" and the "receptive mode."[23] The "active mode," as its name implies, is concerned with activity, with manipulation, and with directly influencing the environment. Thinking in the active mode is more logical, and attention is more focused with a heightened awareness of boundaries. It is the mode for *doing,* for making things happen.

The "receptive mode," on the other hand, is more concerned with intake from the environment. Thinking in the receptive mode tends to be synthetic rather than analytic, and the attention is more diffuse. This mode is more concerned with letting things happen. It should not, however, be confused with passivity: It is merely a different way of engaging the world. It is probably our emphasis on rationality and the left hemisphere that has led to a predominance of the "active mode" —we in the West are continually making the world respond to our needs. The opposite of this is the Taoist concept of *Wui-Wei*, of letting things be, a surrendering to Nature and flowing with change rather than continually pitting oneself against it.

LEFT–RIGHT ASSOCIATIONS

Psychologist Robert Ornstein has taken this polarity further, suggesting that Western thinking is left-hemisphere dominant, whereas Eastern thinking is right-hemisphere dominant.[24] The evidence for this is, however, very meager. Ornstein also believes that many of our so-called unconscious mental processes reside in the right hemisphere, and he points out that in many societies the left side of the body is associated with unconscious processes and with other functions attributed to the right hemisphere. This is probably a gross oversimplification of the division. As we have seen, mental functions do not seem to fall into such a neat separation between the left and right. Nevertheless, the parallels with the right–left symbolism found in nearly every culture of the world is fascinating.

The right side of the body, or the right hand (corresponding to the left side of the brain, remember), is generally associated with the good, the sacred, the pure; with life, joy, medicine, and health; with heaven and progress. The left is associated with evil, the profane and the impure, with death, sorrow, poison, and illness; with hell and with regression. The right symbolizes masculinity, lucidity, and adaptability; the sun, daytime, and light. The left symbolizes femininity, obscurity, and passivity, the moon, nighttime, and darkness. In China the right is yang, the creative and the firm; the left is yin, the receptive and the yielding. Yang is summer, the time of life and growth; yin is the winter, the time of hibernation and recession. In most cultures the right hand is used for religious offerings and for taking food, and it is the right hand that is shaken in greeting. Christ sat at God's right hand and the *good* thief was crucified on Christ's right. In alchemy the right is associated with the king and with Mars; the left with the queen and with Venus.

In many languages, the words for right and left have other meanings. In English *right* also means "correct." *Sinister* comes from the Latin *sinistra,* "left." In French the word *droit,* "right," also means "straight, not twisted or perverse"; similarly with the Armenian for "right," *adj.* In Italian *destro,* as well as signifying the right hand, also means "the right moment" and is sometimes used in the sense of being clever. The Arabic *yamine* has the second meaning of "prosperity," and also "oath." In many of the Bantu languages of West Africa (Swahili, Nyanja, Lomwe, and Suto, for example) the word for "right" is also the word for "male" (*mkono wa kuume,* "the male hand" in Swahili), and the word for "left" is also the word for "female."[25]

Probably the most detailed left-right symbolism is found in the Tantric writings of northern India. These are fascinating in that although they were written many hundreds of years ago, they foreshadow much of what we are now discovering about the left and right

Figure 20 Cross-cultural associations with left and right, paralleling some of the attributes of right and left hemispheres.

RIGHT (Left brain)	LEFT (Right brain)
Male	Female
West	East
Conscious	Unconscious
Good	Evil
Sacred	Profane
Pure	Impure
Life	Death
Joy	Sorrow
Medicine	Poison
Health	Sickness
Progress	Regress
Heaven	Hell
Light	Dark
Sun	Moon
Day	Night
Yang	Yin
Active	Passive

hemispheres of the brain. Tantric writings associate the left nostril with the moon and with feminine qualities, and the right nostril with the sun and masculinity. They maintain that the breath rarely flows through both nostrils equally, for a while it flows predominantly through the left and then for a while through the right, the changeover taking place once every twenty minutes or so in the healthy person. When the sun breath is flowing—that is, when the right nostril is dominant—one is advised to undertake the actions involving speech and instruction, as well as combat and physical exertion. These correspond to the linguistic functions associated with the left hemisphere, and the "active," competitive mode. When, on the other hand, the moon breath is dominant, one is advised to engage in painting, composing, listening to music, and other creative and artistic activities—that is, with functions associated more with the right hemisphere. The Tantrists also claim that when a person gains enlightenment, that is to say, when he is fully aware both inwardly and outwardly, the breath is found flowing equally in both nostrils. This presumably reflects the fact that such a person would be using both hemispheres of the brain in balance, rather than temporarily suppressing one in order to make full use of the other.

In terms of brain functioning a synthesis of the qualities associated with the left and right hemispheres implies a greater communication between the two hemispheres via the corpus callosum. Over its evolution the human brain has undergone a steady thickening of the corpus callosum. As a species we seem to be moving in the direction of greater communication between the two halves. A similar phenomenon seems to be happening at the level of individual evolution, personal development of awareness resulting in an increased communication between the hemispheres. There has over the past decade or so been widespread growth of interest in techniques of meditation and personal development. One such technique, which has attracted considerable attention from the scientific world, largely as a result of the wide availability of subjects, is the Transcendental Meditation technique. Much of the research has concentrated on changes taking place in the brain itself, and in 1975, Dr. Bernard Glueck, working at the Institute of Living in Hartford, Connecticut, found that the electroencephalogram (EEG) patterns of subjects practicing this technique showed an increased synchrony between the left and right sides of the brain—in other words, both sides appeared to be functioning together—which he suggested showed a much greater communication through the corpus callosum.[26]

This effect has since been borne out in a number of other laboratories in Europe and America.[27]

There are thus two principal ways in which the functioning of the right side of the brain can be brought into balance with that of the left. The meditation approach quiets the brain's activity and increases the communication between the two halves, permitting the right to function along with the left. The educational approach focuses more on developing the actual skills associated with the right. This latter approach is the one that will underlie most of the advice given in Part Two on how to make the most of your brain. The two approaches are not, however, in conflict: They are in fact complementary, the best results being achieved by following up both approaches. The one increases the brain's efficiency. The other helps you use that increased efficiency more fully still.

Figure 21

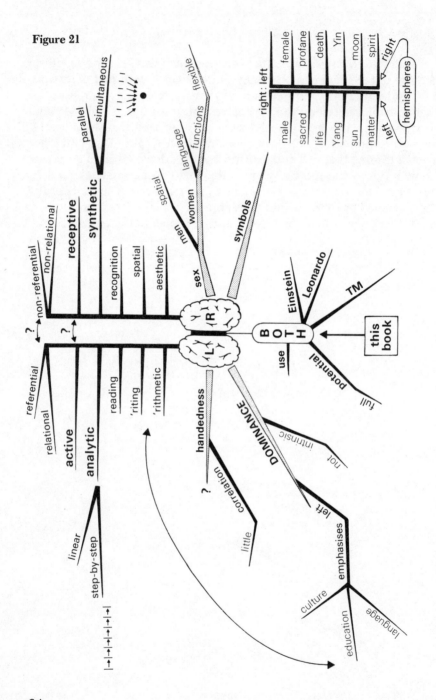

5.
The Ever-
Adaptable Brain

Do mental abilities decrease with age?
Do older people lose memory for recent events?
Can the adult brain compensate for serious damage?
Can the brain be reeducated after an accident?
Can neurons reproduce after all?
How can you make the most of your brain?

It is a common misconception that mental faculties begin to decline after about the age of twenty. Charts of mental abilities are often drawn to look like line *b* in Figure 22. There is said to be a steady increase in ability throughout childhood and youth, followed by a gradual falling off during adulthood. Several lines of research, however, show that this is not the case; one's mental potential continues to increase steadily throughout life, only beginning to tail off after about the age of sixty— and even this tailing off may not be necessary.

One reason sometimes cited for this supposed decline is that neurons are steadily dying off and never being replaced. This is itself a doubtful statement, but even if it were true, it is extremely unlikely that it would have any effect on mental abilities for the following reasons:

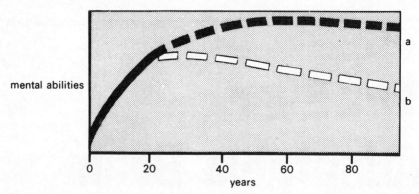

Figure 22 Growth of mental ability with age. (a) Potential continued growth with age. (b) Common misconception of mental ability decreasing after about 20 years.

1.   The brain contains some ten to twelve billion neurons, and even if neurons did die at the rate of a thousand a day less than 1 percent would be lost over an entire lifetime. In this respect the human brain deteriorates more slowly than any other organ in the body!

2.   When brain damage is very gradual, the loss of function is considerably reduced. To remove less than 1 percent of the brain's material cell by cell over a lifetime would have a negligible effect, if any, on mental abilities. Each time one cell died, the brain would be able to recover from the loss immediately.

3.   Since the cells that die would be distributed fairly evenly throughout the brain, their loss is unlikely to affect any specific function. Indeed, since there is already a very large degree of redundancy in the nervous system, it is most unlikely that the loss of this small number of cells would be noticed at all, whether it occurred slowly over a lifetime or in one instant.

Researchers have often been misled into assuming that mental abilities decrease with age because they failed to take into account the development of education over the years. A twenty-year-old person will probably have received a better education than a person of seventy. Thus a straight comparison of the current mental abilities of the two age groups would be measuring the difference in educational backgrounds as well as any intrinsic deterioration. When psychologists began to perform longitudinal studies—that is, studies that followed specific individuals throughout their lives—they found that as far as IQ was concerned there was no deterioration with age. Their scores on intelligence tests appeared to remain stable until the age of seventy. The only noticeable decrease in abilities was that after sixty, people were slower at tasks that involved physical movement as well as mental functioning.[1] In cases where intelligence and other mental abilities have been found to be declining, it was usually because of some sickness or physiological malfunction: It was not a deterioration of the brain itself.

Oxygen is essential to brain function. Although the brain amounts to only about 2 percent of the body's weight, it consumes 25 percent of the body's oxygen intake. If the oxygen supply is reduced, brain function suffers. If the supply is completely cut off for more than two or three minutes, the brain begins to deteriorate irreversibly.

As a person grows older, the arteries to the head, as well as those to the heart, may become clogged by arteriosclerosis as fats begin to build up inside the artery walls. In one study it was found that in people between fifty and eighty years old there was, on average, a 50-percent blockage of the arteries feeding the brain. This can seriously affect mental function. When the arteries of elderly patients were cleaned out, it was found that their IQ scores increased significantly—by 4.6 points on verbal comprehension, and by 12 points on perceptual organization. Measurements of their personality revealed a significant reduction in anxiety, suspicion, distress, disorientation, and feelings of nervousness.[2] Thus a major factor in mental deterioration may be simply the restriction of the oxygen supply to the brain.

Another factor that can decrease the oxygen available to the brain and so lead to a decrease in intellectual ability is high blood pressure. At Duke University a group of eighty-seven people in their sixties were studied over a period of ten years. Every two and a half years they were given a collection of psychological and physiological tests, including a measurement of blood pressure. It was found that those people who had very high blood pressure suffered a marked loss in mental abilities, whereas those with normal blood pressure showed no decline.[3]

Deliberately enriching the brain's supply of oxygen can also reverse any apparent deterioration of function in old people. Brief periods spent in an oxygen chamber can lead to a remarkable intellectual revitalization. Patients given short treatments twice a day for just fifteen days have been found to become more active, ask for reading material, and generally begin to become much more alert. Many were so improved that they were sent home.⁴

Expectancy and belief are confounding factors in any study of the effects of aging. If people are given to believe that mental potential is going to decrease after twenty, then it is very likely that it will. And if they are then told that they are doing as well as can be expected, and to take it easy, the decline will be reinforced. The human mind is remarkably adept at materializing its own beliefs, and graphs such as line *b* in Figure 22, if publicized in the national press as true (as they have been), soon appear to substantiate their own false conclusions.

Conversely, the realization that there is an enormous latent potential in the human brain that can be continually unfolded throughout adult life and even through old age can lead to the pattern of continued development shown in line *a* in Figure 22.

The choice is yours.

AGING AND MEMORY

Older people often claim that their memory for recent events is getting poorer, although they may be able to remember clearly events from their childhood.

Long-term memory is based largely on minute chemical changes in the brain and, chemically speaking, the brain is still very much prepared for learning through most of adulthood. RNA, a complex molecule intimately involved in the process of learning, does not decrease with age. In fact the RNA content in the brain is generally *increasing* throughout life: It usually does not show signs of decreasing until the sixties or seventies.⁵ So chemically there is no reason why learning abilities should decrease after the age of twenty.

In fact there is little experimental evidence to suggest that memory does decrease with age in the manner claimed. Many of the studies show the opposite. People of various ages have been tested on recall and recognition of prominent newspaper events that occurred during a period of about forty years preceding the study, and of photographs of well-known faces over a thirty-year span. In these cases no evidence has been found of the older people showing increased forgetting for recent events compared with earlier ones.⁶

Other studies have investigated whether there is any evidence of "living in the past" as far as *personal* memories are concerned. People were asked to name personal associations to common words and then estimate the original date of that association. It was found that the average age of remembered events tends to keep pace with chronological age. There is a slowly increasing lag such that the memories of a person aged one hundred would tend to cluster around the age of eighty. But this hardly constitutes living in the past: It is simply due to the fact that their long span of memory lowers the average age for remembered events. The fact that it is lowered to eighty rather than fifty or lower implies that the recalled episodes were coming more from the latter part of their lives.[7]

A possible reason why memory for recent events may appear to deteriorate in older people is that the brain remembers better those things that are especially outstanding. In childhood there are many more new, remarkable, and outstanding experiences than there are later in life, and these more "special" events are better remembered. Thus a person in a routine situation who does not encounter so much novel material may well find that things are not being remembered as well. In this case deliberately paying attention to what is going on and maintaining an interest in it can lead to a great improvement of memory. Every situation is unique. Be fully conscious of its uniqueness and your memory will not fail you.

RECOVERY OF FUNCTION

In chapter 2 it was shown that the human brain appears to be remarkably adaptable during the first two years of life. If some area of the young brain is damaged, or even removed, other areas of the brain will take over the functions of the damaged area and the child will usually grow up without any noticeable impairment.

There have been many instances of young children who were born with only one hemisphere, or who have had one side removed for medical reasons soon after birth. In such cases the remaining half of the brain has been found to take on the functions of the missing half as well as its own functions.[8] Children are occasionally born with no corpus callosum connecting the two hemispheres—a phenomenon known as agenesis. Yet most of these children grow up normally with no deterioration in function.[9] It appears that the brain compensates for the missing nerve fibers by rerouting the communications between the left and right hemispheres through other pathways lower down in the brain.

Such effects have been known for a long time and have usually
been explained by the fact that the brain is still growing and therefore
able to adjust to damage to any of its structures. But it has generally
been assumed that when the adult brain, or even that of a child over
three or four years old, receives similar damage, there cannot be a full
recovery of function, although the undamaged areas of the brain may
compensate to some extent for the damaged parts. It is, however, now
being realized that the adult brain can also show considerable plasticity.
It appears to be capable of remarkable readjustment and compensation,
and, given suitable rich and varied stimulation, will continue growing
and developing right through life.

There are many instances of people who have had large parts of
their brain damaged or destroyed, and who were at first seriously in-
capacitated, but who over time recovered many of the functions lost
at the time of injury. A typical case is of the American soldier who
received a massive brain wound in the Korean War. He lost all of the
area in the left hemisphere normally associated with speech. When
examined three months after the injury, he could speak only very
laboriously, in two-word sentences. When asked to read the phrase
"New York University College of Medicine," all that he could produce
was "doctors—little doctors." Yet when he was reexamined eight
years later and shown the same phrase he said, without the slightest
difficulty, "Is there a catch? It says 'New York University College of
Medicine.' "[10] The latent linguistic abilities of the right hemisphere,
which normally are suppressed by the stronger language faculty of
the left, appeared to take over and develop to such an extent that the
right hemisphere could carry on most of the functions previously gov-
erned by the left.

In the foregoing case the recovery happened without any specific program of retraining. When a brain-injured person is given
special retraining immediately after the injury, the spontaneous recovery of function is greatly enhanced. A young sailor in World War
II suffered a severe injury to the verbal cortex in the left hemisphere and as a result was only able to utter a few grunts. Instead of
being left to fend for himself, he was given an intensive retraining
program. After only one month the sailor had begun to speak again.
But he spoke his first few words in his original hillbilly dialect,
whereas the lady therapist spoke in a Yankee accent. At this point
the trainer wanted to resign because, she asserted, he was evidently
faking his condition.[11] She had, however misinterpreted his recov-

ery, which in this case would appear to be not a complete relearning of language so much as a fuller development of language areas, which had, up till then, been dormant.

In another case, examined at length by the Russian psychologist Aleksandr Luria, a young soldier who had received a severe head wound suffered impairment of vision, loss of memory and the ability to speak, read, or write. Reduced almost to infancy, the man resolved to reeducate himself all over again. Through continual perserverance he taught himself to recall and understand, to speak, then to read, and finally to write.[12] And he did all this without large parts of his brain and at a time in life when it had generally been thought that the brain was very set in its functions.

The more immediately the retraining follows the injury, the more effective it is. In cases where the retraining had to be delayed for several months the patients did not make such a quick nor such a successful recovery.[13]

A large number of small injuries have been found to be much less damaging than one major injury, even though the total effect of tiny injuries may destroy more brain tissue than the one sudden injury. Damage to the left hemisphere, for example, does not disrupt linguistic functions so seriously if the damage develops very slowly.[14] This fascinating aspect of gradual damage was demonstrated by removing the motor cortex of a monkey in small increments. After each small piece was removed, the monkey was given intensive exercise and training in walking, and even when hardly any of its motor cortex remained, the animal could still stand and walk.

Some of these findings have been applied with good effect to people who have had a stroke. After a stroke a person may be paralyzed to the extent that he is confined to a wheelchair and is often unable to speak coherently. In the past, very little was done in the way of retraining, and recovery was slow. Today, however, stroke patients are given maximum encouragement to exercise their limbs, taught to walk again, and given intensive speech therapy to help them regain their verbal abilities. Again, the sooner the retraining, the more effective it is.

These principles have also been used in helping young children overcome brain damage. Two American psychologists, Glen Doman and Carl Delecato, established the Institute for the Achievement of Human Potential in Philadelphia to help children who were physically handicapped as a result of some brain injury. Previously it was thought that such children rarely, if ever, overcame their defects. Doman and Delecato's approach concentrated on training the parents in how best to help their handicapped child cope with and surmount their problems. The parents of a partially paralyzed child would be shown how to manipulate his limbs so as to help the brain learn better how to control them. As a result many, though not all, such children started crawling and walking. Others who were mute began to speak, and in many cases IQ scores increased dramatically. In one case a child with a whole hemisphere missing was brought up to the level of the normal child of his age.[16]

Doman realized that if such recoveries were possible with brain-damaged children, even more should be possible with normal children. So he went on to apply his methods to ordinary children, and with equally astounding results. Many children have learned to read by the age of two and showed a greater general emotional development than other children of the same age.[17]

A similar approach has been taken by Moshe Feldenkreis from Israel. He believes in reeducating the motor areas of the brain by manipulating the muscles, thus giving the brain direct experience of how it should control them. At a demonstration of his technique in London, he took a fifty-year-old man who had been a spastic all his life and, by very gently moving the limbs this way and that, taught the brain a much smoother control of the muscles. After just one hour of such treatment the man stood up and walked smoothly just like a normal person, tears of joy running down his face. A miracle? No. Simply the combination of a very sensitive therapist and an awareness of the possibilities open to the adult human brain given the correct retraining.[18]

Another interesting example of recovery of function concerns the split-brain patients discussed in the previous chapter. At the time of the operation there appeared to be a distinct localization of function—verbal skills, for example, residing predominantly in the left hemisphere and visual-spatial skills in the right. Ten years after the original operations, however, each side of the brain had largely recovered from the loss of the other half. The left side had developed visual-spatial skills and other faculties associated with the right hemisphere, whereas the right had developed linguistic abilities. This recovery occurred without any retraining. When suitable reeducation *is* given, the right hemisphere can learn to read and write much faster—in less than six months.[19]

NEURON REGENERATION

The brain's ability to recover from serious injury raises the question of whether or not neurons can regenerate themselves. Until recently this possibility was not generally accepted, it being thought that recovery of function was due principally to the development of innate potentials in other areas of the brain and to gradual recovery from shock caused by the injury. Recent findings, however, suggest that after damage neurons may well be capable of growing new fibers and even of reproducing themselves.

Studies of the effects of brain damage in rats show that the damaged areas do not remain empty but that nearby neurons move into the damaged area, filling up the vacancy.[20] Damage to the visual system of hamsters has been found to lead to a positive redirection of nerve fibers and with them the formation of many new synapses, all of which functioned competently.[21] Other studies have shown that when axons in certain areas of the brain are cut, the end that is still attached to the cell body rapidly starts growing large numbers of tiny sprouts. These sprouts spread out through the nervous system reestablishing contacts with the stranded synapses until all the original connections are restored.[22] Although it was known that such regeneration could occur in the peripheral nerves running from the muscles and sensory organs to the brain, this was the first time it had been found in the brain itself.

There is also the possibility that neurons may actually reproduce themselves after damage. Although neurons do not normally multiply, they do, nevertheless, have the genetic potential for reproduction. In some way this potential is being inhibited in the normal nervous system. Experiments suggest this inhibiting factor may be connected with the electrical state of the cell. Neurons subjected to electrical depolarization (i.e., reduction of the electrical potential across the cell wall) will sometimes begin to divide and reproduce just as other cells do.[23] Neurons can also be induced to reproduce themselves if placed in a medium enriched in potassium ions.[24] This change in ion concentration affects the cellular membranes in the same way as direct electrical depolarization.

These are exciting findings and ones that may revolutionize our thinking about neurons. It has not yet been ascertained whether or not such regeneration can occur in the normal nervous system, but the brain always appears to make the maximum use of the possibilities open to it and one of the most likely places to find such changes in nerve cell membranes would be in damaged tissue.

MAKING THE MOST OF YOUR BRAIN

The research on recovery of function gives a most instructive insight into the adult brain's latent potentials for continued development. If the seriously injured brain is capable of such remarkable recoveries, new areas developing the damaged faculties and neurons growing to regenerate damaged connections, what is the normal intact brain capable of? Can the adult brain draw upon these latent faculties of growth and development without having to go through the traumas of brain injury?

The answer is almost certainly yes.

Moreover, since the healthy intact brain is not handicapped by injured areas and missing connections, its potential for further development is considerably greater than that of the damaged brain. In order to help this natural potential unfold, there are two things you should do:

1.   Use your brain

2.   Care for your brain

Using Your Brain.   The adult brain, like the young child's, thrives on experience. If we are to make the fullest use of its innate potential and continue to grow in mental abilities throughout life, it is essential we give our brains as rich, as varied, and as stimulating an environment as possible. One of the principal reasons that mental faculties appear to drop off after about the age of twenty is that formal education ceases around this age and we do not provide the brain with so many challenges and exercises. After leaving school, or college, many people stop using their brains as much, and with this comes an apparent decline of the brain's potential. Like any other organ, the brain atrophies if not in constant use.

Education, coming from the Latin *e-ducare,* means literally "to lead out," to bring out one's full potential. If the full potential has not been developed by the age of twenty—and it never has—then education should continue. There should be continued learning, continued mental challenges, and continued mental exercise.

The extent to which enriched stimulation can affect the structure of rat brains has been demonstrated by the work of Mark Rosenzweig's team at the University of California. They put groups of rats in environments full of such playthings as ladders, wheels, ramps, rungs, etc., and found that the richer surroundings led to an increase in both the weight and the thickness of the cerebral cortex. Further work at the University of California showed that fully mature rats gained as great an increase in the weight of their cortex as did young rats.[25]

Rosenzweig and his team have since investigated whether the increased growth in the brain came merely from seeing an enriched surrounding or from actively interacting with the environment. They divided their rats into three groups: "enriched" rats, who were allowed to play freely in their complex environment; "observer" rats, who were able to see the enriched environment but not interact with it; and a control group, who lived in an impoverished environment. After one month of this treatment the animals' brains were examined. It was found that the "observer" rats, who had merely perceived the enriched environment but not interacted with it, did not show the same significant increase in brain weight as did the "enriched" rats—in fact, they did not differ significantly from the impoverished group.[26]

One reason rats are often used as experimental animals is that their nervous system is in many basic ways similar to the human nervous system. Applying Rosenzweig's work to the human situation, we might infer that just living in an enriched environment is not enough—we need to interact with it actively in as many ways as possible if our brains are to benefit from it. Watching television may, if you watch the right channels, provide diverse stimulation, but it is generally passive stimulation and is not going to be of great benefit to the brain's development. Much better is directly interacting with the world, with other good minds, investigating new fields (and integrating them with the old), exercising your mind whenever possible, drawing on your resources, setting yourself challenges, and enjoying it all.

The truth of this is borne out by people who have continued with their education throughout life. Research scientists, university lecturers, and polymaths who have applied themselves to numerous problems and continually drawn upon their resources and their knowledge of many different fields of study show no apparent deterioration in mental abilities. They show thriving alert minds right through into old age. Albert Einstein, one of the most creative intellects of human history, pursued his theoretical work right up until his death at the age of seventy-seven. Bertrand Russell, the philosopher, mathematician, historian, politician, and polemic, displayed an outstanding memory, was still writing at a prodigious pace and playing a major role in world affairs at the age of ninety-five. Similarly Carl Jung's mind was very alert and productive in his old age. Michelangelo was still creating masterpieces at the age of eighty—and at a time when the average life expectancy was only thirty-five. Rembrandt was at his apex in the final years of his life. Cezanne, Turner, and Picasso likewise maintained their talents in old age. Gauguin did not begin painting till he was thirty-five but continued for the rest of his life. Bach, Brahms, Haydn, Tchaikovsky, and Britten were all composing excellent work in their last years. George Bernard Shaw's mind was as acute and penetrating at the age of ninety-four as it was at thirty. Similarly, Wordsworth, Tennyson, and D. H. Lawrence showed little if any deterioration of mental abilities in their later years.

The moral is: If you want to get the most from your brain, use it; make the most of it!

Some of the ways in which this can be done will be discussed in Part Two.

Caring for Your Brain. Regular exercise is invaluable to the brain. In the short term it increases the oxygen supply, and in the long term helps keep the arteries clear. In a six-year-long Canadian study of three hundred school children it was found that those who did additional physical exercise each day and were fitter physically also received higher grades in their academic work.[27] Exercise can also directly affect personality. Regular jogging and physical training lead not only to physical fitness but also to increased emotional stability, increased imagination, and increased self-sufficiency.[28]

Regular rest is also vital for mental functioning. The human nervous system works on a regular alternation of action and rest and is accurately attuned to this cycle. Disrupting the cycle disrupts the brain's natural daily rhythms. During sleep, particularly during dreaming periods, proteins and other chemicals in the brain used up during the day are being replenished. The body also grows during sleep. As adults we may cease growing taller, but the cells in the body are continually being replaced, and most of this growth takes place during the night.

Rest is valuable during the day as well. Taking regular breaks during reading or study improves both comprehension and memory. In addition, such techniques of deep relaxation as Transcendental Meditation, when practiced as a regular part of the daily routine, have been shown to lead to fuller use of mental abilities.

In a simple measure of reaction time, people were asked to press a button as soon as a light came on, and it was found that those practicing TM had reacted faster—0.3 seconds as compared with 0.5 seconds for the control group.[29] Another study measured meditators' ability to guide a metal ball through a complex maze by tilting the board on which the ball rolls. This game requires accurate perception as well as quick and accurate motor responses. Subjects who had been practicing TM performed much better at the task than other people, and their performance increased after a meditation period.[30] Other work has shown that the intelligence growth rate of young children increases with TM. Learning ability, memory, problem solving, and creativity also improve.[31]

As far as food is concerned, a regular, well-balanced diet is good for brain functioning in general. In particular, vitamin E, which increases cell oxygenization, helps nerve cells to make better use of the oxygen available. (The best sources of vitamin E are whole wheat, whole grains and cold-pressed vegetable oils made from seeds—e.g., sunflower seed oil.) Vitamin B and vitamin C can increase mental alertness, and vitamin D helps the assimilation of minerals such as calcium, magnesium, and iodine, which in turn increase alertness. Most vitamins can be obtained from fresh vegetables and fruit. Vegetables should be eaten raw sometimes, as part of a salad, say, since some of the vitamins are decomposed by cooking, especially by stewing.

Natural foods are generally more nourishing than preprocessed goods. Moreover artificial preservatives and dyes have in several cases been shown to be harmful to the brain. Other things to avoid are too much sugar and starch, which can lead to mental dullness, and excess caffeine, alcohol, and other unnecessary drugs.

Food requires thought as much as thought requires food. So think before you eat, and you will eat and think better.

Figure 23

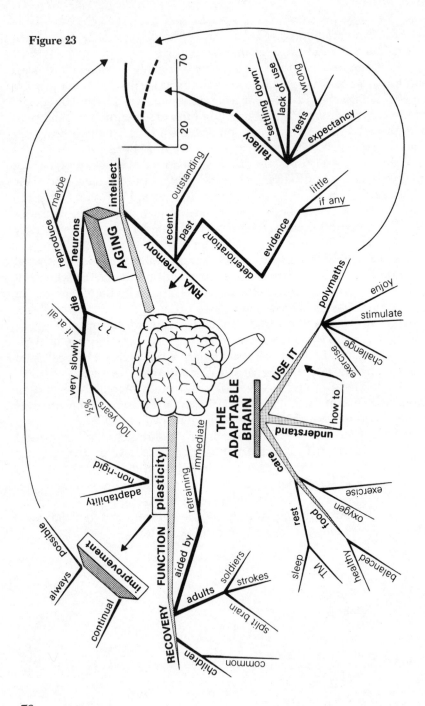

Part Two
FUNCTION AND POTENTIAL

6.
The Psychology of Memory

Are there different types of memory?
How quickly do we forget?
Can unforgetting occur?
What do we remember best?
Is it good to break study with rest periods?
Does warming up first help?
Why are outstanding things remembered best?
Does "chunking" help?

Memory is undoubtedly one of the most important human faculties. Without it there would be no learning from experience, no intellectual functioning, no development of language, nor any of the qualities that are generally associated with being human. Yet, with the possible exception of consciousness itself, memory remains the most mysterious of the mind's faculties. Despite the fact that more research has been devoted to the study of memory than to any other mental function, comparatively little is known about how the mind remembers things, and why it also appears to forget.

Memory is often thought of as the ability to recall past events. If someone were asked to remember what he ate for lunch yesterday, he would probably be able to give a brief description, and if we were to check back with what he had actually eaten, it would be possible to see how well he had "remembered" it.

Memory, however, is more than just the ability to recall. If the same person were asked what he ate for lunch a year ago, he would probably be very unlikely to recall it. Yet if we could remind him of what he actually ate, he might well say, "Ah yes, now I remember." He would recognize the items and could still be said to have retained some memory of the event. Thus retention does not necessarily imply recall.

If, after reminding him of an event or situation—in this case a luncheon—he still failed to recognize it, this would not necessarily mean that he had no memory of it. It might well happen that under hypnosis he would be able to recall details of the meal perfectly. There may be many events and experiences that are recorded in memory but that cannot immediately be recalled or recognized. Indeed, as will be shown in chapter 12, there is growing evidence that the brain may record everything that is ever experienced.

THE VARIETIES OF MEMORABLE EXPERIENCES

Memory can be divided into several different types:

Episodic Memory. The memory for past episodes and events in one's life, such as tripping over the cat.

Factual Memory. The memory for facts, such as that the Battle of Hastings took place in 1066, or that Einstein formulated the theory of relativity. These are not actual episodes in one's life, though they will have been learned as the result of numerous little episodes at school, in reading, and at other times.

Semantic Memory. The memory for meaning. We remember that a "butterfly" is an insect with four large brightly colored wings, and that "smooth" describes a certain tactile sensation, as well as having several other meanings. The average person remembers several hundred thousand words and meanings.

Sensory Memory. Most people have a strong visual memory, being able, whether they believe it or not, to remember several thousand faces, probably seeing most of them clearly "in the mind's eye." Many will also be able to remember the sound of favorite pieces of music, or the smell of some tasty dish.

Skills. Skills also involve memory. A person remembers how to get dressed, drive a car, or throw a ball. Even walking and speaking are skills learned early on in life.

Instinctive Memory. The newborn baby "remembers" to suck at its mother's breast, and the adult brain "remembers" how to breathe, sleep, digest, etc. The bases of many such memories are inherited and stored in the genes. This genetic memory also specifies many individual characteristics, both physical and mental.

Collective Memory. Psychologists such as Carl Jung have suggested that we may also have access to collective race memories. These appear, mainly in dreams, as archetypal symbols that are very similar for large numbers of people, though outside their normal experience of life.

Past-Life Memory. Some people appear to be able to "remember" events from before their birth, sometimes from many centuries before. Under hypnosis it is possible to examine this phenomenon more fully, and it is often found that the "memories" do correlate with actual happenings in the life of an individual in the past—though the subject may have no knowledge of that individual's existence.

There is hardly a moment in our lives when memory is not playing a crucial role, and the more we understand how it functions, the more we can help ourselves at work, at home, in play, and in study, both with others and on our own.

THE EBBINGHAUS EXPERIMENTS

The first experimental investigations of memory were carried out by Hermann Ebbinghaus in Germany from 1879 to 1885. Ebbinghaus realized that memory is powerfully affected by meaning and association, and in order to control for these factors, he decided to use words that had no meaning or association. So he made up lists of nonsense syllables. Using himself as a subject, he spent six years in arduous experiments learning and relearning thousands of such lists.

His method was to take a list of nonsense syllables (e.g., TAJ, ZIN, DEC, RAX, DAK, JAF, HUQ) and set about remembering it by what he called the anticipation method. He would first read the list through to himself at a steady rate. Then, going back to the beginning, he would try to anticipate the first word, check whether his anticipation was correct, then try to anticipate the second word, and then the third, and so on until the end of the list. Having gone through the list once, he would go back to the beginning and start again. He repeated this procedure until he could go through the whole list anticipating each syllable correctly, recording how long the whole process took.

In a typical experiment he learned eight lists of thirteen nonsense syllables. After a given lapse of time he learned one of the lists again. By comparing the relearning time with the original learning time, he was able to estimate how much of the original had been retained. By relearning different lists after differing intervals of time, he was able to trace how retention decayed. In order to analyze the results statistically, he collected many sets of results, subjecting himself to the lengthy learning procedure no less than 163 times!

Ebbinghaus's results are summarized in Figure 24. They show a rapid initial decrease in memory followed by a gradual tailing off over the following days and nights. Most forgetting occurs immediately after learning. It will be seen that even one hour afterward more than half the original had been forgotten. Nine hours afterward about 60 percent of the original had been lost, and one month afterward 80 percent had gone.[1]

Ebbinghaus also investigated how the amount of time spent in learning affected retention. In some cases he stopped going through the lists before learning was complete; in others he kept on going through them even after having learned them perfectly. When he retested himself twenty-four hours later, he found that the more trials there were in the original learning, the less trials were needed to relearn the lists. Even when he had continued going through the lists after the

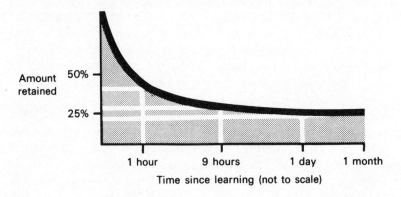

Figure 24 Curve of forgetting, after Ebbinghaus.

learning was complete, he found that relearning was still easier and that the extra trials had not been wasted.

One of Ebbinghaus's major contributions to psychology was to show that a seemingly insoluble problem could be approached experimentally, provided the situation was reduced to a few measurable essentials. In using nonsense syllables he had attempted to eliminate the effect of meaning and association, which are difficult factors to evaluate. Yet in this also lies a clue for the further development of memory. By stripping away meaning and association Ebbinghaus had effectively stripped away all that was most valuable to memory.

Numerous other experimenters since Ebbinghaus have found the same general curve of forgetting; but they have also found that the more meaning, organization, and association there is in the material, the less steep is the curve. And shortly we shall see that, by taking the opposite approach to Ebbinghaus and making the maximum use of these other factors, it is possible to produce a "forgetting" curve that does not decay with time but remains a straight line near the 100-percent level. That is to say, there is virtually no forgetting.

THE REMINISCENCE EFFECT

There is one major modification that should be added to the general curve of forgetting. For a short period after the initial learning the memory may improve a little rather than decrease. This effect, which is the opposite to forgetting, is known as the reminiscence effect. It has been found that children who were given a poem to learn but not allowed to learn it to perfection remembered it better a day after learning than they did initially, often being able to recall lines they had not been able to remember at the time of learning.[2]

The reminiscence effect has been looked at by a number of different psychologists and in a number of different situations. Although it is a fairly common occurrence, it is not present in all learning situations. It seems to depend upon the nature of the material being learned, the method of testing, and the activities a person is engaged in between the initial learning and the retesting.

The time between learning and reminiscence also varies considerably. In a paired-associate test, in which subjects are presented with a list of paired words and tested for recall a little time later by being given the first word of the pair and asked to name the second, it is found that the reminiscence effect is strongest after about half a minute.[3] In learning lists of nonsense syllables, reminiscence has been found to be highest after about one minute.[4] Memory for photographs of faces was found to be best one and a half minutes after the initial viewing.[5] And in mechanical tasks reminiscence has been found to occur ten minutes after the initial learning.[6] It has also been found that the more meaningful the material and the greater a person's interest in it, the stronger is the effect. It is, for example, stronger with poems than with lists of abstract words, and stronger still if the poem is an interesting one.[7]

The exact reasons for the reminiscence effect are still not clear. Numerous theories have been put forward over the last fifty years, but none have satisfactorily explained all aspects of the phenomenon.[8] Inhibition theories suggest that during the initial learning recall performance is impeded by the task of learning, but that this effect dissipates afterward. According to this hypothesis it is not an improvement in retention that is being observed but a temporary improvement in recall. Consolidation theory, on the other hand, suggests that during the rest period the memory trace itself is being strengthened. The memory is being integrated and reinforced with other memories, and this unconscious processing adds to the permanence and strength of the record.

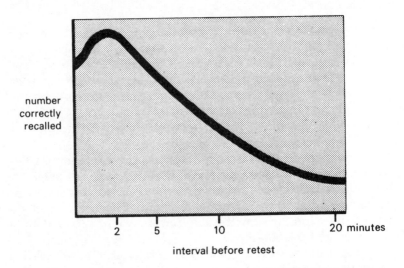

Figure 25 Forgetting curve for nonsense syllables showing reminiscence after 2 minutes. The improvement in recall is usually between 5 and 10 percent.

AN EXPERIMENT

Before going on to investigate how memory works, it will be useful for you to perform a simple experiment. The results will illustrate several important factors in memory. First, find yourself a pencil or something else to write with. Then read through the following list of words just once. Do not study them, just read each to yourself:

water, life, dog, line, home, mouse,
field, balls, rabbit, apple, sheep, head,
bone, year, goat, Maharishi, hill,
oar, donkey, shape, crop, wind, pig,
tool, cow, door, stone, flower, cat.

On the next page you will find a blank space. Write there as many of the words as you can remember, in whatever order they come to you. (If you feel bad about writing in books, a sheet of paper will do.)

PRIMACY AND RECENCY

You are unlikely to have recalled the whole of the list (for those who have, we shall be dealing with photographic memory shortly). Among the words that you have written down you will probably find that there are more from the beginning and end of the list. You are more likely to have recalled *water, life, flower,* and *cat* than *year* and *wind.* The increased probability of recalling the first two or three items is called the *primacy effect;* and that of recalling the last few items is called the *recency effect.* The two effects are shown together in Figure 26, in what is called a serial position curve.

The exact shape of the curve depends on a number of variables, such as the length of the list, the nature of the list—whether it is words, pictures, prose, or the learning of skills—and how much the person organizes the material to be learned and thereby improves memory throughout. In some cases primacy is the strongest effect, in others recency.[9] In any event, the general finding that the beginning and end of a learning session are remembered better occurs again and again in many different learning situations.

In the case of lectures the curve has been found to be more like that of Figure 27. Memory is good for material at the beginning of the

Write below as many words as you can remember from the list on the previous page.

lecture, being best a few minutes after the start. It gradually tails off during the lecture, but improves markedly again at the end.[10]

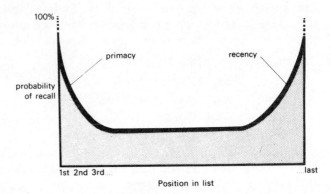

Figure 26 Serial position curve showing primacy and recency effects.

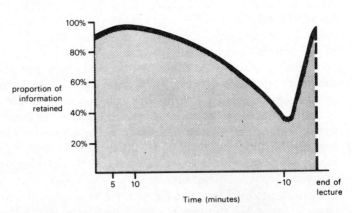

Figure 27 Recall during lecture. Memory for the beginning and end of lecture is almost perfect, but it tails off increasingly rapidly in the middle. (From E. J. Thomas, *Studies in Adult Education*, April, 1972. Reprinted with permission.)

DISTRIBUTION OF LEARNING

Ebbinghaus found that when he introduced short rest intervals between successive periods of practice, his learning efficiency improved. This was puzzling at first: It was expected that the rest periods would lead to forgetting and hence to reduced learning. The reason for the increase, it was later realized, lay partly in the reminiscence effect.

Immediately after learning, the memory was actually improving, so that when he returned to the task, more rather than less of the material was available as a basis for further learning. Supporting evidence for this comes from the finding that the greater the reminiscence effect, the greater the value of taking short breaks.[11]

The primacy and recency effects are two other factors that enhance the value of taking breaks. A single period of learning benefits from primacy and recency only at the start and finish. If the session is broken into a number of smaller blocks, with short breaks in between, there are more times at which primacy and recency effects can occur.

THE WARM-UP EFFECT

In physical activity a person always performs better when he has had a chance to warm up a little. The same is true of most mental activities. A warm-up effect is especially noticeable in learning where it has been found that retention is enhanced if a person has performed a similar task immediately beforehand. If, for example, people are given three lists of paired adjectives to learn (e.g. *blue–round; soft–high; . . .*) they will learn the second list faster than the first, and the third faster than the second, despite the fact that the lists are unrelated.[12]

A brief warm-up just before relearning has also been found to be very beneficial. In one experiment two groups of subjects were given lists of paired adjectives to learn. After twenty-four hours one group was given a short warm-up task before relearning, the other was not. The surprising thing was not that the warm-up group showed better retention, but that they showed *no forgetting, even improving slightly!*[13] In this case it would appear that, in addition to having a warm-up effect, the short practice before relearning had reestablished the appropriate mental "set" (see page 203)—that is, their minds were "set" for the particular task to come. The implication is that much apparent forgetting may be simply due to changing one "set" for another.

THE VON RESTORFF EFFECT

In the memory experiment you did earlier most of you will have recalled *Maharishi*—it stood out from the rest of the list. This tendency to remember outstanding elements in a list is called the von Restorff effect.

Von Restorff found that three digit numbers were better learned if presented within a list of nonsense syllables than if surrounded by other numbers.[14] Thus in the first of the following lists the three-digit number is remembered better than the nonsense syllables, while in the second list the nonsense syllable is remembered better than the numbers:

TAJ	532
ZIN	147
DEC	938
RAX	HUQ
378	706
DAK	594
JAF	821

The effect has since been found to be true in any situation in which items stand out in some way from those around them, or are in any way surprising. Thus a brightly colored picture is better remembered than the black and white ones surrounding it, and the tall girl with husky voice will stick in your memory better than many other people.

One possible explanation is that the outstanding elements increase a person's attention, which in turn leads to better memory. An investigation of this possibility measured the galvanic skin response, a physiological measure of arousal, which was indeed found to increase significantly when the outstanding item was presented, though this does not prove conclusively that the increased arousal was also responsible for the improved recall.[15]

You may possibly find that you also remembered the words *goat* and *hill*—words positioned on either side of *Maharishi*. The higher arousal created by the outstanding word also effects the retention of those words close to it in the learning sequence. Thus the serial position curve of Figure 26 can be modified to include high retention for outstanding items and their neighbors:

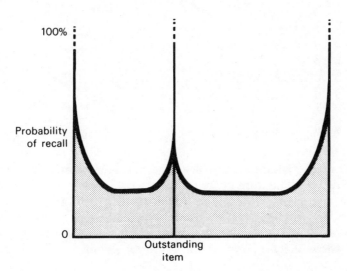

Figure 28 High recall of outstanding items, and increased recall of their neighbors.

THE MAGIC NUMBER SEVEN

In a memorable paper called "The Magic Number Seven, Plus or Minus Two," George Miller from Harvard showed that the immediate memory span appears to be limited in the number of items that it can hold.[16] He briefly presented people with short lists and immediately asked them to recall as many as they could. He found that whatever the items—whether they were numbers, words, colors, musical tunes, or any other items—most people could not correctly recall lists that had more than about seven items in them. To see this for yourself try remembering each of the following sequences of numbers. Just read each line through at a normal reading pace. Don't study them or try to remember them, just read each line through quickly and then look away or close your eyes and see how much of it you can remember. Or even better, if you have somebody else around, get them to read each list quickly aloud to you and see how many you remember each time.

```
3  8  7  4
5  1  3  4  9
6  2  8  7  4  1
9  5  0  2  1  3  6
2  9  4  0  1  7  5  8
3  0  1  4  9  6  8  2  5
1  4  9  2  5  3  1  7  8  4
```

It doesn't matter what the items are, whether they are numbers, words, or anything else. The immediate memory span seems to be somewhere around seven items. Thus if the list of words given on page 87 had been only seven words long or less, you would probably have recalled it all correctly and in the correct order. As it was, you probably only recalled a few of them, and even then probably not in the order presented.

Miller suggested that the immediate memory span was not limited by the amount of information contained in each item, but by the number of "chunks" that had to be remembered. In this respect, *4, dog,* and ☐ are all single chunks. Immediate memory seems to have the capacity for about seven separate chunks, and anything much more than this is lost.

Since it is the number of chunks that limits the immediate memory rather than the actual information content, it follows that effective memory span can be increased by reorganizing the material into larger (but not more) chunks. In his article Miller quotes an experiment by Sidney Smith in which he taught twenty subjects to recode items into larger chunks. He started with strings of binary digits—that is, strings of zeroes and ones—and found an average memory span of nine digits. Subjects were then taught to recode the digits in pairs renaming 00 as 0, 01 as 1, 10 as 2, and 11 as 3. Thus 10110100 would be recoded as 2, 3, 1, 0, and reduced from eight to four chunks. Once subjects had mastered the recoding, their binary digit span nearly doubled. Grouping in triplets, and recoding as the numbers 0 through to 7, they could increase their spans still further. Since the immediate memory span is seven, one would expect a capacity of around twenty-one binary digits after recoding in triplets. The increase was not, however, quite this large. This was possibly due to the extra load imposed by the encoding process itself.

To go further required considerable study, so Smith decided to follow the Ebbinghaus tradition and use himself as a subject. He learned recoding systems for binary digits in groups of four and groups of five, in the manner shown in Figure 29. His immediate memory span was larger than most people's, and he was able to remember about fourteen binary digits. When the digits were encoded in pairs, he could remember eighteen binary digits (nine chunks); in triplets, he could remember thirty-two binary digits (ten chunks); in quadruplets, forty (ten chunks). No extra value was gained from recoding in groups of five; his maximum span stayed at forty, (see Figure 30).

Now this is not just trickery. The mind remembers the number of chunks rather than the total amount of information. So organizing material into chunks is in fact helping the memory. Chunking is so natural that most people do it anyway without realizing it. Given the number 572317482, a person would probably regroup it as 572,317,482 and remember it as five hundred and seventy-two million, three hundred and seventeen thousand, four hundred and eighty-two. In doing this not only has a nine-figure number become three groups of three, but the individual digits have been given different tags—572 has become five hundred and seventy-two million rather than just five-seven-two million—which again helps memory. This is why we usually split telephone numbers up into several chunks; in the United States as 418-325-7162, and in many European countries as 41 83 25-71-62. Chunking in this way makes it easier to remember the list of ten digits, and when it comes to recalling a number, one recalls it chunk by chunk—area code, followed by exchange, followed by number.

Shown a long word such as *antidisestablishmentarianism,* people do not generally remember it as a sequence of twenty-eight letters— that would far exceed most people's immediate memory span. Instead, the letters are grouped together and stored as a number of larger units, probably something like *anti-dis-establish-ment-arian-ism.* Each part, being a familiar pattern, is treated as a single chunk. As children, most people did not learn the alphabet as a monotonous sequence from *A* to *Z*, but as organized units and subunits. The exact organization varies from one person to another; for some it may be *abcd, efg, hijk, lmnop, qrs, tuv, wx-yz;* for others, *abc, de-fg, hi-jk, lm, no-pq, rs-tu, vw-xyz.* This chunking reduced it to a smaller number of parts, and the patterns and rhythms set up also helped make it much easier to learn.

When listening to a story, people do not usually remember every word that is spoken: They build up themes and subthemes, extracting the essential features of the story. It is these larger units

Binary digits:	1 0 1 1 0 1 0 0 1 1 1 0
Grouped in twos:	10 – 11 – 01 – 00 – 11 – 10
Recoded as:	2 3 1 0 3 2
Grouped in threes:	101 – 101 – 001 – 110
Recoded as:	5 5 1 6
Grouped in fours:	1011 – 0100 – 1110
Recoded as:	11 4 14

Figure 29 Recoding of binary digits (sequences of 0s and 1s in twos, threes, and fours). Each pair of binary digits can be equated with a number between 0 and 3 (inclusive); each triplet with a number between 0 and 7; and each quadruplet with a number between 0 and 15. Recoding in this way decreases the number of "chunks" to be remembered. "11, 4, 14" is more easily retained than "101101001110."

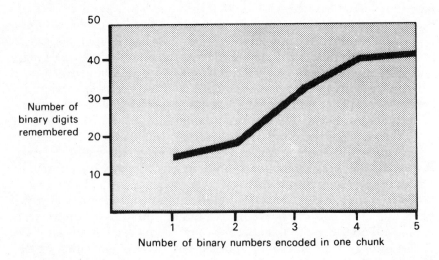

Number of binary digits remembered

Number of binary numbers encoded in one chunk

Figure 30 Effect of recoding into larger chunks on immediate memory span for binary numbers.

that are remembered. When later the story is recalled, these ideas are expanded, with varying degrees of success, into a word-by-word account.

APPLICATIONS AND ADVICE

Breaks. Any period of study or learning is best broken down into smaller chunks, with short breaks between each session. The actual size of each chunk will depend upon the type of material being studied. In practice, it is found that somewhere between fifteen and forty-five minutes is the best. If the chunk becomes too small, there is not sufficient meaning and internal coherence to gain a proper understanding of the material, and if it is too large, the full benefit of taking breaks is lost.

As to the question of how long the break should be, something of the order of five to ten minutes is best. It has been found that learning improves when the time between blocks is increased from thirty seconds to ten minutes, but no further improvement is gained by increasing the break period further.[17]

This finding can be understood in terms of the reminiscence effect. After a few minutes break, recall of the material actually will

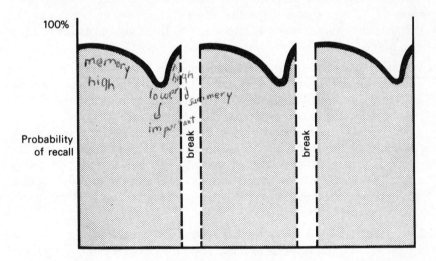

Figure 31 Retention curve when regular short breaks are taken.

have risen. Thus when one returns to study, he will remember *more* of the previous session than if he had simply gone straight ahead without a break, and comprehension and memory of the next section will be correspondingly improved. When regular short breaks are taken, the retention curve of Figure 27 changes to look like that of Figure 31.

The first thing to do when you sit down for a period of study is to plan the time, deciding how often you are going to break and when. And having done so, keep approximately to the schedule.

At certain times when you should be taking a break the study may be going excellently and it might seem tempting to continue on. In fact it is still better to take a break. It has been found that interrupting a task in which a person has become involved can lead to higher recall of the material—an effect known as the Zeigarnik effect after its discoverer.[18] Also, despite the fact that the understanding may be very good, the later recall of the material will be worse if the mind is not given a short break. *Understanding is not the same as remembering.*

During the breaks themselves you should take a complete rest from the type of work under study. If you merely switch to something similar, not only is the mind not given a real break, but numerous interfering associations will be made that will impede later recall. The best thing to do is to relax both mentally and physically and take some fresh air. The rest also helps the mind consolidate and organize the information gained, and it is important to let it get on with this in its own way.

Warm-Up. As far as study is concerned, a few minutes spent reviewing previous knowledge of the field and establishing what you want to know will have the dual effect both of warming you up to study and of "setting" your mind to the particular field concerned.

This also applies to the short breaks taken during a session. On returning to the study always spend a minute or two going over the previous session(s)—even though you only stopped five minutes previously. This quick review warms you up again and reestablishes mental set, bringing the memory of the previous section, now at maximum reminiscence, to the fore.

Lecturing, Giving Talks. Including regular breaks in a teaching or lecturing situation is going to make the subject more enjoyable as well as better remembered.

Since people will tend to recall the beginnings and ends of the session, it is best to try to arrange the material so that the most important points come when the memory is particularly high (see Figure 24). The high recall at the end can be used both to summarize the main points and to present a preview of important points to come after the break or in the next lecture.

In the middle of the lecture, particularly during the second half, when memory is at its lowest, it is good to give greater emphasis to important points, making them more outstanding—perhaps with visual aids or examples—to compensate for the lower recall.

The von Restorff Effect. This can be used to improve memory in a number of ways. Whenever you want to remember something, deliberately make the idea *stand out:*

- Exaggerate it. The more bizarre an idea is, the more arousing it is, and the more clear will be the memory.
- In writing or note taking, use outlining, bold print, color, and anything else that will make important points stand out.
- When reading, underline important points.
- Everything is unique. Emphasize its uniqueness in your mind, how it is different from everything else.

Figure 32

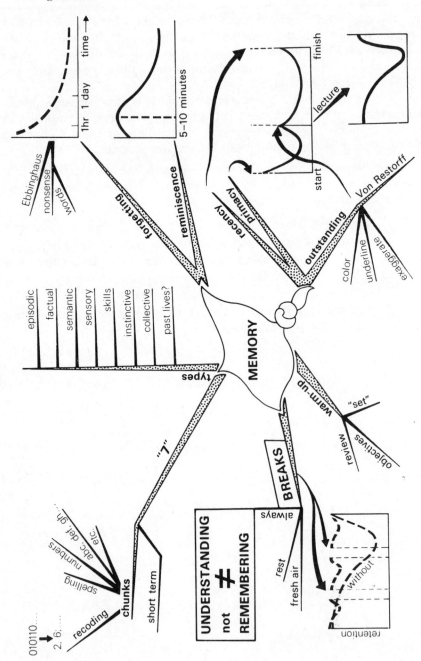

7.
Association and Organization in Memory

Why are associations important in memory?
Why is organization important?
How does principle seeking help memory?
Is principle seeking better than rote learning?
Why are meaning and significance important?
Does sleep learning work?

The power of association was realized by Sir Francis Galton in 1879. That year effectively marked the birth of experimental psychology: In Germany, Wilhelm Wundt, from Leipzig, established the first laboratory exclusively devoted to psychological studies, while Ebbinghaus was beginning his six-year experiment on the rate of forgetting. In the same year Sir Francis Galton took a walk down Pall Mall in London, a length of some 450 yards, and while he walked, he let his mind generate associations to everything he saw. During the walk he counted some three hundred objects on which his attention rested for a while, and recorded a considerably greater number of associative images. He wrote afterward:[1] "Samples of my whole life had passed before me. . . . Many bygone incidents, which I have never suspected to have formed part of my stock of thoughts, had been glanced at as objects too familiar to awaken the attention. I saw at once that the brain was vastly more active than I had previously believed it to be, and I was perfectly amazed at the unexpected width of the field of its everyday operations."

Many of us have probably received similar insights into the role of association in memory. When we cannot remember a friend's name, we may go through the alphabet trying first *A,* then *B,* then *C* and so on until the name is suddenly remembered. There may be places we have visited long ago about which we now appear to remember very little, yet if we were to revisit the place and see a few of the buildings and hear and smell the place again, we would probably find a whole flood of detailed memories streaming back. Or, in trying to recall a passage in a book, we may well find it easier first to recall when and where we read the book, where on the page the passage was, and other associations.

If it were not for the cues provided by association, one would have difficulty recalling anything. Memory would be like a vast library without a catalogue. Associations give some information about which part of the memory we should be looking in, and the more associations there are, the more specific the search can be. Associations may come from any direction and from any sense. Any one item in memory will probably have hundreds, perhaps thousands, of different associations.

The more associations we make when learning material, the easier it is to remember that material. Indeed, so powerful is the role of association that almost nothing will destroy it. The only things that will interfere with it are other stronger associations—apart, that is, from barbiturate overdoses, brain surgery, electric shock therapy, etc.

CONTEXT DEPENDENCY

The environment in which the learning takes place provides very important associations. As Victor Hugo once remarked, "Nothing awakes a reminiscence like an odor." Most people have probably used such environmental associations at one time or another to "jog" their memories. A typical example would be of the person who, while cleaning his teeth, thinks of a friend he should call. A minute later, when he gets to the phone, he finds he has completely forgotten who it was. He racks his brain but cannot recall it. So he goes back into the bathroom, but still he has no clue. He stands by the basin again: still nothing. So, checking that no one is looking, he starts cleaning his teeth again, and suddenly the memory comes back.

The seventeenth-century British philosopher John Locke quoted a particularly curious example of environmental association in the case of a certain young man learning to dance.[2]

> Having learned to dance, and that to great perfection, there happened to stand an old trunk in the room where he learned. The idea of this remarkable piece of household stuff had so mixed itself with the turns and steps of all his dances, that though in that chamber he could dance excellently well, yet it was only while that trunk was there; nor could he perform well in any other place, unless that or some other such trunk had its due position in the room.

There are many legendary anecdotes of a person having had a hard night's drinking and waking up with no memory whatsoever of the previous night's fun and games. But later, perhaps the next evening, when he gets drunk again, his memories come flooding back. This phenomenon was tested by giving people a number of tasks to learn—some while they were under the influence of alcohol, and some while they were sober. It was found that what was learned after drinking alcohol was remembered best when again under its influence.[3] Other experiments have shown the same to be true with people given heavy amphetamine or barbiturate doses.[4]

In an investigation of the effects of environment on memory, people were given lists of nonsense syllables to learn. Some of the subjects were then tested on the lists in the same room, others in a different room. It was found that memory was best with subjects tested in the same room as that in which they had originally learned the material.[5]

In another experiment sixteen divers were given lists of forty words to learn either while they were ashore or while they were ten feet down in the sea. When they were later tested on the lists, it was found that lists learned while underwater were recalled better underwater, and lists learned on land were recalled better on land.[6]

SUBJECTIVE ORGANIZATION

It has long been known that if a person is given a list of words to remember, he will later tend to recall them in clusters—words of similar meaning, or of the same sound, often being recalled together.[7] If you turn back to the words you recalled in the memory experiment on page

87, you will probably find that the names of animals may have been recalled in clusters. Yet if you look at the original list, you will see they were all separated from each other.

When subjects were given lists containing words from a few specific categories—for example, names of animals, vegetables, or professions—not only did they tend to recall items in clusters, but the more clustering that occurred, the better was the person's recall.[8] This suggests that a considerable degree of internal organization of the material is taking place, either consciously or unconsciously. This internal ordering is called *subjective organization.*

Endel Tulving from the University of Toronto devised an ingenious experiment by which to measure the degree of subjective organization taking place. He took sixteen words and constructed sixteen different listings of these words such that each word appeared only once in each of the sixteen different positions, and was followed by and preceded by each other word just once. Each list was read out aloud just once, and immediately after hearing it, the subjects were asked to recall as many words as possible from that list. This procedure was repeated with each of the sixteen lists. Tulving then analyzed the order in which the words had been recalled on each test, and he found the following results:[9]

1. Many of the words were followed or preceded by the same words on a number of different occasions, showing that a degree of subjective organization had taken place.

2. Subjective organization of the material increased as the experiment progressed, although the words were in a different order each time.

3. There was a positive correlation between the degree of subjective organization and the ability to recall the list—the greater the organization, the better the recall.

When we try to remember some new information, often we may repeat it again and again to ourselves. The phenomenon of subjective organization suggests that it is not the repetition itself that is helpful for memorizing, but that through repetition the mind is constructing patterns and imposing its own organization on the material. In addition, the repetition gives the mind a chance to make associative links where associations are not already obvious. Subjective organization is also enhanced by relaxation. This is yet another important reason for taking regular breaks during study.

The importance and the power of organization is shown by the fact that just the instruction to organize material is sufficient for it to be remembered. In one study subjects were given one hundred cards, on each of which was printed a word. Some of the subjects were told only to sort the cards into categories, while others were instructed to memorize the cards. When they later tried to recall the cards, the subjects who had merely been instructed to categorize the cards did just as well as those who had been told to try to remember them.[10]

PRINCIPLE SEEKING

Following are three lists of ten numbers (each therefore longer than the average immediate memory span of seven items). Study each list and memorize it in such a way that you could be sure of still remembering it correctly were you to be asked for it tomorrow morning.

(a)	0	1	2	3	4	5	6	7	8	9
(b)	8	6	4	2	0	9	7	5	3	1
(c)	1	8	4	5	7	2	0	9	3	6

The first list is easy; the sequence is already well known. To remember it you remember not the numbers themselves but the pattern —the digits 0–9 in their normal order.

The second is still moderately easy, once you see the principle underlying the sequence. It is the even numbers backward followed by the odd numbers backward, and again you remember the pattern rather than the numbers themselves.

The third is more difficult because the pattern is not so obvious. If you were to commit it to memory, you might do so by breaking it up into chunks. Or you may repeat the numbers over and over again allowing your mind, either consciously or unconsciously, to impose some organization upon them. Alternatively you may study the sequence further to discover the pattern and remember the rule. In the long run this will still be the most effective method.*

*The rule is: Add 3 to the first to get the third, add 3 to that to get the fifth, and so on for every other number. Subtract 3 from the second to get the fourth, subtract 3 from that to get the sixth, and so on. Ignore any "tens" digits. The odd items start with 1 (easy to remember) and continue from there by adding 3. The even items start with 8 and continue from there by subtracting 3. Got it?

George Karona, who wrote a whole book on the role of organization in memory, describes an experiment in which students were divided into two groups; one half was told to learn a sequence of numbers
by rote, the other half was told to look for the principle. Both were
given three minutes in which to do so. At the end of the three minutes
there was little difference between the groups; 33 percent of the rote
memorizers and 38 percent of the principle seekers recalled it perfectly. Three weeks later, however, the situation was very different.
None of the memorizers could recall the list successfully, whereas 23
percent of the principle seekers still knew it perfectly.[11]

We continually use underlying principles and rules in remembering everyday facts. Most people do not remember by rote which years
are leap years. Instead we usually remember the principle that leap
years are those that are exactly divisible by four. And we may remember the additional principle that the centuries themselves are not the
leap years, unless the century year is itself divisible by four hundred.

For the same reason long-distance information in the American
telephone network was chosen to be 555-1212 rather than 641-8752.
The pattern underlying the first number will be seen at a glance and
remembered easily.

Another example of principle seeking is the remarkable memory
of chess masters for board positions. If a chess position is shown to a
novice for five seconds, he will probably only be able to put six or eight
pieces back in their correct positions. A chess master, on the other hand,
will probably be able to put 90 percent or more of the pieces back
correctly. Whereas the novice tries to remember twenty or thirty individual chess pieces, the master sees the positions in terms of a few major
configurations—that is, he has sought the underlying principles of the
positions, and it is the configurations he remembers, not the positions.
This is shown by the finding that when the pieces are just placed randomly on the board so that they no longer represent an actual game,
the master does no better than the novice on this test.[12] Remembering
the configurations rather than the positions themselves also has the
advantage of reducing the information to a smaller number of chunks.

If you try playing chess blindfolded, or without a board and pieces,
so that you have to rely solely on memory, you will notice that the
configurations—lines of "power," areas of weakness—are remembered
as much as, if not more than, the positions themselves. A blindfolded
game is within the capacity of most average chess players and is an
excellent mental exercise. For a while it was thought that to play three

blindfolded games simultaneously was one of the greatest exertions of which the human memory was capable. But in 1933 Alexander Alekhine played thirty-two, in 1943 Najdorf played forty, and in 1960 the Belgian Master Koltanovski took on *fifty-six* simultaneous games blindfolded, winning fifty and drawing the other six[13]—a revealing glimpse into the fantastic capabilities of the human mind and memory.

MEANING AND ATTENTION

Another important way in which memory is organized is in terms of meaning. Meaning is an essential part of all thought processes, and it is meaning that gives order to experience. Indeed, the process of perception is ultimately one of extracting meaning from the environment. If there is only shallow processing of the material, little significance is extracted and the memory is poor. If the processing is deeper, more meaning is extracted, more meaningful connections are made with other ideas, and the memory is much stronger.[14]

Deeper processing requires conscious involvement with the material. If the mind is not attending, information will "go in one ear and out the other." The trace it leaves may well be too faint to be recalled in normal circumstances. The more that you consciously attend to something, the greater will be the depth of processing. The greater the depth of processing, the more meaningful the material becomes. The more meaningful it becomes, the better the memory. And the better the memory, the more opportunity there will be to make meaningful connections with new material in the future.

ASSOCIATIVE NETWORKS

Memory is not recorded like a movie film or tape recording, with each idea linked to the next in a well-defined temporal sequence. The information is recorded in vast interconnecting networks. Each idea or image has hundreds, perhaps thousands, of associations and is connected to numerous other points in the mental network.

There is now considerable interest in theories that regard human memory as a vast, intricately interconnected network. According to such models it is not letters, syllables, or words that are recorded, but concepts and propositions. The propositions are then related in various ways to other propositions, forming an associative or semantic network. According to such a model the act of encoding an event—in other words, the act of memorizing—is simply that of forming new links in the network, that is, making new associations.[15]

Such models not only tie in with most of the experimental findings on memory, they also explain the incredible versatility and flexibility of memory.

Memory is not like a container that gradually fills up, it is more like a tree growing hooks onto which the memories are hung. Everything you remember is another set of hooks on which more new memories can be attached. So the capacity of memory keeps on growing. The more you know, the more you can know.

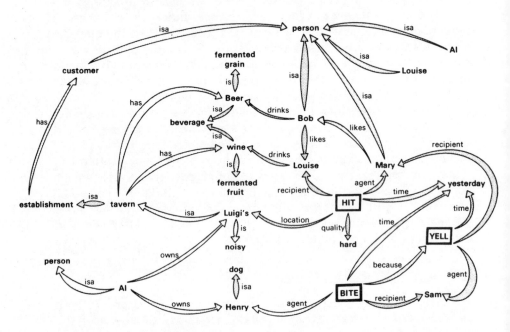

Figure 33 Semantic network representing a small set of interactions among Bob, Louise, Mary, Al, Henry, and Sam at Luigi's. The people and objects in the interactions are linked by lines showing their relationships, and the main activities are in circles. You can "read" it by starting with "Al," who owns Luigi's, a tavern...and Al's dog, Henry, bit Sam because.... (From R. H. Lindsay and D. A. Norman, *Human Information Processing*, New York and London: Academic Press, 1972. Used with permission.)

SLEEP LEARNING AND SUGGESTOPEDEA

In the fifties and early sixties there was a lot of interest in what was called sleep learning. The idea was that by playing a tape of material to be learned to a sleeping person, a large amount of the information could be digested and remembered. Experiments at the University of Florida showed that the average recall for five nights of material presented during deep sleep was 13 percent.[16] These and other experiments have concluded that learning occurs during sleep only to the extent that the subject is partially conscious. It therefore tends to disrupt sleep, and for this reason it has largely fallen from favor.

A related learning technique that is at present increasing in popularity is one known as suggestopedia. It was originally developed by Georgi Lozanof in Sophia, Bulgaria, in the 1960s. The technique used draws heavily upon yoga and hypnosis and incorporates such factors as deep relaxation, music, and psychodrama. The subject sits quietly in a chair and is taken to a very relaxed state. Then carefully chosen baroque music is played while the instructor (or tape) presents the material to be learned in the background. The student does not try to listen to the study material, the attention remains on the music. It is claimed that in this relaxed state the mind is able to absorb information much more readily and that material that would normally take two years at college can be learned in two or three months using suggestopedia. It has been claimed that this rapid assimilation of knowledge can be attributed to the enhancement of the activity in the brain's right hemisphere.[17]

APPLICATIONS AND ADVICE

Since the context of the original learning is an important associative cue to memory, it follows that the more distinctive and memorable you make the learning situation, the better will be your memory of the material studied. By becoming more conscious of the surroundings rather than just letting them slip by passively, and by deliberately associating the material studied with the situation itself, you will be forging stronger associative links and making it difficult for the material to be forgotten.

Also, by deliberately forming clear associations between ideas, you will be able to remember them much more easily. Advice on how to do this will be given in chapter 9.

For the purposes of recall, organization can be just as effective as deliberate learning. It is also much less tiring and considerably more enjoyable. If you can find any general pattern or rule in the things you need to recall, the recall will come much more easily and last a lot longer. Without looking back, see if you can remember the three lists of numbers given earlier in this chapter. (Hint for the third list: It began with 1.) If there is no obvious organization or order, try making up a rule that fits; creative ideas are usually remembered well.

There is no danger of your memory filling up. Indeed, the more you remember, the easier you will find it is to remember new things.

Figure 34

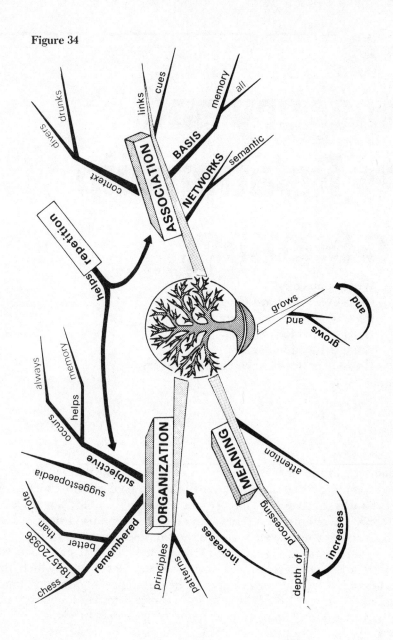

8.
Imagery and Its Relationship to Memory

What is imagery?
Does everyone have imagery?
How do images help memory?
Is visual memory perfect?
What is eidetic imagery?
Do only children have eidetic imagery?

Imagery is a sensory-type experience in the mind without an actual corresponding situation providing the immediate sense stimulus. One of the earliest surveys of imagery was conducted by Sir Francis Galton in 1883. He circulated a questionnaire to one hundred men, a large proportion of whom were distinguished in science or some other field. They were asked to recall their breakfast table as it had been that morning, and to describe the vividness and detail with which they could conjure up the experiences of hearing, smelling, tasting, touching, and feelings of cold, hunger, drowsiness, etc. He found an enormous variation in the degree of reported imagery. In some cases the subject's description was as lucid as the original scene, as clear and rich in detail as if the breakfast table were still in front of him. Other people had much vaguer images, and some reported no imagery whatsoever and did not believe it was even possible.[1]

Recent studies are now suggesting that everybody does in fact possess a considerable degree of imagery, whether, paradoxically, they are aware of it or not. In a study of five hundred people everyone reported having images of some kind. Ninety-seven percent reported visual images and 92 percent auditory images.[2] And even these figures are probably too low. If those few people who do not report visual imagery are asked to describe something, such as the Taj Mahal, they tend to break off in middescription to comment, "Yes, I *do* have visual imagery."[3]

To create a mental image is to "imagine," and the power of imagination is almost limitless. Although the situation has never been seen before, it is not difficult to imagine a green cat driving a car, making the sound of a brass band, and smelling of roses. This ability to put common images together in the mind to create new images is invaluable, if not essential to the process of memory.

IMAGERY AND MEMORY

Most people use imagery in memory quite naturally, often starting very early on in life. Some have various images associated with numbers. Often this involves a spatial arrangement of the numbers. They

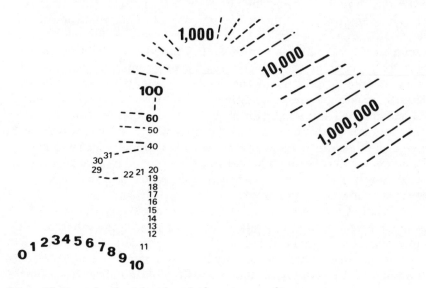

Figure 35 Example of number-form laid out in mental space.

may be strung out in a line, the line weaving its way through space, perhaps receding from the observer the higher the number. The individual numbers may vary in size, important points such as 10, 100, 500 and 1,000 appearing bigger than the others. Or they may vary in color, each number or group of numbers being a particular color. It has been found that about 80 percent of the population have some such "number form." Many people have similar forms for the alphabet, for the days of the week, the months of the year, etc.

This imagery may not appear very useful to the adult, but it was undoubtedly of immense benefit in early childhood. It probably helped one to learn the numbers, the alphabet, days of the week, etc. Although young children are not usually taught to use imagery, the mind finds it much easier to attach sensory associations of one form or another to abstract concepts and remember the image patterns created. It is in effect creating an additional degree of organization.

INTERACTIVE IMAGES

To investigate the power of imagery in memory, students were given twelve pairs of unrelated nouns, such as *dog* and *bicycle,* and told to associate the two by imagining a visual scene in which these two objects interacted in some way or another. Thus a person might imagine a dog riding a bicycle, being hit by a bicycle, or urinating on a bicycle. They were also given twelve pairs of words that they simply repeated aloud three times. In both conditions the time allowed for each pair was the same—eight seconds. Immediate recall tests showed that 80 percent of the imaged pairs were remembered correctly, whereas only 33 percent of the repeated pairs were remembered.[4] Thus by creating strong associative images the subjects had increased their recall two and a half times.

Another study investigated the importance of vividness in such imagery. When the images were vague and indistinct, recall was around 70 percent (still very much higher than that gained by rote repetition), but when they were "seen" vividly and distinctly, as if they were real, recall was around 95 percent.[5]

Other experiments on verbal memory have shown that words that evoke a strong mental image are far more easily remembered.[6] The more vivid the imagery, it seems, the more stable is the memory.

Imagery is valuable in memory because it strengthens associations and links. If the imagery does not actually link the ideas, it is of little value. This was shown by giving lists of word pairs, such as *dog–bicycle,* to two groups of people. The first group were told to create a strong visual image in which the two objects interacted in some way. The second group were also told to create a strong visual image but with the objects separated; for example, the objects could be pictured as being on opposite walls of a room. Recall tests showed that those who had produced strong *interactive* images recalled 71 percent of the words, whereas those who had formed separated images recalled only 46 percent of the words, which is only a little better than the 33 percent scored by rote repetition.

Imagery is most effective, therefore, when it is as vivid as possible and as interactive as possible.

Even when people claim to be poor visualizers, imagery can still be very valuable in helping memory. In fact, poor visualizers and good visualizers show the same improvement in memory when instructed to use imagery. The only difference is that the good visualizers tend to be much more confident of their memory than poor visualizers.[8]

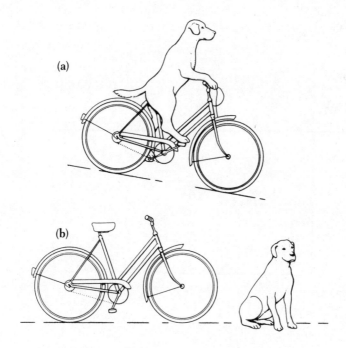

Figure 36 Dog-bicycle (a) connected, (b) disconnected.

VISUAL MEMORY

Visual images are generally much better remembered than words. So much so that visual recognition is practically perfect. In fact there is only one study that shows picture memory to be poor, and in that study the pictures were deliberately constructed to be as misleading as possible.[9]

In order to assess the potential of visual memory, subjects were shown a series of 2,560 photographic slides at the rate of one every ten seconds. These seven hours of viewing were split over several consecutive days. One hour after the last slide had been shown, the subjects were tested for recognition by showing them 280 pairs of slides in which one member of each pair was a picture from the original series, while the other was from a similar set but had never been shown to the subject. They recognized 85 to 95 percent of the original slides correctly. These high scores were maintained even when the presentation rate was speeded up to one every second, and even when the pictures were shown as a mirror image so that the right-hand side became the left-hand side. The experimenter commented that "these experiments with pictorial stimuli suggest that recognition of pictures is essentially

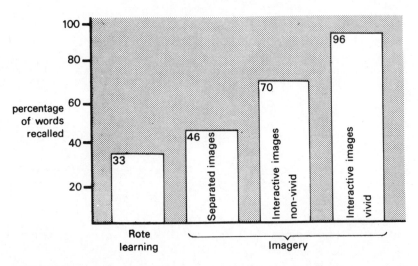

Figure 37 Effectiveness of imagery over rote learning of word pairs, and value of interactive and vivid images.

perfect. The results would probably have been the same if we had used 25,000 pictures instead of 2,500."[10]

In the foregoing experiment the pictures were recognized after an average interval of one and a half days. In another experiment subjects were tested immediately after presentation of some six hundred pictures, and recognition was then found to be 98 percent correct! Subsequent work in Canada expanded on this, presenting subjects with ten thousand pictures and measuring the extent to which the vividness of the picture affected recall. With vivid pictures the subjects were recalling 99.6 percent correctly.[11] When these results were extrapolated, it was estimated that if the subjects had been shown a million pictures rather than ten thousand, they would have recognized 986,300 of them!

These subjects were also tested on the effect of having to recognize the picture from a selection of thirty-two alternatives instead of having to recognize the correct picture from just a pair. This obviously made the task more difficult, but even with thirty-two alternatives, subjects were still 92 percent correct. Again it was concluded that "the capacity of recognition memory for pictures is almost limitless, when measured under appropriate conditions."[12]

PHOTOGRAPHIC MEMORY

Some people are able to look at a page of print for just a few seconds, then close the book and read it all back as if they were looking at a photograph of the page in their mind. The technical term for this ability is eidetic imagery, coming from the Greek *eidos* meaning "form" or "that which is seen." Eidetic imagery was widely studied up until about 1930, but virtually no more work at all was done on the subject until the recent interest in the role of imagery in memory.

The first work in this field was carried out by Galton in 1880. He studied boys from Charterhouse School and found that 18 out of 172 had the ability to see vivid eidetic images.[13] The work was taken further in the early part of this century by E. R. Jaensch in Germany and G. W. Allport in Cambridge, England.

Allport worked with children, generally in the ten-to-thirteen year age range. In a typical study he would place a picture on a dark gray background and leave it there for thirty-five seconds while the child looked at it carefully. The picture was then removed and the child was asked to look at the gray background alone and report what he saw.

Allport found that a large number of children behaved as if they were still actually seeing the picture, as if they had somehow remembered it photographically.[14] Most people have a very strong memory for pictures, but the imaging these children displayed differed from normal visual imagery in a number of respects.

1. The eidetic images were external, "out there." They were actually seen to be resting on the gray background on which the picture had originally been placed. And if the gray surface was folded or bent, then the eidetic image was likewise folded or bent.

2. The eidetic image was much clearer and stronger than a normal image. It tended to obscure the background it was projected against, rather as if a thin film containing a picture had been laid upon the background.

3. The eidetic image was much more persistent than a normal image. The children could maintain it for many minutes and in several cases come back to it weeks, or even months later. In this respect it differed from a visual afterimage—the sort of image you get from staring at a bright light bulb for a few seconds. Afterimages tend to fade rapidly, after half a minute or so. If particularly strong, they may persist for several minutes but never for weeks or months. In most afterimages the color is reversed—that is to say, one perceives complementary colors: red appears as turquoise, blue as yellow, and green as magenta, and vice versa. There is no such color reversal with the eidetic images. Furthermore, in the original viewing of the picture the children were encouraged to let their eyes rove all over it, whereas to create a good afterimage, it is necessary to keep the attention focused on a particular point of the picture.

4. The children reported a vast amount of detail in the image, often "seeing" items that had not been consciously noticed on the original viewing. Looking at their image, they could count the number of stripes on a zebra, for example, and do so correctly—something that is not possible with normal visual imagery. In one of the studies there was a street scene and in the background was an inn with the word *Gartenwirthschaft* written above the door. This German word was meaningless to the children and was not re-

ported when they first looked at their eidetic image, but when they were asked to look more closely, each of the children with strong eidetic images was able to see the small letters above the door. Some of them could spell the word out correctly, others nearly so. Moreover, they could read the letters off from right to left as easily as from left to right.

Although eidetic imagery has often been called photographic imagery, later experiments showed significant differences between the two. The eidetic image was found to be much more flexible than a photographic image. When, for example, a child was "looking" at an eidetic image of a picture containing a donkey and a manger, it was suggested to the child that the donkey was hungry. Immediately the child "saw" the donkey begin to walk over to the manger, bend his neck, and start eating.[15] In other cases subjects could make certain items in the picture bigger or smaller at will or rotate them to see what they looked like from the other side.

Another difference between eidetic imagery and "photographic" memory is that there may be additions, omissions, and distortions in the eidetic image. Despite the wealth of detail the image is generally not as exact as a photograph would be.

Eidetic images need not be limited to vision. It is possible to have an auditory eidetic imagery. One may, for example, be able to hear a symphony mentally, picking out all the individual instruments; or one may have a tactile eidetic image, being able to feel the image of a piece of fur with full clarity and richness.[16]

Later Work on Eidetic Imagery. Between 1930 and 1968 there were only two studies published on eidetic imagery. Since then there has been a renewed interest in the subject, one of the most remarkable experiments being to use pairs of computer-generated patterns of quasi-random dots. Although they appear to be random, these patterns are so designed that if one pattern is presented to the left eye while the other pattern is presented to the right eye, the two images fuse stereoscopically and a clear shape stands out in the middle of the combined pattern.

Instead of presenting the two patterns simultaneously to the right and left eye one pattern was presented to one eye on one day and the following day the second pattern was presented to the other eye. In one subject the eidetic imagery was so strong that she had retained the first

Figure 38 Two random dot patterns which when fused stereoscopically cause a shape to stand out from the background (from B. Julesz, *The Foundations of Cyclopean Perception*, Chicago: University of Chicago Press, 1971. Used with permission.)

picture in sufficient detail that it fused with the second picture and the hidden shape appeared, even though the eidetic image was being viewed twenty-four hours later.[17]

In a similar experiment children were shown the pictures (a) and (b) of Figure 39. They first looked at (a); then this was removed and they looked at (b). Those with strong eidetic images were able to superimpose the two and see the face depicted in (c). It is very difficult for a child to work out what the combined picture would look like and, indeed, they were often surprised when they suddenly saw the face.[18]

Eidetic imagery seems to be much more common in children than it is in adults. Estimates of its frequency of occurrence vary enormously. Some studies have suggested that 50 percent of children under the age of eleven possess the faculty, while others put the figure as low as 3 or 4 percent, or even zero percent. Such wide variability probably reflects the different types of tests used, the different criteria for eidetic imagery, and the varying cultural backgrounds of the children.

It is also difficult at first to get children to admit to having eidetic imagery. After a few years of schooling they soon become inhibited about saying that they see things which are "not really there"—not really there in the sense that other people cannot go up and touch and objectively verify their experience. People researching into eidetic imagery often have to spend some time with the child, gaining his confi-

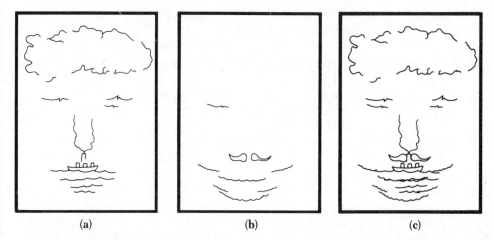

(a)   (b)   (c)

Figure 39 Eidetic children first were shown picture (a); it was then removed and picture (b) was exposed to view; (c) is the picture formed by combining the other two pictures. Eidetic imagers can remember one pattern and project it on to the second pattern at a later date, seeing the hidden shape. None of the children saw a face initially in the first picture, but many of them did when shown the second one, suggesting eidetic memory of the first.

dence, so that he will not feel silly, and not feel he is going to be laughed at or criticized, when he reports what he sees.

Several investigators have looked at the way eidetic images vary with age. Eidetic imagery seems to decrease fairly rapidly after about the age of ten, and by the time children are fourteen, they show about the same frequency of occurrence as do the rest of the adult population —that is, about 2 percent with moderate eidetic imagery and one in a million with very strong eidetic imagery.

This trend probably owes a lot to our educational systems. The emphasis on reading, writing, and arithmetic—that is, on the logical left-hemisphere functions—does not encourage strong visual imagery, which is a right hemisphere function. And, like any faculty not regularly used, eidetic imagery begins to atrophy.

The view that eidetic imagery is educated out of most individuals was first put forward in 1930 by E. R. Jaensch, one of the early researchers on the subject. He found that in special schools in which there was more emphasis on sensory activities, 80 to 90 percent of the children showed eidetic imagery.[19] This view is further supported by recent studies from other cultures in which children are not subjected to a predominantly verbal educational process. In several African cultures it has been found that eidetic imagery is retained through adulthood, with about 50 percent of the population showing the phenomena.[20]

Further evidence that adults may not have completely lost the faculty of eidetic imagery comes from some experiments in hypnosis. Adults under hypnosis were taken back to the age of seven. They were then presented with random-dot stereograms one at a time (see Figure 38), and several were then found to have eidetic imagery—though none of them did in the normal waking state.[21]

APPLICATIONS AND ADVICE

Possibly everyone has the ability of eidetic imagery latent within them, but in nearly all cases it has atrophied through lack of use—or rather, it has been educated *out* of our lives. Regular exercise of imagery by, for example, taking a moment to form clear interactive images of things you wish to recall, or imagining in as much detail as possible a place you were in earlier in the day, can revive some of these lost abilities.

Imagery can be developed by such exercises as the following: Sit comfortably and close your eyes. Relax easily. Now imagine yourself outside a building you know well—a friend's house, or if you are not at home, your own house. See how much of the image you can recall from memory. What is it built from? How many windows are there? What do the windows look like? Imagine the door. What color is it? What design is it? What is it made from? What is the door handle like? And what surrounds the door? Open the door and walk inside. Look at the walls—what color are they? What is on the floor? How does it feel to touch it? What furniture is there? Notice as much as you can. Spend some time just allowing your mind to roam around, letting images come up from memory.

Now imagine yourself picking up some object that is in the room. How does it feel—hard or soft? Is it hot or cold? What does it smell like? What color is it? Really get to know that object as if you were really there, looking at it from different sides and from above and below, using as many of your senses as you can.

When you feel quite comfortable with this exercise, you might try some more creative imagery and imagine yourself inside some solid object. For example, you might imagine yourself inside a brick of the wall, or inside the wood of a piece of furniture. Again imagine how it feels, what it looks like; are there any tastes or smells? Perceive as if you were really inside it.

Another useful exercise is to imagine an object changing in unusual ways. Imagine a glass of water, for example. Imagine it floating in the air in front of you, and then imagine it moving around in whatever manner you desire. Move it up to the ceiling, move it down and around. Imagine it turning upside down and the water staying in. Then try imagining the water changing color, becoming blue, then green, then golden. Let it change size. Imagine the glass becomes as tall as you, or imagine it becoming so small that it can sit on your fingernail.

Such exercises, if practiced regularly, will greatly enhance your power of imagery. As you begin to use imagery more in daily life, your overall memory will improve. And, as we shall see later (chapter 15), the ability to form clear images can also be very useful in setting and achieving personal objectives.

In the animal kingdom, and in primitive man, memory evolved to record the routes and location of food, shelter, mates, and foes. Such a memory naturally uses associative imagery, with the result that associative imagery becomes the backbone of memory. It is only in relatively recent times that man has turned his memory to the recording of phone numbers, addresses, concepts, mathematical formulae, etc., all of which, being poor in imagery, are often poorly remembered. Their retention can, however, be greatly enhanced by the deliberate use of the natural capacities of memory and association, as will be shown in the next chapter.

Figure 40

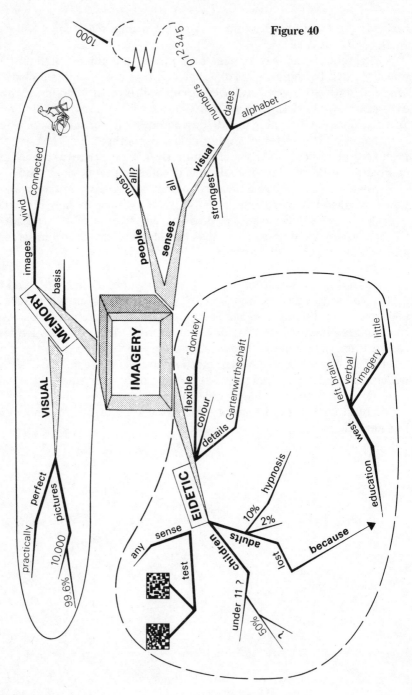

9.
Mnemonics

What are mnemonics?
How do they work?
Who first used them?
How to use simple mnemonic systems
Can they be used for anything?
Are mnemonics cheating?
Do some people have perfect memories?

The word *mnemonic* comes from the Greek *mneme,* "to remember"; a mnemonic is essentially any technique that helps people remember things better. It can be tying a knot in a handkerchief, a rhyme, a visual image, or any other aid.

The basis of virtually all memory techniques is the formation of a strong association. The association can be a link to some well-established memory, a link to a standard set of mental memory pegs, or a link between any previously unrelated ideas that need to be recalled together.

If, for example, you wanted to form a mnemonic between *apple* and *penguin,* you might form an image of a penguin with its head stuck inside a huge apple. You might like to try forming your own image connecting these two objects. Whatever the association, try to make maximum use of the factors that naturally enhance human memory:

Uniqueness. The association should be unique so that there will be no possibility of interference with other associations. It would not be very helpful to imagine a penguin eating an apple. Penguins do eat things (though not apples normally), and the image would not be so outstanding. But an apple eating a penguin, yes!

Exaggeration. The more exaggerated the image, the better. Make the apple huge. The more bizarre and outstanding an image, the more arousing it is and the clearer is the memory that results.

Sensory. For most people the image will be predominantly visual, since visual memory is usually the strongest, but smells, sounds, movements, etc., should be included wherever possible. See the penguin waddle, hear the crunch of snow, smell and taste the apple. The association can also be improved by making the image three-dimensional, in color and as vivid as possible.

Interactive. The connection between the objects should be the prime feature of the image. As we saw previously, disconnected images do not work so well: They must be closely connected. A penguin standing beside an apple is not a good association. It is much better to put it inside the apple.

Simplicity. The simpler the connection, the better. Apples and penguins both survive the cold well, but this would be too sophisticated a link for a mnemonic. Keep it childlike, unencumbered, and unique.

Creativity. Being creative involves you much more in the association and increases the depth of processing. The more original the image, the better will it be remembered. Indeed, the act of creation is essentially the same as that of memorizing— the forging of a link between two previously unassociated ideas.[1]

Sexual and Vulgar. Don't be afraid to make sexual or vulgar connections if they occur to you—and they probably will. Most people find such associations are remembered much better. No one else need ever know of your associations, so there need be no fear of embarrassment. Turn back to the memory experiment you did on page 87 and check whether you recalled the word *balls,* and if so, can you remember any helpful associations you had?

Involvement. Memory is intimately linked with conscious experience. The more strongly you experience something, the better you will remember it. So savor your mental image fully.

EARLY MNEMONIC TECHNIQUES

Mnemonic techniques were extensively used by the ancient Romans and Greeks. The Romans developed what is known as the systems of *loci. Locus* (*loci,* plural) is the Latin word for place and from it we have our word *location.* In the Roman system each item to be remembered was associated with a particular place in the surroundings. A person would first form a standard list of locations that he knew well. Maybe he would take his courtyard and make the pillar on the left the first *locus,* the ledge next to it the second *locus,* the tree the third *locus,* the statue the fourth *locus,* etc. Then, if the first item to be remembered were a horse, he might imagine a horse standing on top of the pillar, or standing up as a pillar. If the second item were a sword, then he could imagine a sword, perhaps standing on its tip on the ledge, at the second *locus.* And so on through the standard set of *loci.* To recall a given list, the person only had to go back and think of the pillar to get the first item, the ledge to remember the second item, and so on.

The Romans are said to have used this system extensively in memorizing speeches. Each of the topics to be remembered was associated with one of the standard places in the person's system so that he was able to give his speech in the correct order by merely running through the sequence in his mind as he spoke. The remnants of this system have descended into our own speech as "In the first place . . ." and "In the second place . . ."

The Greeks used a similar system of linking ideas with places. Our word *topic* comes from the Greek *topos,* which likewise meant "place." The topics to be discussed were the locations in the Greek memory system.

Many others since the early Greeks and Romans have used mnemonics. Thomas Aquinas used mnemonic systems in teaching his monks. They were used by some of the kings of England and France, and by Shakespeare, Francis Bacon, and Leibnitz. Children at school use them without any prompting, and they are the "secret" behind nearly all great "memory men."

PEG WORD SYSTEMS

Modern peg word mnemonics are based on similar principles to the early Roman and Greek systems, but the *loci* are now replaced by a standard set of objects that are each associated with a specific number. Thus the first item is linked to an image associated with 1, the second to an image associated with 2, etc.

In order to make it easy to remember which objects are associated with which numbers, mnemonic principles are applied to the choice of object. There are three principal ways in which this is usually done:

Number-Rhyme.   The objects are chosen to rhyme with the numbers they represent. Thus one might have: 1–gun; 2–shoe; 3–tree; . . . ; 10–hen.

Number-Shape.   Here the shape of the number is the cue: 1–pole; 2–swan; 3–breasts; . . . 10–Laurel and Hardy.

The Major System.   Each digit is associated with a consonant, or similar sounding group of consonants. Most systems are based on a standard framework laid down in the seventeenth century:

1–t, d, th	(t and 1 have one downstroke)
2–n	(two downstrokes)
3–m	(three downstrokes)
4–r	(last letter of four)
5–l	(Roman for 50)
6–j, sh, ch	(j is mirror image of 6)
7–k, g (hard), ng, qu	(k is two 7s back to back)
8–f, v	(f in script looks like 8)
9–p, b	(9 reversed, or rotated)
0–z, s	(zero)

Images are then chosen which begin with the associated consonant— for example, 1–tie; 2–noah; . . .

This system is very powerful in that it can be easily extended to numbers beyond 10. The number 695, for example, would require the consonants, *j, sh* or *ch; p* or *b;* and *l*. Adding vowels, one might produce the word *ch*a*pel* as the key object for 695.

Providing each object is well linked to the item to be remembered, the capacity of such a system is almost limitless. In one study a girl with no special ability in memory was taught a similar system for the numbers one to a hundred. Using this, she was able to recall many lists of this length, usually with no errors whatsoever. In one test she was asked to recall alternate items in the series, which she did correctly. The experimenter then jumbled the list around and made her remember it in a different order, which she again did with almost complete success. Then without warning he asked her to remember the original order. She did so with only two errors.[2]

Another experiment extended the list to a thousand items. The images were presented in five hundred pairs and the subjects asked to form strong interactive images along similar lines to those just mentioned. They were presented with each pair only once. Yet afterward they were able to recall 99 percent of the words perfectly.[3] Subjects who are not instructed to form associative links seldom do better than 5 percent correct. Just one simple system had made recall twenty times better!

OTHER MNEMONICS

Many people use mnemonics spontaneously, probably without even realizing it. A person's name, Joy, for example, may have become stuck in the memory because the person was (or was not) a joyful character. At school one may have found it easier to remember that chalk is calcium carbonate by remembering that all three words begin with *c.* Such associations may seem silly and even trivial at the time, and people will not always admit to them, but it is these incidental and seemingly silly associations that are the very fabric of memory.

A powerful factor in memory is rhythm and rhyme, and these are often used in teaching children. The most obvious are rhymes like:

> *i* before *e,* except after *c,*
> or when sounding like *a*
> as in *neighbor* and *weigh*

and

> Thirty days hath September,
> April, June, and November

Other common mnemonics used at school are ones like the English

Richard of York gained battles in vain

where the first letter of each word stands for the first letter of the colors of the rainbow (red, orange, yellow, green, blue, indigo, violet). And the popular one for distinguishing stalagmites from stalagtites:

When the tights come down, the mites run up.

What makes this particularly good and memorable is not only the rhythm and rhyme, but the little "naughtiness" involved.

Many students use mnemonics to help them remember their basic facts. A zoologist may remember how to distinguish a Bactrian camel from a Dromedary camel by simply turning the initial letters on to their sides: ⋒ has two humps, ⋂ has only one. The imaginativeness and unique visual qualities of this mnemonic ensures that once seen, it is rarely, if ever, forgotten.

Mathematicians may remember the reciprocal of pi (0.318310) by simply remembering the phrase "Can I remember the reciprocal?" In this case the number of letters in each word determines the required numbers: *can* has three letters; *I,* one; *remember,* eight; *the,* three; *reciprocal,* ten.

Physiologists trying to remember the order of nerves that pass through the superior orbital tissues in the skull (lacrimal, frontal, trochlear, lateral, nasociliary, internal, abducens) probably find it easier to remember that "lazy French tarts lie naked in anticipation," the first letters of each word being the first letters of each nerve.

One can also use mnemonics for learning foreign languages. Most of the rules of grammar can be given mnemonic interpretations, and the vocabulary itself is always very much simpler to learn with associative images than by rote repetition. In learning French, for example, you might remember that the word for duck is *canard* by picturing yourself throwing a "can hard" at a duck, and that a rabbit is *lapin* by imagining one lapping a pan. Such associations do not usually give the correct pronunciation and spelling, but they are close enough to remind us of the words, and as such are highly efficient cues.[4]

ARE MNEMONICS CHEATING?

It is sometimes said that memory is of no use unless it comes through a thorough understanding of the material. Certainly understanding is valuable in that it helps to build up meaningful associations between the concept involved and one's whole body of knowledge. But rather than hindering understanding, mnemonics often help enhance it. New information cannot be related to other information if it is not available, and difficult material may be understood later on, if, that is, it has been remembered in the first place.

It has been said that there is no such thing as pure rote learning. Ultimately all memory is by some association or other. Mnemonic techniques are essentially making a fuller use of the brain's own natural memory functions, thus helping it in its task. It is not that mnemonics are cheating, but rather by not consciously using them, one is effectively hindering the learning process. The brain is, in the end, going to form associative connections whether you help it or not.

It is possible that some of the differences in learning proficiency among school children are attributable to the use of different memory strategies. It has been reported that the marked differences in learning between a group of normal children and a group of mentally retarded children can be largely eliminated when both groups are trained in learning methods, particularly in the use of associative mental imagery.[5] This has the somewhat revolutionary implication that "smart" people may simply be those who have discovered for themselves efficient learning strategies, and realized, either consciously or unconsciously, the value of associative imagery in learning.

MNEMONICS AND THE RIGHT HEMISPHERE

Some preliminary work has suggested that the use of mnemonic techniques brings the right hemisphere more into play. Straight verbal learning would tend to be associated with the left hemisphere. Visual imagery, on the other hand, is a function more associated with the right hemisphere. It was found that when one image from a mnemonically linked pair was presented in the left visual field, so that the information went to the right side of the brain, the time taken to remember the association was quicker than when the image was presented to the left side of the brain.[6] This supports the contention that mnemonic processes use the right hemisphere more than the left.

Mnemonic techniques have also been used to help people with brain disease. When the left side of the brain has been damaged and verbal functions impaired, memory often suffers. By learning visual mnemonic techniques, such patients have been able to improve their memory, making greater use of their healthy right hemisphere.[7] The use of mnemonic techniques is not only aiding the brain's own natural memory processes, it is also helping to integrate the functioning of the left and right hemispheres.

Piracetam, a drug originally developed as a possible cure for travel sickness, also appears to lead to improved memory. In the early 1970s experiments showed that it enhanced memory in animals, and it was given the name Nootropyl (meaning "toward mind"). Other studies showed that rats given piracetam appeared to have an increased facilitation of transfer of visual information between the left and right hemispheres.[8] Experiments on students showed that after being given the drug for a fortnight, learning abilities increased by 15 to 20 percent. When asked to distinguish between two series of words, one being presented to the left ear while the other was presented to the right ear, it was found that the students taking piracetam performed better than those taking a placebo, again indicating an increased integration of the left and right hemispheres.[9]

The important difference between this drug and mnemonic techniques, however, is that the drug leads only to a 15- to 20-percent increase, whereas mnemonic techniques improve memory several hundred percent.

"S." The power of associative imagery is brought out clearly in the case of a Russian newspaper reporter, Solomon-Veniaminovich Shereshevskii, who was studied by the Russian psychologist A. R. Luria over the thirty years from 1920 to 1950.[10] "S," as he is usually called for short, was sent to Luria by the editor of the newspaper for which he worked. Each day the editor would give the reporters lists of assignments including details of names, addresses, telephone numbers, etc. The other reporters would all take down copious notes, while "S" remembered everything perfectly without any notes at all. Initially he was surprised at the interest taken in him. He thought there was nothing unusual in the fact that he could easily recall what had been said to him, even right back to when he was a baby. "Did not everybody remember every-thing?" he asked.

Luria tested him in a number of ways, giving him lists of numbers, nonsense syllables, words, passages of foreign languages, and complex mathematical formulae to remember. He found no difference in the ability of "S" to remember, whatever the material. Luria worked up from short lists of twenty to fifty items to lists containing hundreds of items, and found that "S" still continued to remember everything per-fectly.

Not only was there no apparent limit to the capacity of his mem-ory, there was no apparent limit to its durability. Luria would some-times ask "S" to recall lists that he had tested him with fifteen to twenty years earlier. In one experiment "S" was read a list of several hundred repetitive nonsense syllables like these:[11]

ma	va	na	sa	na	va
na	sa	na	ma	va	
sa	na	ma	va	na	
va	sa	na	va	na	ma
na	va	na	va	sa	ma
na	ma	sa	ma	va	na
sa	ma	sa	va	na	
na	sa	ma	va	ma	na
etc.					

This was probably one of the most difficult tests he underwent. There is no obvious pattern and the similarity of the lines makes the task highly confusing. Nevertheless "S" not only recalled the full se-ries perfectly but when, eight years later, without any warning, Luria tested him again, "S" still remembered the list in its entirety, with no error.

In such cases "S" would pause for a moment, then commence "Yes, yes ... this was a series you gave me once when we were in your apartment ... you were sitting at the table and I at the rocking chair ... you were wearing a gray suit and you looked at me like this ... now, then, I can see you saying ..." and then proceed to reel the series off perfectly.[12] This illustrates clearly the important associative clues pro-vided by the environment.

The means by which "S" accomplished these remarkable feats of memory was to use imagery. When he was given a random list of items to remember, he would spontaneously form a strong image of the item and associate it with some object along a road or street that he knew. As he mentally walked down the street, he would associate different items with different objects he encountered. Or if the item strongly suggested another location, he would see himself flying from one place to the other. Alternatively he would build up a story around the items. Thus when Luria asked him to remember a complex mathematical formula

$$ \text{N.} \quad \sqrt{d.^2 \times \frac{85}{vx}} \quad . \quad \sqrt[3]{\frac{276^2.86x}{n^2v.\pi264}} \quad n^2b = sv \frac{1624}{32^2} .r^2s $$

"S" used the following imagery:[13]

> Neiman (N) came out and jabbed at the ground with his cane (.). He looked up at a tall tree, which resembled the square root sign ($\sqrt{}$), and thought to himself: "No wonder the tree has withered and begun to expose its roots. After all, it is here that I built these two houses" (d^2). Once again he poked with his cane (.). Then he said: "The houses are old, I'll have to get rid of them ($\times$). The sale will bring far more money." He had originally invested 85,000 in them (85). Then I see the roof of the house detached (_____), while down below on the street I see a man playing the Termenvox (vx). He's standing near a mailbox, and on the corner there is a large stone (.), which had been put there to keep carts from crushing up against the houses. Here, then, is the square, over there the large tree ($\sqrt{}$) with three jackdaws on it ($\forall$). I simply put the figures 276 here, and a square box containing cigarettes in the "square" (^{2}). . . . . etc.[14]

When he was asked to recall some such sequence, he simply started at the beginning of the journey or story and, going over it in his mind, "read off" the items as he came upon each successive image. In this particular case he was able to recall the mathematical formula in precise detail fifteen years later. When "S" describes his process in words, it may appear very cumbersome and lengthy, but remember that he was not using words in his mind, only images, and the sequence of images could be put together in his mind very compactly and quickly so that he could read off the mathematical formula from the images as fast as he could speak.

Occasionally "S" would appear to forget one of the items, but this turned out to be not a defect in memory so much as a defect in perception. He explained that the reason for the omission was that the image had become hidden in some way. This would occur if he had mentally associated the image with an area of the street that was not well lit and thus when he came to recall it, he could not "see" it clearly. In one case he omitted the word *pencil* from a series. And when this was pointed out to him he replied: "I put the image of the *pencil* near a fence . . . the one down the street. But what happened was that the image fused with that of the fence and I walked right on past without noticing it."[15]

"S" 's power of imagery was related to his remarkable synesthesia. In synesthesia the senses lose their boundaries and begin to merge with each other. Thus visual stimuli may evoke smells, tastes, and tactile sensations as well; and sounds may produce visual images. When presented with a tone at 50 Hz and an amplitude of 100 decibels, "S" saw

> a brown strip against a dark background that had red tongue-like edges. The sense of taste is like that of sweet and sour borscht.

For 100 Hz at 86 decibels, he saw

> a wide strip that appeared to have a reddish-orange hue in the center: from the center outwards the brightness faded with light gradations so that the edges of the strip appeared pink.

And with a 200-Hz note at an amplitude of 64 decibels, he saw

> a velvet cord with fibers jutting out on all sides. The cord was tinged with delicate, pleasant pink-orange hue.[16]

Synesthesia came spontaneously throughout his life. When asked if he would remember his way home from an institute where he had been conducting some experiments, "S" replied: "How could I possibly forget. After all, here is this fence, it has such a salty taste and feels so rough; furthermore it has such a sharp piercing sound."[17]

Synesthesia could also hinder his memory at times. If he were recalling images from a visual scene and Luria was saying yes to each correct recall, he would find that the word *yes* produced a smudge on the visual scene and he would have to move the image in order to see the next item clearly.

Curiously his biggest problem was how to forget. If "S" was recalling lists written on a blackboard, he had to be very careful not to recall lists written on the same blackboard in similar situations at other times. He tried various ways to overcome this difficulty, such as writing the items down on a piece of paper, believing that if he wrote them down, his mind would no longer feel it necessary to remember them. This is in sharp contradiction to most people's habit of writing things down in order to remember them, forming stronger associative bonds and increasing the depth of processing mentioned earlier. The solution that "S" finally adopted was surprisingly simple. He suddenly realized that if he did not want the list to be there, it would not appear. All it needed was for him to realize this, then once he set his mind on forgetting, he forgot.

Another curious feature about his mental processes was that "S" did not abstract information, or look for underlying principles, in the way that most people do. If given the following series to recall:

        1   2   3   4
        2   3   4   5
        3   4   5   6
        4   5   6   7
        5   6   7   8

. . . .

he would proceed to form images of these numbers and associate them with other images in his normal manner. And after much effort and concentration he would proceed to recall the entire series perfectly. He did not make use of the obvious patterns in the numbers.[18]

Normally he found it very difficult to remember people's faces. He saw a face as a continually changing pattern of light and shade, which was never the same from one moment to the next. At different times people had very different expressions on their faces, making it exceedingly difficult for him to fix upon one definite concrete image. He was not remembering the abstraction derived from sensory experience, as most of us do, but was remembering the sensory experiences themselves.

"S" 's capacity may sound fantastic, but he was using abilities common to all of us. Indeed, the fact that he did not make much use of organization and principle seeking shows that even he was not using all his abilities—he was still working at only a fraction of his capacity.

APPLICATIONS AND ADVICE

Try making yourself a very simple peg system along the lines suggested on page 126, either choosing images that rhyme with the numbers, or images that have the same shapes as the numbers. Choose whichever you prefer, though it is best to stick to one system. The images you choose should all be of objects of one form or another, objects that are easily visualized. When you have found some image that links well with each number, you should find that you can remember all of them without any difficulty. If there is some difficulty with any particular one, go back and make sure that the association, that is, the rhyme or shape, is clear and simply connected to the number.

Now think up ten other objects—any objects you like. As you think of each object, link it with a number by forming some visual link and association between the object and the image you have associated with the number. Thus if your first object is an orange and you are using a rhyming system, then you want to link orange with gun (the image associated with number one) and you might imagine a gun shooting oranges or, even more unusual, a gun poking out of an orange. Remember to make the connection as absurd as possible, while keeping it simple along the lines indicated on page 126. Then take the next object you think of and link it with the image you have put to the number 2. Carry on doing this until you have linked ten objects to your peg system.

Now take a blank sheet of paper and write down the numbers 1 to 10 in any order you like and see if you can put an object to each number. First take the number, recall the image that rhymes with it or is of the same shape, and then see if you can recall what object was associated with that image. You will probably find that with very little trouble you will get nine or even ten correct—quite an amazing feat for the average memory (or is it?). If you fail to get any of the objects, or recall any incorrectly, check back and see if the imagery was really that absurd, visual, connective, simple, etc. You will often find your failures very instructive.

Then tomorrow see how many of the list you can still recall; you'll probably be very surprised.

Simple mnemonic systems such as the number-peg system can be very useful in daily life when paper and pencil are not easily available for jotting down lists, etc. Some people remember things they have to do the next day just before they go to sleep at night. They are faced with the choice of either getting out of bed, switching on the light, finding pen and paper, and writing them down, or else simply hoping they will still remember them in the morning. By using a simple associative system, you have only to form good clear associations between ideas and their respective pegs in the system and they will be fixed in the memory. The next morning you simply run through the list to recall the ideas that came the night before. The same applies to ideas that come while you are in the bath, driving the car, or at a dinner party.

It might be thought that only one set of items could be linked to the system at any one time, but the same system can in fact be used for two or three lists simultaneously without one set of items interfering with another. As well as the associations that are made deliberately, there are other very valuable incidental associations being made, such as the situation in which the links were made and the general topic of the list. These incidental connections keep the different lists firmly apart in the mind. One can have lists of shopping, lecture points, things to do, people to phone, etc., all linked to the same set of number rhymes and without any confusion. When lecture points are recalled, the images that come to mind will be those associated with the lecture point —those of the shopping list or people to phone are not being called for and will not come up.

Remembering Faces. One area of memory in which nearly everybody claims to have difficulty is remembering faces. One can be introduced to ten people, and within five minutes one has probably forgotten most of the names. Here again associative imagery is impressively powerful.

Instead of just passively hearing the person's name as you shake hands, you should consciously make a clear and simple association between the name and their face, or any other aspect that stands out or is relevant. Again use as many as possible of the factors that naturally enhance memory in order to make the association as vivid and lasting as possible. Thus if you were remembering first names, you might imagine Robin to have a bright red breast and Cheryl to have huge bunch of cherries hanging from her ears or, even better, from her nipples. With surnames one might imagine Mr. Campbell as sitting in a can of soup, Mrs. Evans floating in the heavens, Dr. Harrison in his surgery holding his hairy son, and Ms. Nixon with nothing but her knicks on.

What is important is to make the association strong and clear; really visualize the image as if it were really happening. And if you can link the image with some distinctive aspect of the person, such as the hair style or face shape, so much the better. This can normally be done in the second or two that it takes to be introduced. If an image does not readily come to mind, ask the person to repeat his name. In fact this is always a good policy, not only does it give you longer to make a good clear association, it forces you to be more conscious of the name.[19] When you use a simple system such as this, you will soon have little difficulty remembering twenty or more names straight off. When you do fail to recall a name, you will almost invariably find it is either because the image was not strong or ridiculous enough, or because you were not paying sufficient attention to the associative process at the time.

Absent-Mindedness. Another common complaint about memory is absent-mindedness. This again can be greatly reduced if you use strong associative imagery. If you find that you are always forgetting where you have put things, then the next time you put something away in a cupboard or drawer, make a strong bizarre image connecting the object and the place you are putting it and you will find it almost impossible to forget.

Absent-mindedness occurs when the mind is absent. You are probably only performing the functions semiconsciously. So become as conscious as possible of the event. If you have a tendency to leave your keys behind, imagine yourself using a huge colored key to open the door to go out. If the image is strong enough, then you will certainly remember your key as you start to go out.

As a general rule, whenever you want to remember something, create a simple image connecting the item with the reason for remembering it, making the link as unique, exaggerated, sensory, and original as possible, and you soon will be amazed at how easy it is to recall things you would otherwise have forgotten.

Figure 41

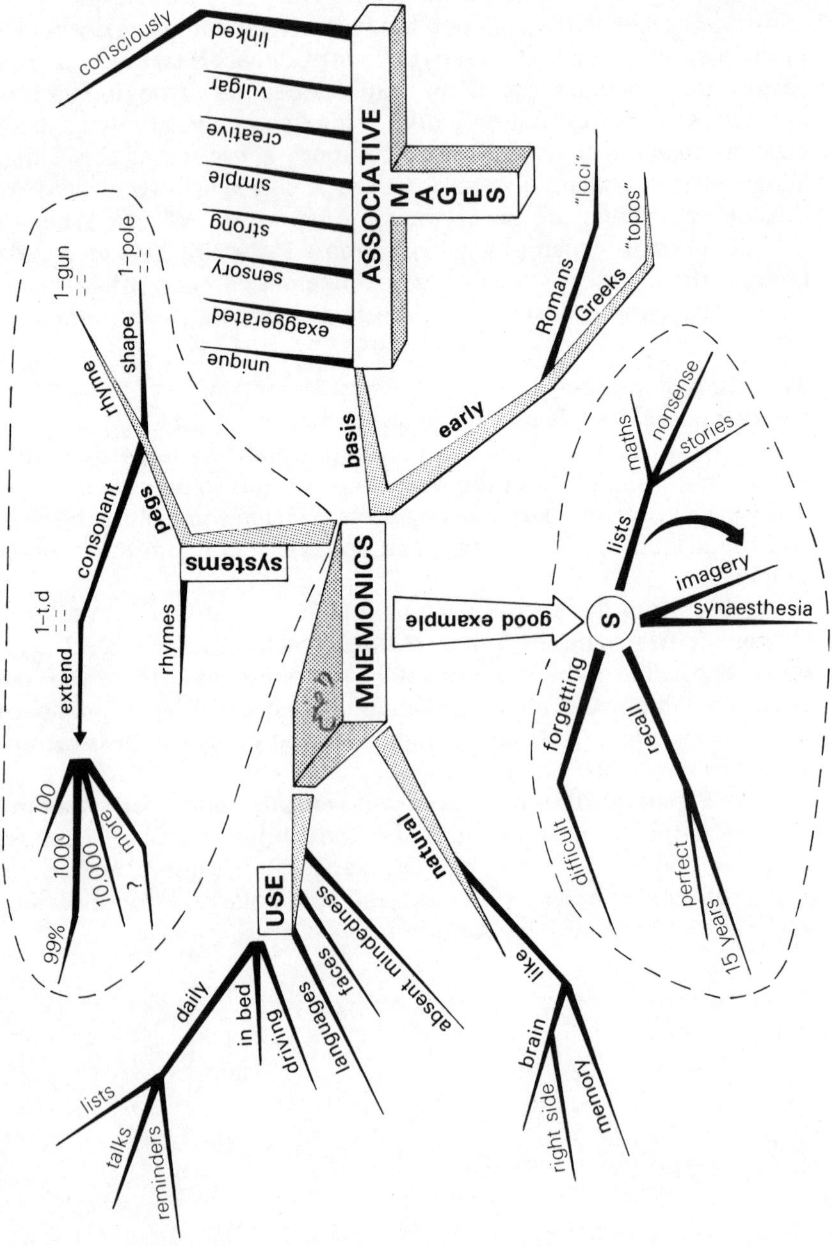
consciously
linked
vulgar
creative
simple
strong
sensory
exaggerated
unique
ASSOCIATIVE
MAGES
"loci"
"topos"
Romans
Greeks
early
basis
MNEMONICS
systems
pegs
rhyme
shape
1–gun
1–pole
consonant
1–t,d
extend
rhymes
100
1000
10,000
more
?
99%
good example
S
lists
maths
nonsense
stories
imagery
synaesthesia
forgetting
difficult
recall
perfect
15 years
natural
like
brain
right side
memory
USE
absent mindedness
faces
languages
driving
in bed
daily
lists
talks
reminders

10.
The Brain's Record of Experience

How are memories stored in the brain?
Can memories be transferred from one individual to another?
Can each memory be associated with a specific chemical?
Is learning the same as memory?
How does consolidation of the memory trace occur?
Why do we forget?
Why is regular review of studies valuable?

One of the first people to consider the subject of memory was Plato, in the fourth century B.C. He proposed what is known as the wax tablet hypothesis. According to Plato's theory, impressions are recorded in the mind in the same way that lines are etched in wax when a pointed object is drawn across its surface. With time the impression wears away, leaving a smooth surface once more. This Plato saw as the process of forgetting.

Since Plato, a wide variety of hypotheses on memory have been offered. For the first part of the present century memory theories were dominated by the idea of the cortical reflex arc. In this theory each memory trace consisted of a particular pathway among the neurons, new memories being laid down as new connections were made between the neurons. Since then, however, it has been realized that the brain does not function like a complex telephone exchange, as the cortical reflex arc theory supposes, nor do neurons appear to make numerous new connections each time a new memory is formed. Current theories suggest that the acquisition of memory is related to the inhibition and facilitation of the synapses throughout the brain. Specific memories are now thought to reside not in a particular synapse or pathway but in the pattern of electrical and chemical changes over the brain as a whole. The two most fruitful lines of research in this direction have been studies of the molecular basis of memory and the application of the principle of holography to memory. This chapter will look at the molecular basis; the next chapter at the holographic theory.

THE MOLECULAR BASIS OF MEMORY

Some of the first experiments to suggest a chemical basis of memory were performed by James McConnell, professor of psychology at Michigan University, in the 1960s. He worked with tiny flatworms (planarians) that he trained to react to light. He conditioned the worms to turn away from light by giving them an electric shock each time they failed to respond. When the worms were trained so that they reacted to the light at least 90 percent of the time, he cut the worms in half. As is common with such creatures the head end of the worm grew a new tail, and the tail end grew a new head. McConnell found not only that the head end still reacted to light, as expected, but also, rather surprisingly, that the tail end, having grown a new head, also reacted to light. He concluded that the learning to avoid light had been stored chemically in individual cells; not only in the brain, but throughout the body.[1]

Now it happens that planarian worms will, when they become very hungry, turn cannibalistic and eat their fellows—providing their victims are cut up into small enough pieces first. This provided McConnell with the chance to test his hypothesis further. If there was a chemical basis to learning that was distributed throughout the body, by training one worm to react to light and then cutting it up and feeding it to another untrained worm, the effect of training might be transferred. To his delight he found that the worms that had eaten the educated victims did significantly better (right from the very first trial) than the worms that had eaten untrained victims.[2]

Whether or not these findings prove a chemical transfer of memory is still a matter of debate. Some workers have failed to replicate

McConnell's results.[3] Others have suggested that there may be some other factor in the experimental procedure that made cannibal worms light sensitive.[4]

Meanwhile McConnell moved on to higher animals. In 1966 he started looking at memory transfer in rats. Rats, however, are not generally cannibalistic, and even if they were, the digestive process would almost certainly destroy any chemicals involved. Instead of feeding the trained rats to other rats McConnell took extracts from the brains of trained rats and injected the extracts directly into the brains of untrained rats. Again he found a very specific transfer of memory to be occurring, the injected rats learning the tasks much faster.[5] Other researchers had similar findings, not only in rats but also in such higher mammals as monkeys. The transfer is generally very specific. Thus if one group of rats is trained to react to the sound of a bell and another group trained to react to a puff of air, then a third group of rats injected with extracts from the bell-trained rats would avoid the sound of a bell but show no reaction to the puff of air, and vice versa.[6]

RNA AND MEMORY

The next step after McConnell's work was to look for the chemical, if any, being transferred. Attention initially turned to RNA (ribonucleic acid). This is a complex organic molecule, containing millions of atoms, which is found in all living cells. It is involved in, among other things, the production of proteins within the living cell. Strands of RNA copy the parts of the genetic code from DNA (deoxyribonucleic acid), and the information contained in the code determines specific sequences of amino acids. When strung together, the amino acids form proteins—the building blocks of life.

Early work showed that the RNA content of neurons increases following learning. Other experiments have since shown that when certain chemicals that inhibit the production of RNA are injected into the brains of animals, the learning is severely impaired or altogether eliminated.[7] Experiments with chemicals that enhance RNA productions have produced an improvement of learning.[8]

Initially it was thought that changes in RNA itself were responsible for memory and learning. It was proposed that a given pattern of electrical impulses impinging on a neuron might produce a slight but permanent change in the structure of the RNA molecules. This would affect the proteins being synthesized, and as a result there would be a change in the cell's functioning. This change would then be the basis of learning.[9] However, it now seems more likely that it is not the RNA itself that is important so much as the increased protein synthesis that results from the increased RNA. Thus many of the early failures to replicate McConnell's transfer experiments may have been due to researchers looking for the transfer of RNA itself, rather than the proteins synthesized by the RNA.

MEMORY MOLECULES

In the 1970s Georges Ungar, at the Baylor College of Medicine in Houston, not only found strong evidence that it is the synthesized proteins that are responsible for the transfer effect; he even managed to identify some of the molecules involved in specific types of learning.

Ungar trained rats to avoid darkness. Normal rats prefer dark areas to light, but in these experiments they received electric shocks every time they went toward a dark area of a box, so they learned to stay in the light area. He then injected extracts from the brains of the trained rats into untrained rats and found, as in similar experiments, that the untrained animals would also start to avoid the dark.

He then set about analyzing the brain extract to find the specific chemical responsible. Combining the extracts from four thousand rats, he found traces of a new protein—a string of some fifteen amino acids. He called this substance scotophobin, from the Greek *skotos,* "darkness," and *phobos,* "fear." To prove that this was indeed the chemical involved in the learning, he had chemists synthesize it from its basic elements. It was found that when the synthetic scotophobin was injected into normal rats, it produced the same avoidance of the dark as did the natural extract.[10] Even more remarkable is the finding by another research group that synthetic scotophobin produces dark avoidance in goldfish as well,[11] implying that it may be a universal coding.

Since then Ungar and his team have discovered an eight-segment chain of amino acids, which they call anelatim and which seems to be the specific chemical responsible for the habituation of rats to the sound of an electric bell. The specificity of the protein is shown by the fact that it was not found when the rats were habituated to the sound of a brass gong rather than an electric bell.[12]

In another series of experiments they analyzed the extracts from the brains of some ten thousand goldfish that had been trained to distinguish between the colors blue and green. They isolated another protein, called chromodiopsin, which appeared to be responsible for this particular color discrimination.[13]

These findings, if they continue to be corroborated, would imply that there may be a specific chemical substance associated with every single skill that it is possible to learn. As far as the number of different proteins are concerned, this is quite possible. Each protein is a string of amino acids, and there are 20 principal amino acids that can occur at any point on the chain. Thus the potential number of combinations is practically infinite. There are, for example, 20 × 20, or 400, different proteins possible containing two amino acids (20 possibilities in the first place and 20 possibilities in the second place). Similarly, there are 8,000 different proteins possible consisting of just three amino acids, and some 33.66 quintillion proteins like scotophobin consisting of fifteen amino acids. And these are still very elementary amino acid chains. Insulin, for example, still a comparatively simple organic substance, contains fifty amino acids, while more complex chains are known to exist containing some several thousand amino acids in sequence. The possible number of different proteins of this length, if written out in the normal way, would have a string of zeroes long enough to fill the next two pages of this book!

IS MEMORY THE SAME AS LEARNING?

Even if it were true that every behavior modification were associated with a protein chain, this would not prove that every *memory* had a similar basis. Learning and memory are not the same thing. Learning, as far as the foregoing experiments were concerned, consisted of training animals to react automatically to a certain given stimulus—a conditioning procedure. Memory, on the other hand, especially in humans, can be taken to include a much broader retention of information. Thus, to say we remember a person's face need only mean that in the right circumstances we might recognize that we have seen the face before. This is very different from the kind of learning that the foregoing experiments have been studying. In human terms, the rat and goldfish experiments are equivalent to training a person to jump in the air every time he saw a specific face until the reaction was so automatic that he would do it whatever the circumstances.

Not only is it extremely unlikely that everyday memory is encoded in the same way that conditioned learning appears to be: It is mathematically impossible. Even given the colossal number of different possible proteins, the variety of different facts we can remember is far greater still (although we cannot record everything simultaneously). This can be seen by observing that if memory worked by one protein encoding the memory for one fact, and the same protein were always used for the same fact, the ability to remember the amino acid sequence of any protein chosen at random would completely exhaust the capacity of such a memory, for the memory of each sequence would require at least one protein to encode it. Thus memory, in its broadest sense, cannot be based on a one-to-one correspondence with specific proteins. It is far more likely that it corresponds to patterns of chemical changes over the brain as a whole—something we shall be looking at further in the next chapter.

CONSOLIDATION

It seems probable that memory is encoded through the direct modification of synapses by proteins synthesized within the cell body. Although neurons produce several times as much protein as any other cell, none of these proteins is secreted: They are all used within the neuron itself. As we saw in chapter 3, many of the proteins travel rapidly down the axons, often at the rate of a few centimeters per day, to arrive at the synapse. The fact that they travel so fast means that very often a protein synthesized in the cell body can be at the synapse within only a few minutes. Thus, if proteins are involved in memory, it would seem that the distinction between short-term and long-term memory may represent the time taken for proteins to arrive at the synapse and consolidate the memory.

Whereas drugs that affect protein synthesis affect long-term memory, drugs that affect only electrical activity, leaving protein synthesis alone, affect only short-term memory.[14] Moreover, drugs that specifically affect the transfer of protein molecules down the axons have also been shown to affect long-term memory. The drug colchicine, for example, appears to block long-term retention by interfering with the microtubules (thin tubes inside the axons that carry the proteins from cell body to synapse), thus preventing the necessary changes at the synapses itself.[15]

Substantial evidence that the synapses are involved in learning has come from two different directions. First, learning can dramatically change the effectiveness of a synapse, decreasing its transmitting ability to zero or enhancing it considerably.[16] And second, the amount of transmitter substance at some synapses varies after learning, decreasing after the first day and then rising over the next week and declining again after two to four weeks.[17]

One possible way in which the proteins may affect the synapse is by occupying vacant sites in the grid system we previously looked at. The proteins would fit into vacant spaces in the grid and so influence the rate at which transmitter substances could be released into the synaptic gap. This would in turn affect the probability of the first neuron conveying an impulse across to the second one. Supporting evidence for this comes from experiments showing that after excitation the number of vacant holes in the grid does change significantly.[18]

A second stage of memory consolidation appears to occur during sleep, in particular during dreaming. Deprivation of dream activity has been found to lead to a decrease in memory for recently acquired material. Conversely, when a lot of learning has taken place, dream time tends to increase in the next night's sleep.[19] Thus, dreaming may

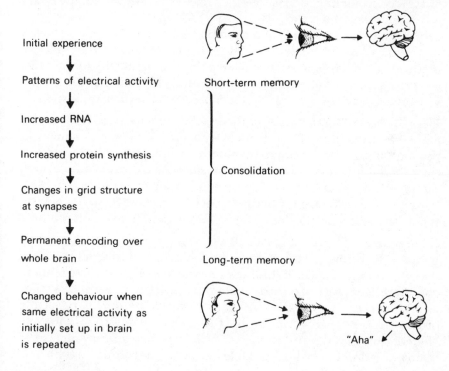

Initial experience

Patterns of electrical activity   Short-term memory

Increased RNA

Increased protein synthesis

Changes in grid structure at synapses   Consolidation

Permanent encoding over whole brain   Long-term memory

Changed behaviour when same electrical activity as initially set up in brain is repeated   "Aha"

Figure 42 Some of the processes probably involved in the encoding of memory.

play an important part in helping to maintain a memory trace.

Proteins themselves last for only a few days and must continually be resynthesized. Therefore, the retention of a permanent memory is likely to involve a more permanent change than just protein synthesis. The protein changes at the synapse probably produce in the longer term permanent structural changes at the synapses, and these modifications may be taking place up to a week or two after the initial experience.

WHY DO WE FORGET?

Evidence from many different sources suggests that, for all practical purposes, our memory is virtually unlimited. Why then do we appear to forget?

Repression.   One of the earliest theories of forgetting was Freud's hypothesis that forgetting is a result of repression. A period that has painful or anxiety-promoting associations is unconsciously repressed. If we cannot remember it, then we do not have to face up to its associations. Very occasionally this can result in a condition known as fugue, in which a person may lose all memory of his past. In mentally healthy people, however, although repression may sometimes occur, it only accounts for a very small amount of our forgetting. You probably cannot recall the last word of the previous chapter, but this is hardly the result of repression.

Decay.   According to the decay theory, the memory trace itself gradually fades with time. Thus, if memory were encoded in changes in protein throughout the brain, then decay would take place as some of the proteins returned to their original state. As the decay progressed, the memory would become fainter and harder to retrieve. Although there is some evidence for decay, especially in short-term memory, it is now thought that interference plays a far greater role in forgetting.

Interference.   The interference theory suggests that forgetting occurs because the memory can no longer be distinguished from all the other memory traces. The trace itself does not necessarily fade, but as more and more memories are accumulated, particularly those with similar associations, or of similar meaning, it becomes harder to recall the original material—in other words, the memories interfere with one another. Interference results not so much from an overcrowding of the memory as from a lack of suitable retrieval cues to distinguish one memory from another.

Search. Related to the interference theory of forgetting is the search theory. According to this, the retrieval of a memory is more of a problem-solving operation. Donald Norman shows that if a person were asked what he was doing on the Monday afternoon in the third week of September two years ago, his response might be as follows:

> Come on. How should I know?
> Okay. Let's see: two years ago. . . .
> I'd be in high school in Pittsburgh. . . .
> That would be my senior year.
> The third week in September—that's just after summer—that would be the fall term. . . .
> Let me see. I think I had chemistry lab on Mondays. . . .
> I don't know. I was probably in the chemistry lab. . . .
> Wait a minute—that would be the second week of school. I remember he started off with the atomic table—a big fancy chart. I thought he was crazy, to make us memorize that thing.
> You know, I think I can remember sitting . . .[20]

As the retrieval process continues and more and more clues are put together, it becomes easier to find the memory, although originally one may have been completely at a loss. According to the search theory, as with the interference theory, forgetting occurs as more and more memories are accumulated without sufficient cues to differentiate between them. Thus, it becomes harder and harder to find any one particular item in memory.

Set. Much apparent forgetting may occur as a result of changed mental preparedness, or "set." As was shown on page 89, a short warm-up task that resets the mind to a particular field can greatly enhance memory. Similarly, putting people back into a situation they were in some time before can invoke many forgotten memories.

APPLICATIONS AND ADVICE

There are several phases of memory consolidation:

1. During the first few minutes, as electrophysiological activity gives rise to protein synthesis

2. Over the next night's dreaming

3. Over the next week or two, as the synaptic changes are made more permanent

Repetition of the initial learning will always enhance memory, and it will be particularly valuable at these crucial stages of memory consolidation. It is therefore always a good plan to establish an organized system of review whenever you undertake any form of study or the remembering of any new material.

A good system is to have your first review of the material about five to ten minutes after the end of study.[21] This not only reinforces the consolidation of protein synthesis, it also makes the best use of the reminiscence effect, since memory is at its highest around this time. Research has shown that a five-minute review at this time considerably improves later recall.[22]

The second period of review should be about twenty-four hours later and should take only two to three minutes. This makes maximum use of the consolidation occurring during sleep, and will compensate for any initial decline in the memory trace.

The third review should be about one week later for two to three minutes. This will make use of the long-term reminiscence effect and stabilize the memory for a much longer period. There should be another review after about one month, again for two to three minutes, and a final review after six months. After this final review most material will be permanently recorded in memory. The consolidation can be further enhanced by appropriate study techniques and note-taking systems so that virtually all the required material can be recalled (see chapter 13).

The effect of such a review program is to reduce greatly the rate

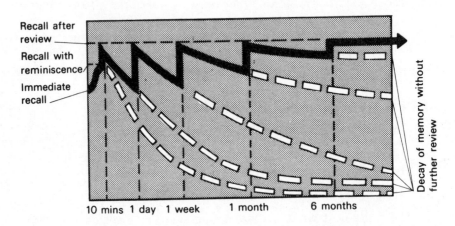

Figure 43 How organized review can keep results at a high level.

of forgetting. Instead of the memory dropping off rapidly by about 80 percent over the first twenty-four hours, it can be reinforced by reviews at the critical consolidation periods and at subsequent intervals, and it can be raised back toward, or even up to, the 100-percent line.

It may be thought that with continual study the reviews would accumulate and take over most of the study time. Actually, this is not the case. Supposing a person studied every day for one hour a day and set up a review program for this study. On any one day he would need to review the work from one day, one week, one month, and six months before.

Review of work done:	Time taken:
1 day before	3–5 minutes
1 week before	2–3 minutes
1 month before	2–3 minutes
6 months before	2–3 minutes
Maximum review time on any one day:	14 minutes

Thus a person spending one hour a day on study would need spend only a *maximum* total of fourteen minutes a day to complete all the necessary reviewing, and improve his memory many times over. This is the maximum because the information may often be recalled as a part of daily life or ongoing program of study, thus producing an automatic review of the material. A person studying as much as six hours a day, every day, still only needs spend a *maximum* of just over an hour each day reviewing the last six months' work in order to fix it permanently in his memory and so gain the greatest value from the study. If the extra 20 percent of time spent reviewing leads to an improvement in long-term memory from 10 percent to 90 percent, the overall gain in efficiency is about 750 percent. *Thus a few minutes devoted to review makes the hours spent studying effective and worthwhile.*

Figure 44

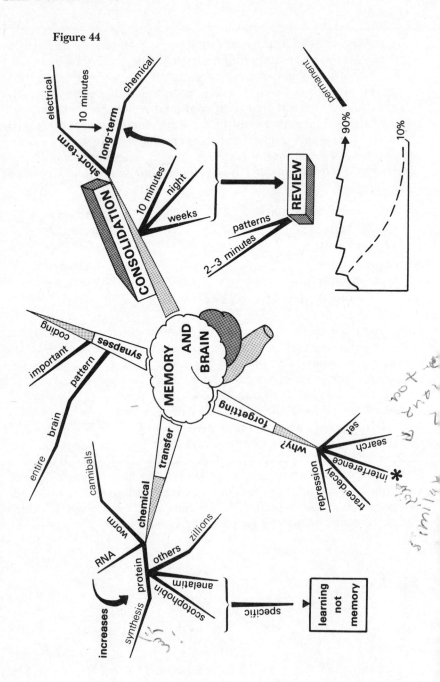

11.
The Holographic Theory of Mind

What is a hologram?
How is it different from a photograph?
Is memory encoded holographically?
Is the mind a hologram?
Is the universe a hologram?

The term *hologram* was first coined by Denis Gabor in 1947 to describe a new photographic process he discovered and for which he was awarded the Nobel Prize in 1971. In a normal photograph the visual information is stored as a direct representation of the image, each point of the photograph corresponding to a particular part of the image. In a hologram the entire photographic plate stores a record of all the wave patterns produced by the object. The whole of the image is encoded at every point, hence the name *holography,* from the Greek *holos,* meaning "whole."

Gabor originally developed holography as a means of improving the resolution of photographs taken with electron microscopes, and the process did not find a wider use until the discovery of lasers some time later. Lasers produce coherent light, that is to say light in which all the

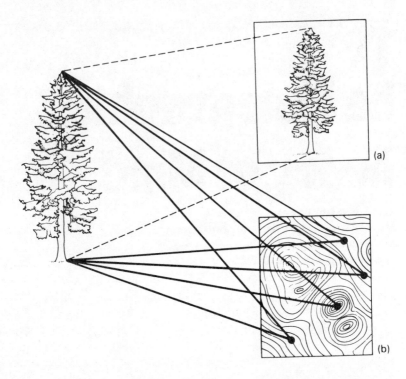

Figure 45 Difference between (a) ordinary photograph and (b) hologram. In an ordinary photograph each point of the object is represented by a specific point of the image. In a hologram the whole of the object is encoded at every point of the image.

waves are in step with each other. With coherent light it is very much easier to construct holograms and apply them to a number of different purposes.

To produce a hologram a laser beam is split in two. One half is directed straight to the photographic plate; the other is shone onto the object and reflected from it to the photographic plate. The plate then records the interference pattern produced by the meeting of the two waves. The image that is so recorded on the photographic plate bears little obvious resemblance to the object itself. If examined minutely, it looks more like fine waving bands of light and dark, something like a zebra's coat (see Figure 47).

To reconstruct the image the hologram is simply reilluminated using the original laser beam, and a three-dimensional image of the original object appears floating in space where the original object was.

Itzhak Bentov provided a good analogy of seeing how a hologram stores information in his fascinating book *Stalking the Wild Pendulum.* [1] Imagine a pan full of water, into which you drop three pebbles. The pebbles produce three sets of circular ripples, each centered on the point where one of the pebbles hit the surface, and these ripples interfere to produce a complex pattern of waves on the surface. Now imagine you were to quick-freeze the surface and lift out the rippled sheet of ice. The whole sheet would contain precise information about where the pebbles struck. If the pattern were carefully analyzed, the different constituent waves could each be traced back to their source. Even if the sheet were shattered, each fragment would still contain all the necessary information. Taking a small section of the surface, you would be able to analyze what ripples had made up the pattern and work out where the three centers were. In a photographic hologram this reconstruction is done automatically by reilluminating with suitable laser light (see Figure 48).

The hologram is the second most sophisticated information storage system known to mankind (the most sophisticated is the living brain). Thousands of different images can be recorded on the same plate, and each of them can be reconstructed from any part of the plate. The reconstructed images are three-dimensional, and looking at the hologram from different angles gives different views of the image.

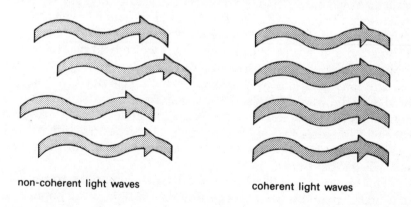

non-coherent light waves   coherent light waves

Figure 46 Noncoherent light (waves out of step) vs. coherent light (waves peak and trough together).

IS MEMORY RECORDED HOLOGRAPHICALLY?

Karl Pribram, from Stanford Medical School, and several other researchers have investigated the possibility that memory may be stored in the brain along holographic principles. In this case individual memories are not stored in specific networks of neurons or at specific synapses but are distributed throughout the whole brain. The fact that different areas of the brain are linked by thousands of parallel pathways provides a basis for the neurological equivalent of coherent activity, and any rhythmic firing would tend to enhance the phenomenon. As the patterns of electrical activity are consolidated by chemical changes, the experience becomes permanently encoded. Any one memory would be encoded as a pattern of chemical changes over trillions of synapses—and possibly glia cells as well—and each synapse would be involved in billions of different memories. Pribram's case is supported by the many striking similarities between human memory and holograms, suggesting that similar principles may indeed underlie both.

Distribution of Memories. Karl Lashley first demonstrated that memory appeared to be distributed throughout the brain rather than localized at specific sites. He trained rats to run mazes and then removed various parts of their brains. But whichever part he removed, he could not remove the memory; by removing successively larger and larger chunks he could only impair the memory to a greater degree. From this he developed two theories: the theory of "mass action," which stated that the intensity of recall depended upon the mass of the brain left intact; and the theory of "equipotentiality," which held that the memory was distributed evenly throughout the brain.

The same phenomena are found in the hologram. The image is stored over the whole plate and every chip from it contains the whole information. The only loss that occurs is a loss in detail and clarity. An image which is reconstructed from a small chip of the hologram will not be as sharp, nor contain as much detail as the original, but the image itself will still be there.

This brings out another important distinction between the human brain and a computer. If just one tiny connection in a computer is altered, the whole informational content may be significantly changed, even upset and destroyed. Both holograms and memory, though, are very resistant to damage.

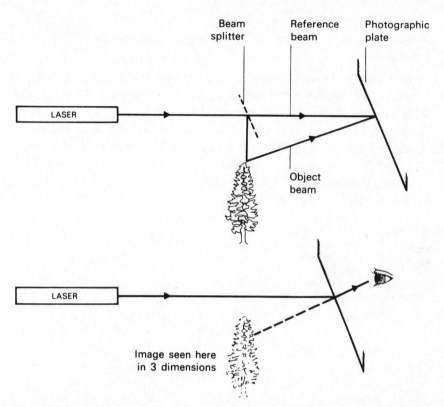

Figure 47 Creation of hologram (top). Light reflected from object meets unreflected light (reference beam) and interference produced is recorded on photographic plate. Reconstruction of image (bottom). When plate is developed and reilluminated with original light, a three-dimensional image is seen standing in position originally occupied by object.

Multiple Images. Many different images can be stored in one holographic plate. Having recorded one image, the plate only has to be rotated by one or two degrees in order to record a second image which will not interfere with the record of the first one. As well as rotating the plate through any number of angles the frequency of the light used can also be changed to record different images. So by varying the angle and the frequency it is possible to record many thousands of complete three-dimensional images on one plate—and of course many thousands are also recorded on each chip. It may sound fantastic, but it is just this kind of fantastic phenomena that we find in the brain—millions of images each stored throughout the brain and each clearly differentiated from the rest.

Initial Conditions and Context. If a holographic plate is illuminated with light of the same frequency and at the same angle as that with which it was originally illuminated, the original image will be reproduced. Change to a different set of initial conditions and a different image is brought out. Earlier it was shown the same is true of memory, that the initial conditions are important cues for retrieving a memory. It is much easier to recall information if a person is put back, either mentally or physically, into the original situation. Thus the

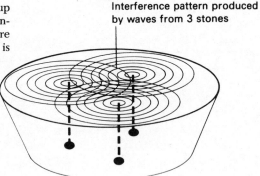

Figure 48 Three pebbles dropped in a bowl of water set up interference patterns which contain all information about where pebbles fell, much as an image is recorded in a hologram.

Interference pattern produced by waves from 3 stones

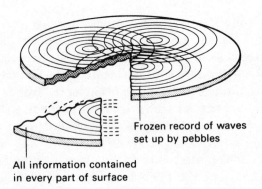

Frozen record of waves set up by pebbles

All information contained in every part of surface

drunk remembers what he did when he gets drunk again, and Locke's young man remembers how to dance only when the trunk is in the room.

Association.   Closely connected with the phenomenon of initial context is that of association. It has been seen how all memories are linked by numerous associative connections, and that by thinking of one half of an association the other half will spontaneously spring to mind. Exactly the same phenomenon occurs in holograms. If, in forming the hologram, the first beam is also reflected off an object instead of going straight to the plate, the interference pattern recorded is that produced by the interaction of the waves from the two objects. On reilluminating the plate with light reflected from one of the objects, the image of the second object is reconstructed. Thus association, one of the most important factors in human memory, is also an intrinsic characteristic of holograms.

Recognition.   When a hologram is illuminated with coherent light reflected from the original object, or something very similar, a bright spot is observed in the hologram rather than an image; the intensity of the spot corresponds to how well the new image resembles the original one. Here we have a close parallel to recognition. When the original object, or something very similar, is perceived, we have a subjective "flash," a sudden bright point in our consciousness, and the stronger the "flash," the clearer the recognition.

Capacity.   One of the most remarkable features of both the hologram and of human memory is their remarkable capacity. Just one cubic centimeter of a photographic hologram can store ten billion bits of information. The human brain is fifteen hundred times as large, and the proteins involved are much smaller than the silver grains in photographic film. Human memory capacity is probably several thousand times greater still. It can probably store something on the order of a quadrillion (1,000,000,000,000,000) bits of information. If all this were given over to memory, the brain would have the ability to record a thousand new bits of information per second for every second from birth onward and still have only used a fraction of its memory potential after seventy-five years. [75 (years) $\times$ 365 (days) $\times$ 24 (hours) $\times$ 60 (minutes) $\times$ 60 (seconds) $\times$ 1,000 (bits per second) = 2,365,200,000,-000.] Some of this capacity is taken up by the brain's programs. But even if they took up 90 percent of the capacity, you would still have enough left to record a hundred bits a second—which is probably sufficient capacity to remember most of the experiences that happen during a lifetime.

IS THE MIND HOLOGRAPHIC?

Not only does memory appear to function on holographic principles, but so does perception. The mathematics of holography involves the use of what are called Fourier transformations. These are mathematical equations that transform the object shape into the coded pattern. Similar transformations occur naturally within human perceptual processes.[2]

A nerve fiber connecting the retina of the eye to the brain is attached to several cells in the retina. These cells constitute its receptive field. The nerve responds differently to different cells in its field, so that if the nerve's activity is recorded while a point of light is moved

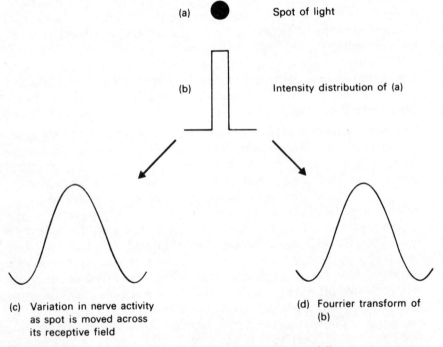

(a) Spot of light

(b) Intensity distribution of (a)

(c) Variation in nerve activity as spot is moved across its receptive field

(d) Fourrier transform of (b)

Figure 49 Response of nerve from retina to spot of light at different points in its receptive field compared with Fourrier Transform of intensity distribution.

across the field, the activity varies as shown in Figure 49. It has been shown that the pattern of activity is in fact the Fourier Transform of the intensity (b).[3] In other words, the brain is making a coded image, and the coding is similar to that which takes place in a hologram.

Other experiments have investigated the electrical response that occurs when the pinpoint of light is replaced by a regularly undulating pattern of light and dark bands. Again it is found that the activity that results relates closely to the Fourier Transform of the input.[4] Research has also shown that hearing, taste, smell, and touch are also analyzed by the same mathematical process.

It has been surmised that the brain probably uses some technique of deconvolution, similar to the processes used to bring out the detail in the blurred photographs of planets radioed back to earth. If the brain did not use some such technique, it would be difficult to understand how we could see as clearly as we do.[5] Such processes are also based on Fourier Transforms. Scientists studying the radar phenomena in bats have found that the only known mechanism that matches the bat's performance is one based on holographic processing. Subsequent research supports the existence of holographic processes in insects, birds, and fish.[6]

IS THE UNIVERSE A HOLOGRAM?

Several scientists have suggested that reality as we know it may be constructed on holographic principles.[7] Physicist David Bohm hypothesizes that the underlying reality is one of pure vibration, a primal frequency realm, which is beyond time and space—analogous to the frequency patterns in a hologram. Any observation or awareness of the world is a concretization of this underlying "reality." A perception by the brain is, in effect, one particular image reconstructed from the infinite number stored in the hologram. It appears to us as real because we can only encompass one particular manifestation at any particular time, and since the hologram is all-pervading, we are usually obliged to see the same "reality" as everyone else.

Such an idea is not new to physics. In the submicroscopic world of quantum physics, objects only have well-defined positions and velocities when they are observed. When not being observed, an object can be in any one of an infinite number of possible states—in fact it is generally said to be in all the states at once. The act of observation, however, forces the mathematical equations to condense out in one particular solution—what mathematicians call the *eigen*-value—and one of the tasks of quantum physicists is to assess the various probabilities of an object appearing in any particular state. If this is so of the submicroscopic world, it is probably also true of the world in which we live our daily lives. It is our being conscious of the world that forces it to adopt a particular reality.

Karl Pribram has argued that a holographic model of "reality" is able to explain telepathy, precognition, clairvoyance, psychokinesis, healing, and most other phenomena that appear to contravene the laws of space and time. These laws are themselves only constructs imposed by our particular concretization of the underlying frequency realm.

This model also makes sense of Jung's phenomenon of synchronicity, in which unrelated events often show striking coincidences. According to a holographic model, there exist underlying patterns and symmetries, but we do not see them because we do not see the realm beyond space and time. The symmetries nevertheless appear in our particular concretization of reality as unexplained coincidences.

Transcendental experiences can also be explained by this model. The person who, deep in meditation, passes beyond the many activities of the mind and experiences a timeless, spaceless realm in which all things are one would appear to be coming into direct contact with the underlying frequency realm. This could explain why people in such states appear to have access to knowledge not available in the ordinary waking state. It would also support the claim sometimes made by people in touch with this level of reality that anything is possible. If we do construct our own reality, it is only a small step to constructing it in any way we imagine. We have only to allow the individual mind and its imagination to resonate with the underlying reality—with the field of all possibilities—for anything to be possible.

Such theories, fascinating as they are, are still highly speculative. The holographic theory of memory itself is not universally accepted. It is still incomplete, and in the future we might see new, even more powerful, theories arising to explain the nature of human consciousness, as the human brain tries to catch up with its own subtleties.

Figure 50

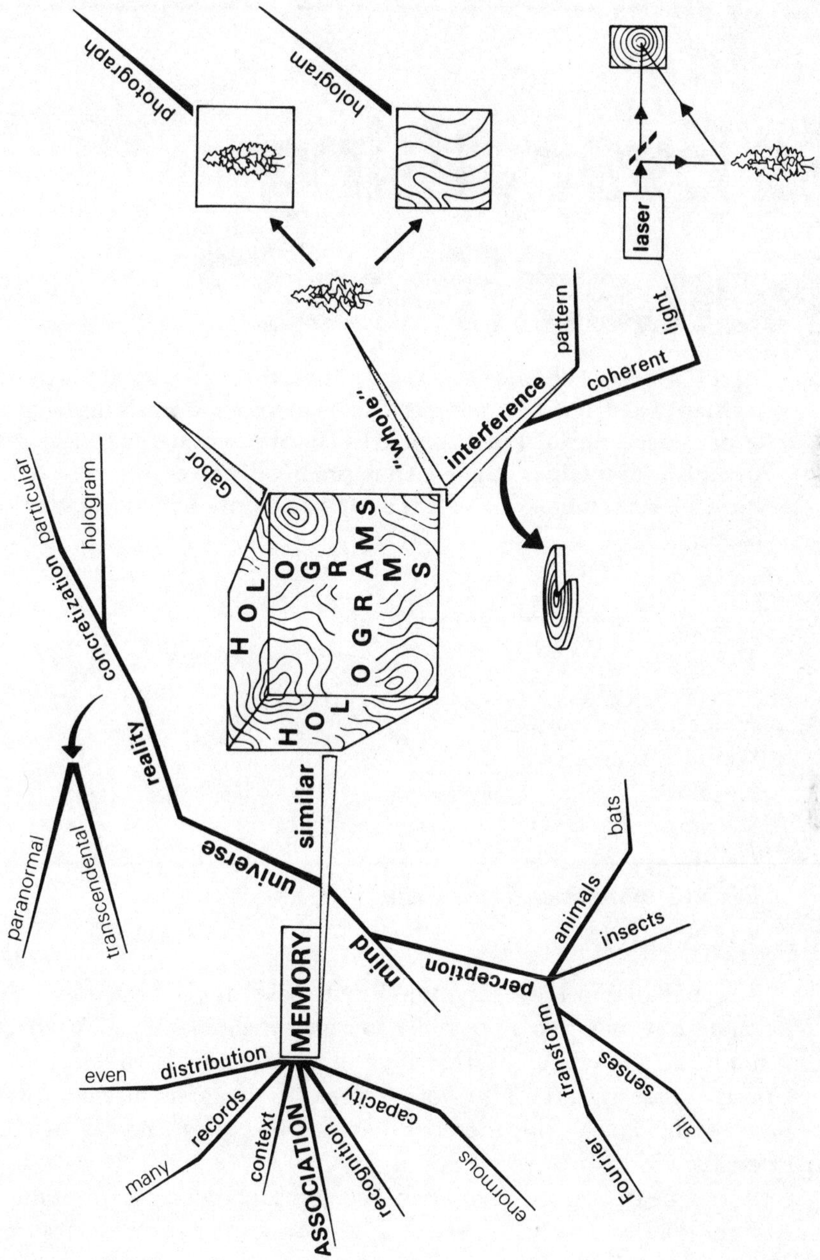
photograph
hologram
laser
light
coherent
pattern
interference
"whole"
Gabor
HOLOGRAMS
particular
hologram
concretization
reality
paranormal
transcendental
universe
similar
mind
MEMORY
perception
animals
bats
insects
transform
senses
all
Fourier
even
distribution
many
records
context
ASSOCIATION
recognition
capacity
enormous

12.

Is Everything Remembered?

In the previous chapter it was seen that, theoretically at least, the human brain has the potential to remember everything that is experienced during a lifetime. This chapter will look at some empirical findings that suggest that practically everything may indeed be remembered. Evidence for this comes from a number of fields:

Recognition
The tip-of-the-tongue phenomenon
Mnemonics
Visual memory
Incidental memory
Memory prodigies
Hypnosis
Dreams
Death-type experiences
Direct stimulation of the brain

RECOGNITION

There is an enormous amount of material that can be recognized, even though it may not be possible to recall it deliberately. A person may not be able to recall intentionally the faces of people whom he met at a party a year ago. Yet if he were to meet them again, he might well recognize the faces. The memory has not been lost; it was merely inaccessible.

It has been argued that such recognition merely represents a partial remembrance of the particular person, but very often in such a situation one will find that he will also notice how the person has changed; or, if it is another person who looks very similar, he may notice that there is something different about the face. He may not be able to pinpoint the difference, but the fact that he notices there is a difference shows that many of the minor details have also been remembered, although they may not be consciously recalled.

Several psychologists have tried to measure the difference between intentional recall and recognition. In one experiment subjects were presented with a list of one hundred words five times. When asked to recall the list, they scored about 30 percent. When, on the other hand, the subjects were asked to recognize the one hundred words mixed with one hundred unrelated words they scored 96 percent correct.[1] This still leaves open the possibility that under more suitable experimental conditions they would have recognized even more, perhaps even 100 percent.

In another experiment people were given lists of words to remember and asked to recall the list three times. It was found that they tended to recall about the same percentage of words on each successive test, but the actual words they recalled varied considerably. Only half of the words recalled appeared in all three tests.[2] This again shows that people remember considerably more than they can recall at any one time.

THE TIP-OF-THE-TONGUE PHENOMENON

One may sometimes be absolutely certain that he knows something yet still not be able to recall it. Often the first letter or even first syllable of a word may be known and it will be "on the tip of the tongue," yet still not recalled.

In a study of this phenomenon experimenters read out definitions of obscure English words and asked people to supply the word. Whenever a person was "seized" by a tip-of-the-tongue state, they asked him to say all the words that came to mind. Although the subjects would have failed on a straight recall test, they were able to produce considerable information about the word—for example, first letters, number of syllables, syllabic stress, suffixes and prefixes—and when they were actually presented with the word, they recognized it immediately.[3]

MNEMONICS

Mnemonic techniques such as those discussed in chapter 9 show that when maximum use is made of imagery and association, memory can be almost perfect. For example, see if you can write down next to the numbers 1 to 10 below the ten items you associated with each of the numbers in the mnemonic exercise given on page 135.

1.
2.
3.
4.
5.
6.
7.
8.
9.
10.

Given a list of one hundred words, few people will be able to recall more than about a quarter of them. Using a simple number-peg system, a person can usually remember all one hundred words perfectly, and in order, and such systems can be easily extended to one thousand words[4] and probably up to ten thousand or more.

VISUAL MEMORY

It was also seen that visual memory is considerably superior to verbal memory. On tests of ten thousand pictures, subjects recognized 99.6 percent of them correctly. As one researcher commented: "The recognition of pictures is *essentially perfect*" (see pages 114–115).

INCIDENTAL MEMORY

In a common type of memory experiment a subject is given a list of words to learn, which he does with varying degrees of success. If, however, some years later, the subject is asked to recall the experiment, he may not remember one of the words. He may well, however, remember the laboratory, what kind of day it was, the clothes he had worn, where he was sitting, who the experimenter was, whether he was friendly or unfriendly, who the other subjects were, and maybe the type of experiment involved. Ironically the person has remembered everything except that which he was asked to remember. One might ask which is the better test of memory capacity: the partial recall of a meaningless, dissociated, nonorganized, boring list of words or the wealth and breadth remembered about the meaningful, multiply associated, interesting events taking place in the environment.

Most psychological tests of memory are misleading if they are taken as an indication of memory capacity. They are generally only elucidating the mechanisms of memory, and in order to elucidate any one particular mechanism, one has to eliminate all other mechanisms that might confound the experiment. Ebbinghaus, for example, in his pioneering experiments mentioned earlier, systematically eliminated all the natural clues and aids to memory in order to measure forgetting. If he had included association, organization, and all the other natural cues, he would probably have found very little, if any, forgetting. Moreover, the majority of memory tests used by psychologists use lists of words or nonsense syllables, yet verbal memory is not nearly so good as visual memory. And few memory experiments would condone the use of mnemonic techniques that helped the person remember. Memory has been studied at its worst, not at its best.

MEMORY PRODIGIES

The remarkable memory of the Russian mnemonist "S" has already been looked at in chapter 9. "S" was not a unique case, although he was one of the most studied cases. Another Russian could memorize 150 poems and recall word for word a story read to him just once several weeks previously. His memory for nonsense syllables appeared perfect, though he did not have any of the synesthesia that "S" did.[5]

The late A. C. Aitken, professor of mathematics at the University of Edinburgh, "easily" remembered the first thousand decimal places of the value of π—forward and backward. Like "S," he could recall lists of words used in memory tests twenty-seven years earlier and had nearly perfect verbatim recall for stories over the same period.[6]

An American named Daniel McCartney, living in the nineteenth century, showed similar prodigious powers. At the age of fifty-four he could still tell instantly what he had been doing on every day since childhood, and could also give the exact date, the weather conditions during the day, and say what he had eaten for breakfast, lunch, and supper on that day. He was also a mathematical prodigy able to give the cube roots of numbers up to millions almost instantly. Yet due to poor vision he could neither read nor write.[7]

Many other similar cases exist, some of them well-known people.

Themistocles remembered the 20,000 names of the citizens of Athens. Xerxes was supposed to be able to recall the 100,000 names of the men in his army. Cardinal Mezzofanti, living in the nineteenth century, was said to be able to speak between seventy and eighty languages, including Latin, Greek, Arabic, Spanish, French, German, Swedish, Portuguese, English, Dutch, Danish, Russian, Polish, Bohemian, Serbian, Hungarian, Turkish, Irish, Welsh, Wallachian, Albanian, Illysian, Sanskrit, Persian, Georgian, Armenian, Hebrew, Chinese, Coptic, Ethiopean, Alyssian, and Amharic. Most of them he could speak fluently.[8]

There were also many Polish Jews called Shass Pollaks who remembered the exact position on the page and the exact page of every word in the twelve large volumes of the Talmud.[9] Indeed, the Talmud was originally handed down solely by memory, as were the even longer Vedic scriptures of ancient India.

HYPNOSIS

Another indication of the phenomenal capacity of human memory comes from experiments on hypnosis. Most people appear to have forgotten much of their early childhood, only a few isolated instances remaining. But in all likelihood the memories have not been erased; it is just that people cannot normally get in contact with them again. When an adult is hypnotized and "taken back" to his early childhood, he will often be able to remember the names of other children in his kindergarten class and be able to give detailed descriptions of them.

David Cheek, from San Francisco, has taken the regression back further and retrieved memories from childbirth itself. He found that his subjects made movements exactly like those of a fetus in childbirth, movements not commonly seen in adults. Cheek himself had been an obstetrician and he conducted an experiment with three adults whom he had delivered twenty years earlier; under hypnosis he took them back to birth. They were then asked for reports of birth experiences, including the positions they took up, which arm extended first, etc. He checked his own notes on the deliveries and found that their descriptions coincided exactly with his own detailed notes of the births.[10]

Cheek also found considerable evidence that people can remember what was said at the time of their birth.[11] As well as throwing more light on the capacity of human memory, this also poses an interesting question: Has language developed sufficiently in the womb for a newborn baby to understand what is being said even if he does not react, or are the words simply stored in memory and understood later?

One of the most amazing examples of memory being retrieved under hypnosis has been reported from Yale University. A bricklayer who ten years previously had worked on a special neo-Gothic building using distinctive bricks was hypnotized and asked to describe a certain brick in a certain wall. He was able to describe the color of the brick, noting that it had been burned a shade too much in the kiln, that it had a purple pebble embedded in the clay in the lower left-hand corner, and that the brick had a slight swelling at the upper right-hand corner that matched the hollow of the brick just above it. The experimenter checked with the actual brick and found that these details, and many others the bricklayer also supplied while under hypnosis, matched perfectly with the brick in question. Moreover, he had laid some two thousand bricks that day, and it is very likely that he would have been able to recall any other of the bricks with equal clarity.[12]

Several police forces are now beginning to use hypnosis in the investigation of crime. In Israel witnesses of terrorist attacks have, under hypnosis, been able to give detailed descriptions of the people involved. Los Angeles police have used hypnosis to solve a number of crimes. In one rape case the victim was able to recall under hypnosis the licence number of her assailant's car.[13]

Under hypnosis people can often recall events that took place while they were apparently unconscious, for example, under an anesthetic during an operation. In one memorable anecdote a woman clearly remembered the surgeon saying, "Well, that takes care of this old bag." She took this to refer to her, though the surgeon was in fact referring to the ovary he had just removed.[14]

In another case reported from Johannesburg a patient accurately recalled that while under deep anesthesia the doctor had exclaimed that it might not be a cyst after all: It may be a cancer![15]

David Cheek likewise found that patients remember a considerable amount of what happens during operations and now uses this to a positive end. He deliberately talks to his patients during anesthesia, giving them positive, optimistic reports on the surgery and suggestions that recovery would be rapid with little pain. He found that the suggestions worked and such patients stayed in the hospital for an average of only eight and a half days, compared with eleven days for patients who were not spoken to under anesthesia.[16]

DREAMS

Further evidence that we may remember far more than we can consciously recall comes from dreams. When people take the trouble to record systematically their own dreams, they may find very detailed memories of the past coming back. Often they may be about episodes they thought had been entirely forgotten. The probable reason why a lot of people do not remember many of their dreams is that there is little association between the world of dreams and the world of daily life. When dreams are suddenly recalled, it is often because of a chance association, and it may well bring back a detailed memory of a dream from several nights or several weeks before. Possibly all our dreams are also recorded in memory, but we do not have the right cues at hand with which to recall them.

DEATH-TYPE EXPERIENCES

Another quite remarkable insight into the capacity of memory comes with the "life review" that some people experience when on the point of death. People who, for example, were rescued from drowning at the very last moment have reported that as they approached death, the whole of their life appeared to flash before them in a moment.

Ten years ago a person suffering a serious heart attack would probably have died. Recent advances in medical treatment have now made it possible to resuscitate a person, even though his heart may have stopped beating for several minutes, and so bring him back from the edge of death. Studies of a number of such cases in which people have temporarily died or been on the brink of death have found many clear instances of this "review" phenomenon. Typical experiences are:

> . . . it was like looking through a volume of my entire life and being able to do it within seconds. It just flashed before me like a motion picture that goes tremendously fast, but I was fully able to see it, and able to comprehend it.

> . . . it shot right by me from the earliest things I can remember right up to the present and it all happened within a short time.

> It was just all there at once, I mean, not one thing at a time, blinking off and on, but it was everything, everything at one time.[17]

An analysis of over a hundred cases of near death from accidents such as mountain-climbing falls, car accidents, and explosions, found that *in half the cases* there was a vivid replay of memory. One woman, who swerved to miss an oncoming car, lost control, and found herself heading toward a bridge pillar, suddenly experienced a dreamlike calm and "saw an endless stream of past experiences—there must have been hundreds—flow through my mind. They were all pleasant. During all of this, time stood still."[18]

Such experiences not only indicate that very little, if anything, is ever forgotten, they also show that the brain can work at speeds many times faster than those to which we are accustomed. Maybe it is because closer to death, the person is freed from the need to keep in touch with the world around him, and the mind starts working at its own natural rate.

DIRECT STIMULATION OF THE BRAIN

Other evidence for the virtually unlimited capacity of human memory comes from the studies of Wilder Penfield and his colleagues at the Montreal Neurological Institute. Because there are no pain receptors inside the brain itself, operations on the brain are often performed with only a local anesthetic to numb the skull, with the patient remaining fully conscious throughout the surgery. During one thousand brain operations between 1936 and 1960, Penfield and his colleagues used this fact to try and ascertain the specific functions of different areas of the cortex. Using fine electrodes they would stimulate a point of the brain with a small electric current and ask the subject to report what he experienced. They found that when they stimulated areas on the side of the brain—what is called the temporal cortex—the patient often reported specific experiences of the past.

The fantastic wealth of detail that Penfield was able to bring forth again suggests that our brains may well be recording everything that happens. The memories elicited were rich in detail, very vivid, and could come from any part of the person's life. Patients would often feel that they were "there," reliving the scene as it happened, often with sight, sound, smell, and touch all present and integrated. One patient, for example, reported:

I was in an office somewhere. I could see the desk. I was there and someone was calling to me—a man leaning on a desk with a pencil in his hand.[19]

Moving the electrode just one millimeter away would usually bring forth a completely different memory.[20]

It is unlikely that the points stimulated were the points at which those specific memories were recorded. The points stimulated were in the "association areas" of the cortex, areas involved in the processing and integration of information, and it is most likely that the stimulation was creating a specific pattern of electrical activity that corresponded to a retrieval cue for a specific memory. The memory itself, though, as we saw in the previous chapter, is very probably distributed throughout the brain.

Each of the lines of evidence discussed in this chapter show that we remember far more than we may ordinarily be aware of. Taken together, they suggest that our memories are vastly greater than we usually imagine. They do not prove we remember everything, but given that the brain has sufficient capacity to do so, it is a possibility.

Figure 51

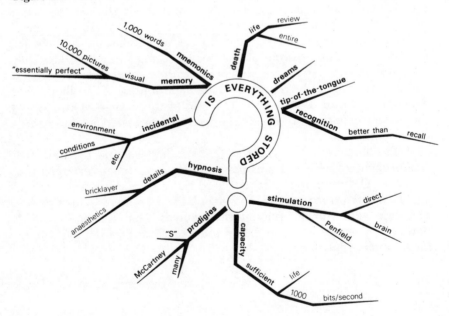

13.
Note Taking

How are ideas linked?
What are key words?
Can note taking be improved?
Are mind maps the answer?
How are mind maps made?
When are mind maps used?

As noted in chapter 1, the human brain is very different from a computer. Whereas a computer works in a linear, step-by-step fashion—albeit very fast—the brain works associatively as well as linearly, carrying on thousands of different processes at the same time, comparing, integrating, and synthesizing as it goes. Thus a person often finds that in conversation his mind is not behaving linearly but racing on in different directions, exploring new ideas and the ramifications of what is being said, and at the same time taking in subtle changes in intonation, body position, facial expression, the eyes, etc., as well as the linear sequence of words.

Association plays a dominant role in nearly every mental function, and words themselves are no exception. Every single word has numerous links attaching it to other ideas and concepts. You have only to take a simple word and start writing down any associations that come to your mind to see that this is true. Given only a minute or two, most people will quickly generate ten or twenty different associations to the word. And these ten or twenty associations are by no means exhaustive. The same word given to ten different people will usually produce sets of associations with very few words in common. Even nonsense syllables have associations. *Boc* is meaningless according to the dictionary, but sit down with a paper and pencil and it is easy to generate several different associations.

Considerable use of this associative power of words is made in creative writing. Part of the art of creative writing is to produce associative images that go beyond the text itself. These offshoots are not linear; they have no well-defined temporal sequence but occur while one is reading, in parallel. Both the writing or reading of such a text tends to make fuller use of the right half of the mind. Scientific writing, on the other hand, tends to be primarily linear, making more use of the left hemisphere. The aim of a scientific paper is not to produce numerous images and send the mind soaring off on other ideas, but to be as specific and linear as possible so that only the one desired idea comes across.

KEY WORDS

We saw earlier that words that had greater significance, had greater meaning, were more outstanding, and generated stronger images were very much easier to remember. When we read, we automatically pick out these more memorable words from the text, and the rest of the material is generally forgotten within a second or two. Thus, take the following sentence: "Astronomers are now suggesting that black holes may not, after all, be entirely black, but may in fact be capable of radiating energy." The key ideas in this sentence, the words that are most memorable and contain the essence of the sentence, are *astronomers, black holes, not black, radiating energy*. The rest of the words are merely grammatical constructions and emphasis; they are not necessary for recall.

Key words tend to be the nouns and verbs in a sentence—though sometimes adjectives and adverbs may be significant enough to become key words. Key words are generally concrete rather than abstract. It has been found that concrete words generate images faster than abstract words—one and a half seconds faster on the average—and that the images they generate are richer and have more associations.[1] For this reason they are better remembered.

In a study by Michael Howe at Exeter University students' notes were examined and the ratio of key words to non–key words measured. It was found that the higher the percentage of key words present in the notes, the better was the recall.[2] Because of their greater meaningful content key words "lock up" more information in memory and are "keys" to recalling the ideas. In the foregoing case you have only to recall the two keys *black holes* and *radiating energy* to unlock the memory of the main idea contained in the sentence.

So that you can get a feel of key words, go back and count how many words in the above three paragraphs of this chapter are actually key words.*

When a young child begins to speak, he starts with key words, stringing them together directly—for example "John ball," or "Susan tired." It is not until later that sentences are expanded and non–key words included to give expressions such as "I want to play with the ball" or "Susan is feeling tired."

We see the same pattern in the historical development of written language. The earlier written languages tended to contain a much higher percentage of key words. This was probably because there was a shortage of material on which to write, scribes being limited to carving on stone or writing on bark or dried leaves; hence it was essential to use words as efficiently as possible. Thus in a Latin sentence there are a higher proportion of nouns and verbs; prepositions, conjunctions, and pronouns are often integrated into the word endings—hence the more complex grammatical structure of Latin. If we go back further to the ancient Indian language of Sanskrit, we find that sentences consist almost entirely of key words. Yet in Sanskrit there is no loss of meaning or significance; if anything, it is more flexible than modern languages.

KEY WORDS AND NOTE TAKING

Although people such as "S" could remember everything that was said without writing anything down, most people find that taking notes helps their recall. Michael Howe in his investigation of students' notes found that items that were noted were six times as likely to be remembered as items that were not written down.[3]

*About thirty.

Taking notes serves several functions besides the simple storage of information. Indeed, simply getting every word down without attention to meaning and significance can often interfere with subsequent memory of the material. In addition to being a means of storing information, taking notes (as opposed to mere copying) performs the valuable functions of

encoding the information;

imposing organization upon the material;

allowing associations, inferences, and interpretations to be jotted down;

bringing attention to what is important; and

bringing attention to what is written.

These are all very valuable for later recall. It has also been shown that the longer the lecture or study session, the more valuable are notes.[4]

The subject of note taking is, however, rarely studied, let alone taught. Thus, although much of a student's life is concerned with the taking of notes, he is seldom, if ever, given much guidance on how best to do so. Most people start out by writing grammatically correct phrases and sentences. Over time they gradually refine these, developing their own shorthand notation and abbreviations in order to make the notes more efficient, making important items outstanding by underlining. Even so, conventional notes still tend to be very cumbersome and inefficient compared with what is possible with key-word notes. When students are asked to take notes in whatever way they have found to be the most efficient and effective, it is usually found that only 5 to 10 percent of the words written are actually key words.

Since it is the key words that are remembered, notes such as those in Figure 52 have a number of serious disadvantages:

1. Time and energy are wasted in taking the notes.

2. Other information may be missed while the student is busy noting.

3. Time is wasted reading the notes.

4. Further time is wasted sorting out key words from irrelevant words.

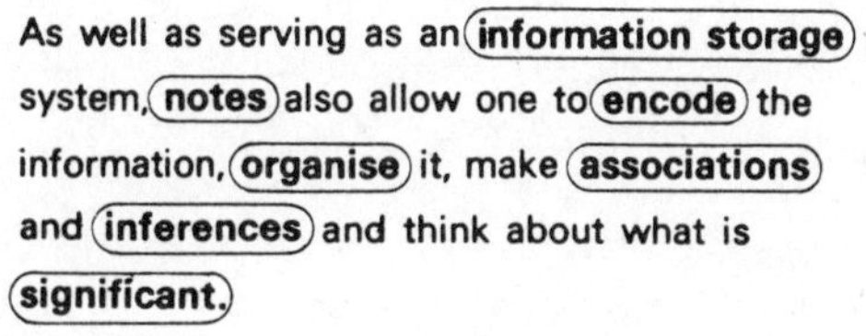

As well as serving as an (information storage) system, (notes) also allow one to (encode) the information, (organise) it, make (associations) and (inferences) and think about what is (significant.)

Figure 52 Conventional linear notes. Only the key concepts (circled) are really necessary.

5. Key words are dissociated (a) visually, (b) in time—this decreases comprehension and memory.

6. The attention wanders more easily.

7. Review is lengthy and laborious.

In short, conventional notes are more like a system to aid forgetting rather than a system to help remembering.

Since we do not remember complete sentences, it is a waste of time to write them down. It is the key words that are recalled, and it is the key words that should be abstracted and recorded. In selecting the key words, a person is brought into active contact with the information. He is not simply copying down material in a semiconscious manner but is becoming immediately aware of the meaning and significance of the ideas, analyzing them, and forming images and associations between them. The memory process is thereby given tremendous help.

MIND MAPS

Most people who have ever had difficulty remembering something from their notes have probably noticed that they may well be able to remember where it had been written on the page, with what other ideas it was associated, and any outstanding visual associations, such as accompanying diagrams. The memory is in fact working excellently, recalling all possible associations, meaningful connections, and outstanding factors. The reason that the recall is difficult is because the notes were not initially made with an awareness of what would be good for recall.

Notes in neat lines may be highly commendable as far as the writing of essays is concerned, but they offer little foothold for memory. In the system of mind maps, developed by Buzan,[5] all the various factors that enhance recall have been brought together in order to produce a much more effective system of note taking. To make a mind map one starts in the center of the paper, with the major idea, and works outward in all directions, producing a growing and organized structure composed of key words and key images. (See, for example, the summary mind maps at the end of each chapter.)

Organization, association, clustering, visual memory, outstandingness, and other phenomena that naturally facilitate human memory can be used to make mind maps more effective in the following ways:

Organization. The brain spontaneously imposes its own subjective organization on all the material it remembers. Even when the material is completely random, subjective organization aids recall. The more we deliberately organize the material, the more we are helping the memory process. In making mind maps the organization is made concrete in the structure of the pattern.

Moreover, the very activity of organizing the material is itself helpful to memory. Having to work out where a given piece of information fits into the pattern as a whole, and how it interconnects with other areas, brings you into more immediate contact with the note-taking process than do straightforward linear notes. This increases the depth of processing and so makes for better memory.

The fact that mind maps often take on an organiclike structure reflects their organized nature. An organism is an organized array of living cells. A billion cells put together in a jar do not create an organism; it is the interrelation and organization of the elements that is important. In the same way, it is the organization and interrelation of

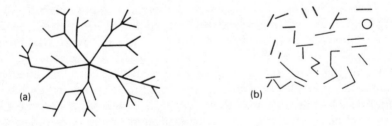

Figure 53 (a) Structured pattern; (b) less structured pattern.

the elements in the notes that give mind maps their organic structure and their value.

Key Words. Key-word notes are far more effective than phrases or sentences. The brain automatically drops the inessentials, and we should do the same in note taking. So only record the key ideas. This has several additional advantages:

1. The bulk is significantly reduced.

2. The recorded words are rich in imagery.

3. The very act of extracting the key words involves you more in understanding the material and further increases the depth of processing.

Association. Since words and ideas that are closely associated are recalled together, it helps memory if they are put together visually in the notes. This reinforces the association and results in a natural clustering of ideas into themes.

Since all the ideas in any one set of notes will be related to the theme of the notes, it is best to start with a key word for the overall theme in the center of the page. The center should be a strong visual image so that everything in the pattern is associated with it.

Clustering. As well as having a well-defined center, a mind map will naturally tend to have a number of subcenters radiating from it, and from these a number of sub-subcenters, and so on. In most practical situations there are seldom more than seven or eight subcenters, so the material can be organized into a number of easily remembered chunks. Similarly, the number of chunks radiating from each subcenter again will usually be within the immediate memory capacity.

Visual Memory. Since visual images are much better recalled than words, the more visual the mind map is made, the better. This can be done in a number of ways:

1. Each word should be printed rather than written in script. This gives the word a clearer visual image, makes it more easily remembered and less likely to be confused with other words. Lower-case letters are better than capitals, since they are more easily read and give better shape recognition.[6] However, where

the word is to be made more outstanding, capitals can be used with good effect.

2. Each of the key words should be printed on a line and each of the lines joined to other lines to give structure to the pattern. The initial inclination might be to join the words up by lines, but this is less flexible. It creates a weaker visual structure than does writing words along the lines themselves, and tends to produce networks that close in on themselves, making additions difficult.

3. Colored images are much better remembered than black and white ones. Therefore, use as many colors as possible in a mind map. Different colors can be used for different themes. They can also be used to make specific parts of the map outstanding. The more daring you are with color, the better.

4. The mind maps can be given depth. The centers and subcenters can be given three-dimensional shapes, providing the map with a more solid visual structure.

5. Use other images besides words. Whenever a simple visual image comes to mind, use it. If diagrams and pictures are part of the material, include them as part of the pattern.

6. Use arrows to link and associate different areas in the pattern.

7. Groups of words can be outlined or their background shaded to hold them together as a unit.

Outstandingness. Whenever an item is outstanding in some way or another, it is better remembered. When you make mind maps, every center should be unique; you should use different key words, different colors, and different shapes. Wherever parts of the pattern stand out, they will be better remembered.

Conscious Involvement. The more you participate actively and consciously in the note-taking process, the better. Mind maps intrinsically are more fun and spontaneously hold the attention more. Wherever possible, think of original ways in which to note the material. The greater the originality and creativity, the greater the interest, and the better the memory. Wherever you have been particularly creative in a pattern, you will always remember that part well. Try to be creative throughout.

With conventional linear notes spontaneous associations have to be held over until you reach the place where they are relevant, and by then the idea may well have been forgotten. Because mind maps are growing the whole time in all directions, associations can be included as soon as they arise. With mind maps the faster you go, the better.

Everybody's memory is a personal affair. We each have our own associations and our own mnemonics. So allow your pattern to be personal, including your own codes and symbols as much as possible. Remember only to use key words and key images. When you look for key words, always remember that they are primarily nouns, and they contain the essential substance of an idea. It might be a good exercise to go back and pick out the key points on mind mapping from the last 4 pages. As you do so, compare them with the mind map in Figure 54, which contains the basic information contained in these pages. As well as showing you how a mind map is created, it will also serve as a very useful review of this section.

WHY USE MIND MAPS?

You will notice that mind maps are reminiscent of the semantic memory structures we looked at on pages 105–106. The similarity is no accident. Since they include as many of the natural memory processes as possible, the mind maps are beginning to take on the same structure as that of the memory itself. A mind map works in the same manner as the brain itself. It is therefore an excellent interface between the brain and the written or spoken word.

Paradoxically one of the greatest advantages of mind maps is that they are seldom needed again. The very act of constructing a map is itself so effective in fixing ideas in memory that very often a whole map can be recalled without going back to it at all. A mind map is so strongly visual and uses so many of the natural functions of memory that frequently it can be simply read off in the "mind's eye."

APPLICATIONS OF MIND MAPS

Whenever information is being taken in, mind maps help organize it into a form that is easily assimilated by the brain and easily remembered. Thus they can be used for noting books, lectures, meetings, interviews, telephone conversations, etc. (fig. 55).

Whenever information is being retrieved from memory, mind maps allow ideas to be quickly noted as they occur, in an organized manner, obviating the relatively laborious process of forming neat sentences and writing them out in full. They therefore serve as a quick and efficient means of review, and so keep recall at a high level.

In a study of note taking in which recall was tested after review, it was found that good notes were "definitely useful for review, but poor notes were not."[7] Howe compared the review value of mind maps using shape, color, boxes, and different letterings with ordinary prose notes and found that recall rose by 50 percent with mind maps.[8]

In another instance a college lecturer in English was concerned that "of the 300 or so books I have read in the last 10 years on Theology, Philosophy, Psychology, Health, Nutrition and Literature, only the haziest of notions of their contents remained in my memory. And yet I had understood almost everything in these books when I read them. . . . [I now realize] understanding is *not* remembering." Using mind maps and a systematic procedure of review and rereview, he reports that "in two days I had three or four patterns of all I needed from the book. . . . It was interesting to find a note at the end of the book saying that it had taken me two weeks to read it in 1969. From two weeks to two days, *with* [mind maps], was quite an improvement."[9]

Because of the large amount of association involved in mind maps, they can be very creative; they tend to generate new ideas and associations that have not been thought of before. Every item in a map is in effect the center of another map, and one could go on generating maps *ad infinitum.*

Mind maps are very valuable in any planning or organization, whether it is of books, reports, lectures, meetings, study, daily tasks, or future activities. In this case do not try to put the material into a linear form until all the relevant information has been retrieved and incorporated into the pattern. Then go over the pattern labeling the branches (1), (2), (3), etc., according to whatever order seems appropriate. By leaving the linearization to last, you avoid the messy problems that arise

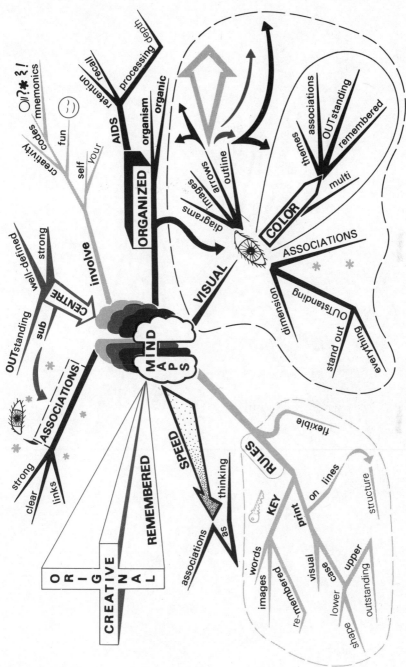

Figure 54 Mind maps on mind-mapping.

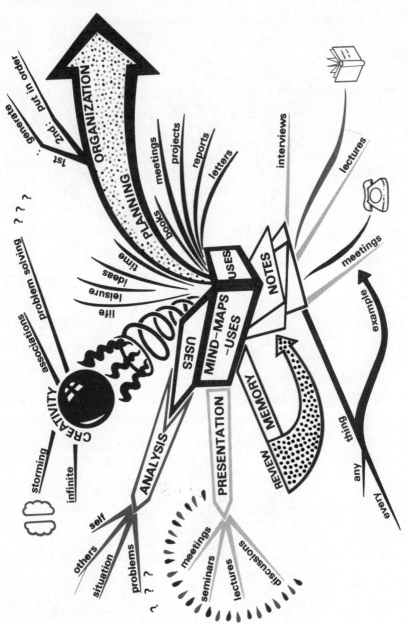

Figure 55

in lists when you start shuffling things around as you recall later points.

The creative potential of a mind map is very useful in brainstorming, either individually or in groups. If you are looking for a solution to a problem, you need only start with the basic problem as the center and generate associations and ideas from it in order to arrive at a large number of different possible approaches, many of which you would never have thought of if you had approached the problem linearly. In this situation do not discard "useless" solutions immediately. Put them into the pattern, as they may themselves later generate useful associations.

Mind maps can also be valuable in giving presentations and lectures. If the key points to be covered are put up in front of the group, it makes it easier for the others to follow. It also helps the lecturer keep to his themes and know where he is going.

Mind maps can be used with great effectiveness in almost any instance where one would normally write or jot down words. Even a book, which is a long linear list of ideas when it appears in print, can be approached as a series of mind maps in the writing stage. This book, for example, was not written from beginning to end as a series of sentences; it was drawn as a set of 7 major mind maps, springing from which came some 150 minor maps. All of the basic work was done in mind-map form. It was only when the book was finally being prepared for printing that it was transposed into a linear form.

In short, mind maps can be used in virtually any situation where there is a flow of information between the mind and the outside world, no matter which direction the flow (figs 55 and 56).

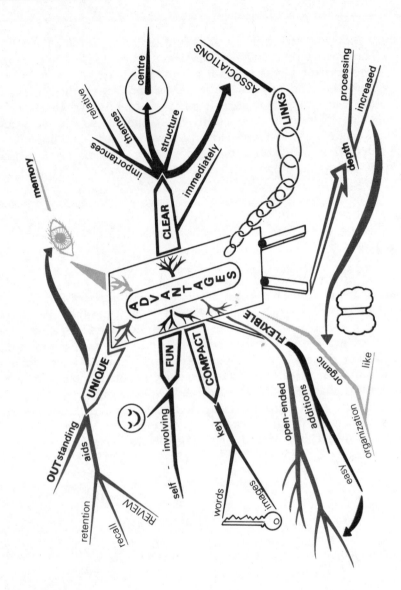

Figure 56

Figure 57

14.
Reading

How do we learn to read?
What do we see when we read?
Why read left to right?
How can reading be speeded up?
And without losing comprehension?
What is the best method of study?

Before 1950 most people were taught to read English by what is called the Alphabet Method. In this system children first learn the twenty-six letters of the alphabet. They then learn particular sounds for each of the letters of the alphabet, having to remember that the same letter can sometimes take different sounds, such as the *c* in *civil* and in *cavil,* and that different letters can sometimes indicate the same sound, such as *g* and *j* in *gib* and *jib.* The children then learn to put the sounds together to make syllables and simple words.

Up to this point the process has been done "out loud" so that the teacher can check on the sounds the children are making. The next step is to teach them to read silently. The children begin by saying the words to themselves, then they are taught to read "silently," and finally to read without moving their lips. They are probably still pointing to the words they read, and so the last stage in this method is to persuade the children to stop pointing at the words and to read with their eyes alone.

Further progress is made by giving the child progressively more complex books, expanding his vocabulary and knowledge of grammar, so that by the time he leaves junior high school he can hopefully read most of the material he encounters.

Unfortunately this method has several disadvantages. A major handicap is the complex relationship of the letters and the sounds they represent, which slow down a child's rate of learning. As one reading teacher put it, "*ay*' is for 'apple,' *bee* is for 'book,' *sea* is for 'confusion.' "

Since the 1950s a wide variety of techniques have evolved that have attempted to overcome the failing of the Alphabet Method. One of the most common of these is the "Look-Say Method." The child is given pictures of a familiar object, such as a cup, and underneath it in large letters is written its name, *cup.* Initially the child is not taught the alphabet but simple words and their associated sounds and meanings. Other techniques have concentrated on adding extra symbols to the normal alphabet so that there is a more direct relationship between the letters and their sounds. In the "Initial Teaching Alphabet," or i.t.a., the twenty-six letters of the English alphabet are augmented by eighteen additional signs so as to cover most of the phonetic range of speech. And in the Diacritical Marking System the normal alphabet is used with additional signs to indicate how letters should be pronounced. In another system, the Color System, the normal twenty-six-letter alphabet is used and each letter is printed in one of forty-eight different colors, each color indicating a specific sound. The current trend is toward combining the best elements of each system, making full use of imagery, color, association, and other factors that help learning.

All these systems undoubtedly have their own advantages, but they are concerned only with teaching basic recognition of letters and words. They do not of themselves help children to increase their "silent reading" speed, to read more effectively, nor to remember what they read.

Children are normally considered to have learned to read once they are reading silently without moving their lips and without tracing the words with their fingers. But in terms of the fantastic amount of visual information that the brain can take in and retain, they are all very poor readers.

Most of us, even as adults, "hear" the words we are reading. We may not go so far as to subvocalize the words—that is, "say" them to ourselves—but the sound of the word is still there. Most people cannot "hear" more than around two hundred to three hundred words per minute, and this rate becomes a limit to our normal reading speed. We have simply not been taught how to read visually. This would speed up our reading to several thousand words per minute. Nor have we been taught how to maximize both our comprehension and our retention of what is read. Learning to read is seen as learning to recognize the letters and put them into words. Yet these are really only the first stages in the reading process.

The word *reading* comes from the Anglo-Saxon *raedan,* "to advise oneself." It does not mean just the ability to interpret the symbols on a page and know the words they form; it is also the ability to advise oneself of the meaning and significance of what is being seen. Buzan, who advocates a similar broader interpretation of reading, defines it as a seven-stage process:

1. Assimilation of the visual data by the eye

2. Recognition of the letters and words

3. Understanding; relating the words being read to the meaning of the passage as a whole

4. Comprehension; relating the information to one's whole body of knowledge

5. Storing the information in memory efficiently and effectively

6. Recalling the information where and when it is needed

7. Making effective use of the information and communicating it successfully to others; and also communicating it to oneself, that is, thinking clearly[1]

By this definition we can see that most standard approaches to reading deal mainly with the first two stages. Comprehension tests may measure the third and fourth to some extent, but children are given little help on *how* to comprehend and integrate the material properly, nor on how to ensure it is remembered.

THE EYE AND ITS MOVEMENTS

In order to understand how we read and how reading may be improved, we must first look a little at how the eye works.

Light entering the eye is focused by the lens onto the retina, which lines the inside of the eye. The retina itself consists of hundreds of millions of tiny cells responsive to light—equivalent to the population of the U.S.A. squeezed onto a postage stamp. Some cells, the cones, respond to specific colors; others, the rods, to the overall light intensity. These cells are connected to a web of nerves extending over the retina, and these nerves relay information directly back to the brain. In fact, the retina is not really separate from the brain, it should be properly thought of as an extension of the cortex.

The center of the retina, called the fovea, is a small area in which the cells are much more tightly packed. These two thousand cones are packed into an area less than one tenth of a millimeter square. The perception of images falling on the fovea is much sharper and finer than elsewhere on the retina. When we are looking directly at something,

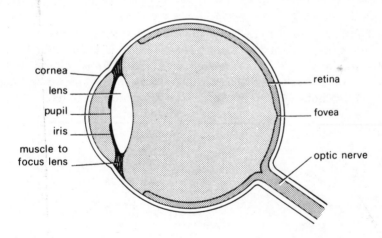

Figure 58 Simplified diagram of the human eye. The retina contains several hundred million light-sensitive cells. They are most closely packed at the fovea, the center of the visual field where vision is most acute (a quarter of a million cells per square millimeter).

the light from that object is falling on the fovea. The fovea sees less than one forty-thousandth of the total visual field. If you are looking at a line of print from a distance of two feet, only about three letters are in this central field of vision, and only those few letters are seen perfectly at any one time. The further images are from the fovea, the less clear the vision becomes, until at the periphery of the visual field you receive only very faint visual impressions.

The fact that we see most clearly that which we are looking at directly has two important implications for reading:

1. The eye must move along the text so that different parts of the line are brought into focus at the fovea.

2. To see anything clearly, the eye actually has to stop moving for a fraction of a second in order that a still image can rest on the fovea and be transmitted back to the brain.

Thus the eye takes short gulps of information. In between it is not actually seeing anything; it is moving from one point to another. We do not notice these jumps because the information is held over in the brain and integrated from one fixation to the next so that we can perceive a smooth flow.

The first person to discover that the eye did not move smoothly was Professor Javal, at the University of Paris, in 1879—that historic year again. Javal called these movements *saccades,* French for "jerks," and since then psychologists have talked of these movements as "saccadic eye movements." The eye is rarely still for more than half a second.

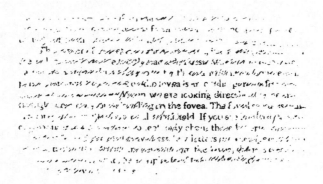

Figure 59 Print as seen by the eye.

Even when you feel the eye is completely still (as when you look steadily at the period at the end of this sentence), it will in fact be making a number of small movements around the dot. In fact, if the eye were not continually shifting in this way, the image would rapidly fade and disappear.

EYE MOVEMENTS IN READING

The first attempts to carry out a detailed study on the speed of the eye movements, the duration of the stopovers, and the number of fixations per line were by Edmund Huey, who published his pioneering work, *The Psychology and Pedagogy of Reading,* in 1908.[2] To this day it remains one of the most comprehensive and accessible studies on reading.

Huey found that the eye takes about a quarter of a second to move from one point of fixation to the next. Thus it is limited to about four fixations per second. Each fixation of an average reader will take in two or three words, so that to read a line of this book probably takes between three and six fixations. The duration of the stops and the length of the jumps will vary considerably, according to both the material being read and the individual's skill. The more skilled the reader, the more will be taken in by a single fixation.

You can see for yourself the way the eye moves during reading by asking a friend to read from a book, holding it up in the manner shown in Figure 60 so that you can watch the eyes as they move along the line.

The visual information is picked up by the eye in a few hundredths of a second, and is quickly sent on its way to the brain. The brain itself takes between a quarter and a half of a second to process and recognize the visual data. While this is taking place, the eye is already moving on to the next point of fixation, and often on to further fixation points. Thus the eye will usually be a phrase or two ahead of what one is conscious of reading.

Although the sharpest perception occurs at the fovea, images that are off-center are still seen but less clearly. This off-center vision is called peripheral vision. We often talk of it as "seeing out of the corner of the eye."

Peripheral vision performs a most valuable function during reading. Words that lie ahead of the current point of fixation will be partially received by the eye and transmitted to the brain. On the basis of this slightly blurred view of what is coming, the brain will tell the eye where

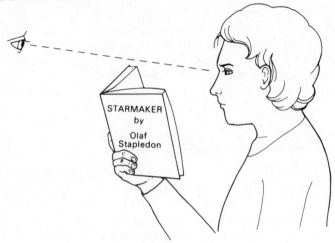

Figure 60 Watch someone reading and observe his eye movements.

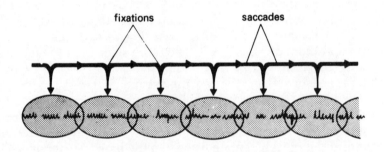

Figure 61 The eye moves along a line of print in steps, taking in the section of the line which is at the center of vision at each fixation.

to move to next. Thus the eye does not move along the line in a regular series of jumps but skips redundant words and concentrates on the most useful and distinguishing parts of the text.

Most readers do not continue to read along the line in a steady sequence. Much of the time their eyes are jumping back to check on words already "read," and even on words in the preceding line. This back-skipping is called regression. Generally the more skilled the reader, the less regression there is. In a study of five thousand readers it was found that 25 percent of the eye movements made by children were regressive, as were 15 percent of those made by adults.[3] Many of these regressive movements are unnecessary. They are not based on lack of comprehension so much as apprehension and fear that one may have missed something.

Huey found that the fixation points tend to be concentrated toward the middle of a line of print. When the eye goes to a new line, it does not usually start at the beginning; instead it starts a word or two in from the edge. The brain has a good idea of what is to come from the sense of the previous lines and only needs to check with peripheral vision that the first few words are as anticipated. Similarly the eye usually makes its last fixation a word or two short of the end of a line, again making use of peripheral vision to check that the last few words are as expected.

WHY READ LEFT TO RIGHT?

What we see to our left (the left visual field) falls on the right retina of each eye and is transmitted to the right side of the brain. Conversely, the right visual field of each eye is transmitted to the left side of the

Figure 62 Typical eye movements down a page of print, concentrated more toward center of page.

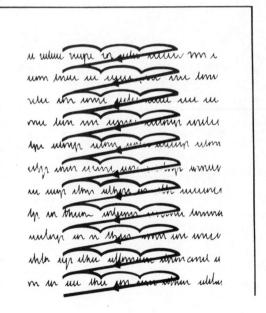

brain. Since the left hemisphere is better at verbal tasks, whatever lies in the right visual field will have its verbal content processed more quickly than that which lies in the left. Experiments have shown that when words are briefly flashed to either the left or right visual fields, the words flashed to the right are recognized more quickly than those flashed to the left.[6]

If a person is reading from left to right, the material that has not yet been read, but which is nevertheless being processed peripherally, is being received by the left side of the brain, more specialized at verbal processing. Reading right to left, on the other hand, results in the material yet to be read being processed by the right hemisphere, which is not as good at verbal tasks, with the result that the brain would have a poorer idea of what is to come.

This implies that it is intrinsically easier to read languages written from left to right. Studies of different systems have shown that not only is left-right reading more efficient, it is also better for the brain itself. The two halves of the brain of the left-to-right readers become more adept at working together and better able to integrate verbal and spatial tasks. The two halves of the right-to-left readers' brains did not work together so well.[5]

Figure 63 Schematic diagram of the visual processing of a line of text. When reading left to right, the material yet to be read is taken in with peripheral vision and analyzed for content by the linguistic left hemisphere. This helps the brain decide the best next point of fixation and increases the efficiency of reading.

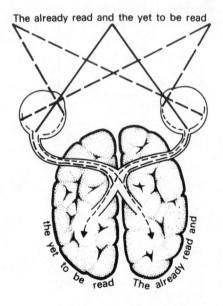

The already read and the yet to be read

the yet to be read
The already read and

RECOGNITION

Once the visual information has been received by the brain, it has to be recognized and given meaning. As soon as the data arrive at the visual cortex at the back of the brain, they undergo feature analysis. The data are broken up into their basic constituents of lines, curves, and angles, the whole process taking only a few hundreths of a second.

To some extent, letters are recognized on this basis. Experiments have shown that when letters are briefly flashed onto a screen and a person is asked to call out what the letter was, any wrong letters called out tend to be letters with similar features; a *P*, for example, may be confused with a *B*, or an *F*.[6] Further evidence for feature recognition comes from the finding that when a person is required to search for a particular letter among a series of letters, he takes much longer when the other letters contain similar features to the letter searched for.[7]

Feature analysis cannot, however, explain how *A* ⤳*A A a A* ᴋ are all easily recognized as the letter *A*. Here the features involved vary considerably from one typeface to the next. It appears that letters are also recognized holistically, that is, as informational wholes in their own right.

Not only are individual letters recognized holistically, but common words are often recognized and treated as single units. As far back as 1886 it was discovered that people were better at recognizing a series of letters flashed briefly before them if the letters formed meaningful words.[8] It has also been found that a person who is a little too far away from a word to be able to recognize the individual letters can still recognize the word as a whole.[9] Words can also be recognized when they are in peripheral vision and the individual letters are too blurred to be recognized.[10] As with letters, words that have their own characteristic shape are more easily recognized than words with shapes similar to others.

Earlier it was shown that immediate memory span depends on the number of "chunks" rather than the information content. The same is true of reading. When we read, we can take in about five chunks at a time. A chunk may be a single letter, a syllable, a word, or even a small phrase. The more meaningful the material, the easier it is to understand, and the larger will be the chunks. Strings of random letters such as *krplztgf* are read very slowly, letter by letter. Nonsense words such as *bidnolleck* that approximate English words in structure will probably be read syllable by syllable. A phrase such as *the differentiated effects of temporal neocortical resections on overtrained and nonovertrained visual habits in monkeys (sic)* that is difficult to understand will be read word by word. But an easy passage will be "chunked" into groups of words and phrases.

REDUNDANCY

There is a large amount of redundancy in printed English, and much of the material can often be omitted without any loss in meaning. Much of each letter's structure is redundant and phrases can still be read even though parts of each letter may be missing. The brain knows that only certain arrangements of lines and curves are going to occur and fits in the letters according to the general gist of the whole thing. It is this redundancy that allows a pharmacist to read a doctor's prescription. The reason many people find doctor's prescriptions illegible is that they are searching for the correct word out of millions of possibilities. The pharmacist making up the prescription has only to pick the right word from a few hundred possibilities. This means that the writing need contain less information and that more of it is redundant.

Not only can parts of the letters be omitted, but whole letters can be dropped. Sntncs wtht vwls cn b rd, and so can th.se wi.h eve.y fif.h let.er mi.sing. Similarly every fifth word . . . be omitted from a . . . without losing the meaning. The general meaning and grammatical structure of a sentence, help the reader anticipate what is to follow. A sentence that begins "We write more words than necessary for . . ." is unlikely to be followed by words such as *cat, visitors, plastic,* or *philodendron.* It is much more likely to be followed by such words as *comprehension, recognition,* or *understanding.* The reader has to determine merely whether the word is one out of ten rather than one out of millions. Only a little information is needed, and this information can usually be gained from peripheral vision, without having to fixate upon the word itself.

By helping us anticipate what is to come, redundancy speeds up the reading process. We read what we expert to read, and the faster, more expect reader will probably have corrected the errors in this sentence without realizing it.

A very simple and convenient way of examining the normal reading process is to read material upside down. This slows down the process sufficiently for you to begin to become aware of the operations involved.

At first it seems very strange. You may start by reading syllable by syllable, much as a child does at first, then after a few lines you begin to take in complete words more easily, and later simple phrases become readable. As you continue, you will find your reading speeding up and will probably notice that you do not read the whole of a word—probably the first letter or two and the last letter or two are sufficient and you guess at the rest, only coming back to it if in the light of the rest of the sentence you realize your guess was wrong. And where you come across phrases that are very common, you will find yourself reading them quite rapidly. You may also begin to notice how the eye fixates on the most distinguishing features of a word or phrase. By slowing down the reading process in this manner you become directly aware of the importance of context. If you continue to practice like this for ten minutes or more, you will find reading steadily speeding up as you get more proficient at reading larger chunks at a time.

SKILLED READING

Reading speed can be increased considerably by

eliminating regression;
expanding the focus of fixation;
making greater use of peripheral vision;
making greater use of redundancy;
increasing motivation;
previewing the material; and
using the right side of the brain as much as the left.

Early speed-reading techniques were based on tachistoscope training. A tachistoscope is an instrument for presenting very brief flashes of a picture. In speed-reading techniques the tachistoscope gives a brief glimpse of a few words from a line and then moves on to show the next few words. Regression becomes impossible, and since more words are included in each flash, the subject is forced to take in progressively larger units with each fixation. Using such techniques it is possible to increase a person's reading speed from 250 or so words per minute to 500 or 600 words per minute.

Doubling your reading speed may sound a considerable achievement, but it is not, in fact, that large an increase. With modern techniques of skilled reading it is possible to increase your rate to 2,000 or more words per minute. Two limiting factors in the tachistoscopic approach are that it does not develop peripheral vision, nor does it make use of many of the findings about how we assimilate and recognize written material.[11]

VISUAL GUIDES

A visual guide is a pointer, such as the blunt end of a pencil or a fingertip, moved along underneath a line of print. To many people it might seem a backward step to start using a visual guide again. Were we not taught very early on at school that pointing to the words as we read only slows us down? How then is it being claimed to speed up reading?

Try moving your finger backward and forward as fast as possible. You will probably find you can do so at least five times a second, which is ten times faster than the eyes normally move along a line of print. So following the finger cannot in itself slow down reading. The reason children are discouraged from pointing to the words as they read them is that stopping to point *at each individual word* can indeed slow up the process. But if instead of pointing at each word the finger is moved along smoothly underneath the line of text, it can actually speed up reading.

A visual guide improves reading in three ways:

1. If the eye is trained to follow the visual guide, then most unnecessary back-skipping is eliminated.

2. Deliberately speeding up the visual guide will help the eye to move along faster.

3. The number of fixations is limited to about four or five per second. As the eye moves faster, it is encouraged to take in more words with each fixation. This increases the meaningful content of the material so that comprehension actually improves.

A visual guide used in this way in practical situations has been found to increase reading speeds by an average of 50 percent.[12] In one study it was shown that a visual guide halved regression (from 1.37 back-skips per ten words to 0.77) and increased the span of fixation by 60 percent (from 2.15 words to 3.50 words). Together these two improvements led to an increase in speed from 274 words per minute to 465 words per minute.[13] This is already approaching the level normally attained by several weeks of tachistoscopic training!

EXPANDED FOCUS

Since written English is highly redundant, a large proportion of the information in a text can be absorbed through peripheral vision. Words that are highly likely to occur in a given context do not have to be checked by looking directly at them—peripheral vision can check that they are what is expected even while the eye is fixating elsewhere. Thus, many skilled readers do not read along each line but read from side to side of the center of the page, taking in most of a line in one glance.

The central area of clear vision extends not only in a horizontal direction but also vertically. Although we may not realize it, when we look at a word in a line, we are also getting a fairly clear impression of the words a line or two above and below. Very fast readers make use of this and can take in two or more lines with one fixation.

Visual guides are again very useful for developing peripheral vision. Instead of moving the guide along individual lines, move it down the middle of the page, following it with the eye. The high redundancy in written language often allows you to use the incomplete peripheral information and still gain as much understanding as you would by fixating on each word or phrase.

Making a fuller use of peripheral vision, the skilled reader is able to get a better idea of the general sense of what is to follow, and this also helps to speed up reading. Furthermore, with this broader overview it is easier to understand and integrate the material. This is why many people find that as soon as they start speed reading, their comprehension actually increases. They have a broader perspective of what they are reading, and since they are reading faster, the short-term memory for what has just been read goes back several sentences further and those words being read are understood within a larger immediate context.

The importance of context in aiding both understanding and speed becomes apparent if you try reading the following passage as it stands:

> With hocked gems financing him, our hero bravely defied all
> scornful laughter that tried to prevent his scheme. "Your eyes

deceive," he said. "It is like an egg, not a table." Now three sturdy sisters sought proof. Forging along, sometimes through calm vastness, yet more often over turbulent peaks and valleys, days became weeks as many doubters spread fearful rumors about the edge. At last, from nowhere welcomed winged creatures appeared, signifying momentous success.

Each sentence is simple enough; the grammar is straightforward, and the words are common. The reason you probably found yourself reading it slowly was because you simply had very little idea of what it was about. And if you did manage to make sense of it, it was probably only after much time spent reading it several times through (or of looking down here first). But once you know that it is about Christopher Columbus discovering America, you can read it much more easily, much faster, and remember it better.

In addition to the redundancy in letters and words mentioned earlier, whole phrases, and even sentences, are sometimes redundant. Often sentences are only elaborating on other sentences or putting them in different words; they can be omitted without loss of meaning. The efficient reader will recognize this from various clues in the text and skip ahead, checking with just a glance or two that no new information is being added. Since the main theme of a paragraph is often stated at the start, many skilled readers read only the first sentence of a paragraph, doing so with one or two fixations, merely checking the rest of the text with peripheral vision.

Obviously the degree to which skimming is possible depends largely on the type of text being read. In very condensed concise passages it may well be necessary to read every sentence. Conversely, with highly redundant material it may not even be necessary to check each paragraph. The important thing is to be flexible. Go slowly when you need to and fast whenever you want to and the material allows you to.

HIGH-SPEED TRAINING

In high-speed training the reader is forced to scan pages of print at speeds many times faster than normal reading. The reader starts by moving the visual guide as fast as physically possible along each line, not worrying if very little is absorbed. Then he begins moving the guide down the page, increasing the pace every few minutes until he is spending only one second on each page. At this speed very little, if anything will be absorbed. After about five minutes of high-speed training, the person goes back to reading at what he takes to be a normal speed. He will probably find, however, that he is reading at double his usual speed and yet with the same or even greater comprehension.

This training breaks the habit of reading at a set pace. It is rather like driving down a highway at eighty miles an hour for a long period, and then being asked to slow down to thirty miles an hour. If you try to do this without looking at the speedometer, you will probably think you are at thirty when in fact you are still doing fifty.

High-speed training has two other advantages: It encourages you to see the key words in the text; and it brings the right side of the brain into the reading process.

When you first start high-speed training, spending only a second on each page of the book, everything seems to be a blur and nothing is absorbed. But after a few minutes an interesting phenomenon may occur. You may find that a few of the words are in fact being seen. This by itself is not remarkable. What is significant is that the words that are being picked out are generally the nouns and verbs in the text. Moreover they are often the key nouns and verbs. The fact that these words are being picked out implies that, although the page of print is not being consciously read in detail, most of the page is nevertheless being processed by the brain. And being processed in only a second! The high-speed training develops this ability to extract the relevant words from a page.

A person learning to read finds it easy to stop saying the words aloud and not difficult to stop subvocalizing (moving the throat); but many people find it difficult to stop hearing the words they are reading, and this limits their speed to 250 or so words per minute. High-speed training breaks the habit. At a page a second you cannot hear many of the words, but you can still take in the page visually, for visual processing is many times faster. This shift in processing corresponds to a shift from the left hemisphere to the right. When you slow down again to "normal" speeds, the right hemisphere stays enlivened, words continue to be taken in visually, and reading is correspondingly faster. It is only when the shift is made from auditory to visual reading that high speeds become possible. Indeed, it could be said that until you have made this shift, you have not fully learned to read.

Florence Schale, at Northwest University, has integrated many of these different approaches to skilled reading and taught them to large numbers of people. She found that most people were capable of reading at what would normally be considered very high speeds: two thousand or more words per minute. In a study of fifteen hundred people she also found fifteen people who, after suitable training, were capable of reading at even higher rates of twenty thousand words per minute—and still with a comprehension rate of 70 percent or more! (Seventy percent is good: People reading at "normal" speeds or two hundred or three hundred words per minute seldom score better than this.) The most advanced subjects were able to take in two columns of print simultaneously by scanning down the center of the page. The readers themselves did not claim to have "photographic" memory, but they reported that the key words in the passages stood out and that they read enough key words to complete the thoughts of the passage meaningfully. One subject, a fifteen-year-old girl, could even scan material at the rate of eighty thousand words per minute, with 100 percent comprehension![14]

APPLICATION TO STUDY

It is of little value to be able to read at two thousand or even twenty thousand words per minute if half an hour later 90 percent of the information has been forgotten. Reading, as was expressed in the expanded definition on page 188, includes not only the assimilation and recognition of the written material but also understanding, comprehension, retention, recall, and communication.

The principal reason many people find themselves forgetting what they have read is that as children they were rarely given guidance on memory and study. The most common approach to study of a new text is a linear one, typified as the "start and slog" approach. The reader opens the book at page 1 and reads the book through to the end—if, that is, he does not give up out of boredom or fatigue halfway through. This might seem the obvious approach, since most books do appear to start inside the front cover and end just before the back cover. But a linear approach is, in fact, an inefficient use of both the reader's time and knowledge and has a number of serious disadvantages:

- Time is wasted going over material that is already familiar.
- Time is wasted covering material that is irrelevant to the study in question.
- Time may be wasted wading through large chunks of text only to find that the author has conveniently summed up the essence of a chapter in a short summary at the end.

- The reader has no overall perspective until he *finishes* the text, and possibly not even then.
- Association and organization are poor, and this leads to poor recall of the information.
- Any information that is retained is usually disorganized; it is seldom well integrated with the rest of the book nor with the reader's whole body of knowledge.
- Motivation is low and the reader tends to become bored, dull, and tired. The more tired he becomes, the less efficiently he reads, the less he remembers, and the less motivated he will be to read again.

Numerous books have been written on the subject of study, and nearly all agree that a book should be approached as a whole. The reader should start with some sort of plan and overview in order to get a general feel of the ground, setting definite goals and aims, selecting relevant portions, and rejecting irrelevant ones. A linear approach to study is like going shopping by systematically walking along each street, going into every store, and walking through every floor of each store picking up here and there any items required. Holistic study, on the other hand, parallels the normal activity of shopping. One prepares a list of what is required, goes only down the relevant streets, window-shopping as one goes to get a preview of what is available, selecting the few stores that contain all that one needs.

In approaching any sort of study, the following practices will all be valuable:

1. **Plan the session.** Do not just rush into the text, but set aside a definite time and definite areas to be covered.

2. **Review your current knowledge of the subject.** This increases expectancy of what is to come, bringing to the fore the relevant mental hooks, which improves the retention of what is being read. The best way to do this is to make a quick mind map of your current knowledge.

3. **Establish objectives.** This sets the right mental hooks in advance. In addition it helps you select the relevant and reject the irrelevant.

4.   **Overview the material.**   This clarifies the aims and goals and gives you an overall perspective of the subject covered. It also makes use of the "warm-up" effect (see page 89). During overview you should not be reading any of the text itself. Look at:

> **Title and subtitle.**   They are not trivial. Their implications may affect your approach to the book.
>
> **Author.**   If he is known to you already, you have a good idea of the level at which the book will be pitched. You may not need a popularization, for example.
>
> **Date of publication.**   This will indicate whether the material is up to date, where that is pertinent.
>
> **Table of contents.**   Study them carefully. You will begin to have a general feel for the layout of the book and which parts are going to be of greatest interest and relevance.
>
> **Index.**   Indexes are not only valuable for finding passages. Quickly running through the index at this stage will give you a fuller idea of the topics covered and how much attention is paid to each.
>
> **Diagram, pictures, graphs, and other visuals.**   Visual information is better absorbed and remembered than verbal information (see pages 114–115) and often summarizes large portions of text.
>
> **Dust-jacket flaps/back cover.**   These provide a good overview.
>
> **Preface.**   Nearly always written last, it will, if short, often provide an excellent summary, and usually a statement of purpose for the book and/or a note on the author's perspective on the subject.

All the foregoing will probably take a minute of two yet will save you many times this. You will begin to know how much of the book is going to be valuable and will not be wasting time on irrelevancies, repetitions, and that which you already know. If, for example, you practice hang-gliding as a regular hobby and pick up a book entitled *A Guide to Hang-Gliding,* you may well find after a minute's overview that there is nothing in the book new to you.

You will have effectively read the book in a minute and need spend no more time with it.

5. **Preview.** Get a close feel for the book as a whole by flipping through, looking at:

> Beginnings and ends of chapters.
> Subsection headings.
> Summaries the author may have provided.
> Anything else which catches the eye—bold print, italicized sections, etc.

6. **Practice high-speed training.** It is good to precede in-depth study with five minutes of high-speed reading. This not only increases "normal" reading speed but encourages the use of the right side of the brain. During the high-speed training you will be unconsciously absorbing a considerable amount of the text. An extra five minutes here can save an hour or more later.

7. **Study in depth.** This is the stage for filling in details not provided by the overview and preview. Again treat the book as a whole. It will often be more effective to go through the book quickly ten times, gradually building up knowledge, than to slog through from the beginning. Psychologists call this the lag effect. It has been found that when the same information is repeated during the same learning session, the material is better remembered the more separated are the repeated presentations.[15] In addition, difficult passages may often become clear in the light of later sections. In other instances the mind may be working subconsciously on the argument and spontaneously come up with an understanding of it later on. Flexibility is of utmost importance here; different types of books will require different approaches.

8. **Mark and underline.** Despite most people's inhibitions, marking books can be very valuable. Mark the text in preparation for notetaking. If the book is not yours, use a *soft* lead pencil and remove the marks later with a soft eraser; it would take a forensic expert to discover you. If it is your own book, do not be afraid to use different colored pens; it helps memory and distinguishes different themes and topics.

Underlining key words, or otherwise making them more outstanding, has been found to greatly enhance students' performances, resulting in better short-term and long-term comprehension than does straight reading,[16] and also that students who regularly use underlining during reading score significantly higher on recall than those who do not.[17]

9.   **Be prepared to reject.**   Omit sections that are

  irrelevant;
  already familiar;
  padding;
  repetition;
  outdated; or
  excess examples.

Also reject false arguments. Robert Thouless, in *Straight and Crooked Thinking,*[18] lists thirty-eight dishonest tricks to watch out for. Some of the principal ones are:
  using emotive words to bias the reader
  quoting well-known names to "prove" a point
  denigration of opponents rather than their arguments
  generalization from the particular
  false premises
  undefined sources
  proving by analogy
  misuse of statistics

10.   **Take regular breaks.**   Taking a five-minute break every thirty or forty minutes increases retention of the material. Break regularly even when the study is going excellently. *Understanding well is not necessarily remembering well.* After each break take a minute to review the previous work. This consolidates the retention. Rest during the break. Especially rest the eyes by cupping them in your palms. The hand should not touch the eye but simply form a little dome over it. This practice soothes the eyes and gives them complete rest.[19]

11.   **Make mind maps.**   Mind maps increase comprehension and integration of knowledge; they are easier and quicker to make than

conventional notes, are better remembered, and are more fun. After you finish a book, take a five-minute break; then go through the book making detailed pattern notes, relating points to previous knowledge wherever possible. Remember to use color, imagination, outstanding features, shape, outlining, absurdities, etc., as much as possible.

12. **Review.** Regular review consolidates memory. Making detailed mind maps serves as the first immediate review and makes maximum use of the reminiscence effect. It helps integrate the material and gives an overall perspective. Review again, after one day, one week, one month, and six months, by running through your pattern in your head. This ensures that you will remember virtually everything.

The best way to review is again to use mind maps, as described in the previous chapter. At the end of a study session, if you're not already working with a mind map, it is good to prepare comprehensive notes in map form.

The preparation of the mind map can count as the first review, and once that is completed, many of the details will already be firmly implanted in your memory. At the subsequent reviews it is enough to go over the pattern mentally, checking that you can still recall all the details, referring back to the pattern whenever you are vague.

A good way to organize all the reviews is to keep a file of all your mind maps. Each map should be marked with the date of its next review, and they should all be ordered by date. Each day look at the top of the file to see if there are any for review. Once you have reviewed them, put a new date on them and reinsert in the corresponding place in the file. In this way the patterns will automatically arrive at the top as they are needed.

Or, if the patterns are filed by subject, go through all the files regularly to see whether any patterns are due for review.

THE BEST CONDITIONS FOR STUDY

Heat. Most central heating systems keep the temperature between 68 and 70 degrees Fahrenheit. This may be comfortable as far as the body is concerned, allowing a person to work with only a shirt or cotton dress, but it is a little too warm for the brain. The brain works best when the surroundings are at a temperature of 65 degrees Fahrenheit (18 degrees Celsius). You may need to put some more clothes on if you have been used to working in warmer conditions, but it will be worth it in terms of increased mental clarity.

Light. The human eye is capable of a remarkable range of adaptation, being able to accommodate variations in intensity of several million fold. Once the eye has adjusted, it can read under the brightest sunlight or by a dim candle flame. In order not to put too heavy a strain on the eyes, however, something in between is more advisable—shade on a bright day, or a well-lit room at night.

Natural daylight is better than artificial illumination. It contains the full range of the visible spectrum and is much more restful as a result. Artificial light tends to give an unbalanced spectrum, and some forms of fluorescent lighting may be limited to a very narrow band of wavelengths. This puts an undue strain on certain cells in the retina and leads to more rapid fatiguing of the eye.

Daylight also has the advantage of providing a diffuse illumination. If you are working out of the direct rays of the sun, the light is coming from many different directions and does not cast harsh shadows across the page. If possible, windows should be to your left (for right-handed people) so that a shadow of your writing hand will not fall across the page. It is best not to work directly in front of a window, for every time you glance up out of the window, the eyes are forced to make a rapid accommodation to the change in light intensity, and this can result in eye strain.

Similarly with artificial light, it is best to work in as diffuse a light as possible, one reflected from the ceiling and the wall rather than directed straight onto the paper. This gives a greater evenness of light and avoids tiresome reflections from any shiny objects there may be on the desk. If spotlights are used, they should be used in conjunction with a good general illumination. A single spotlight may help to concentrate the attention on the page, but it is not good for the eyes. It creates a very uneven brightness over the table itself, which means that every time you glance away, the eyes again have to accommodate to a rapid change in intensity, this time to darkness rather than brightness.

Posture. The fatigue felt after a period of study is partly mental fatigue, partly eye fatigue, and partly a result of muscular effort and tension. The least tiring study position is an upright one with the back very slightly bent forward. Sitting with an absolutely straight back can, if you are not used to it, add tension to the back muscles.

Chairs should be high enough that the thigh is horizontal and the lower leg at a right angle to it with the feet resting comfortably on the floor. If the seat is too high the chair edge exerts pressure on the leg obstructing blood circulation. If too low, the thighs are tilted up and the weight of body pressing down on the top of the thigh again causes tiring pressure.

This does not mean you have to have chairs made especially for you. A little adjustment with cushions or foot rests will usually be sufficient.

Table height should also be attended to. Too low and you will begin to slouch, with tension and fatigue in the back. Too high and your arms will be pushing up into your shoulders.

Thus reading in its broadest sense is far more than recognizing letters and putting them together to form sentences. Reading also needs to be efficient. We need to be able to go faster where we need to, comprehend better, remember what we have read, and apply it usefully in long term. Moreover, as much attention needs to be paid to how and where we study as to the art of reading itself if the best use is to be made of the time spent reading.

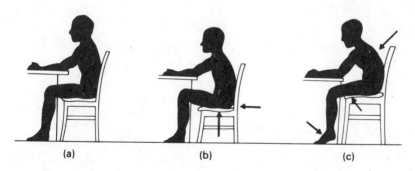

Figure 64 Sitting positions (a) good; (b), (c) bad (arrows show tension points).

Figure 65

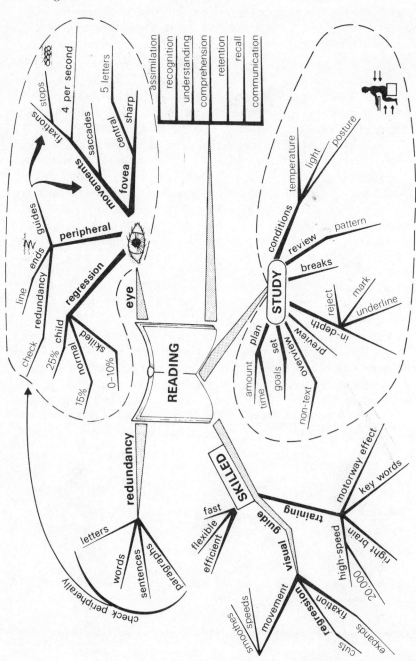

15.
Belief and Set

What is mental "set"?
How does belief affect our lives?
Can it actually change people and society?
Does positive thinking work?
How much is it used in sports?
Can it cure illnesses?
Can a person alter his body's functioning through "set"?
Can one also alter the world around one?

If you have just bought a new coat, you may start noticing a lot more people wearing the same or similar coats. The number of such coats may not have increased significantly, but your mind has become tuned to these particular coats and picks them out from the crowd. This is an example of what psychologists call set. The mind will tend to pick out whatever it is "set" for.

If we are expecting someone to call us on the telephone, we will immediately recognize their voice on the other end. If, on the other-hand, we are not expecting them and have not heard from them for some time, it may be a little while before we recognize the voice. Or again, the postman may be easily recognized when we see him standing outside the door early in the morning, but it may be much harder to recognize him when we meet him on a holiday in Spain. These are examples of negative set—missing that which is not expected.

Psychologists have measured the role of set in perception by asking people to recognize words flashed briefly before them and giving them different expectancies of what was to come. In one experiment, subjects were very briefly shown the name of an animal, such as *horse.* One group was told that they were going to see the name of an animal, another group that they were going to see the name of a flower, and a third group that they were just going to see a word. Those who were expecting to see the name of an animal recognized the word most quickly and made the least errors. Those who were expecting any word did second best. And those who were expecting to see the name of a flower did worst of all, reacting more slowly and making more mistakes.[1]

In a similar experiment using single letters it was found that if the flashes are made very brief indeed, the subject could still be correct nearly every time if the choice was between two letters, for example, *A* or *B,* but almost always incorrect when the choice was one out of twenty-six.[2]

Thus, set can be deceiving in that you may sometimes see what you expect to see even when it is not there. Magicians rely heavily upon this. They get you to expect them to do one thing, and you see them doing that—for example, burning your five-dollar bill—even though they are really doing something different. Because of your set you miss the little "tricks."

Set will often continue for some time after the initial expectation. When people are asked to recall as many names as possible beginning with a certain letter—*T,* say—they will still be set for names beginning with *T* several hours after the experiment has ended. The task remains at the "back of the mind" and as soon as a *T* name appears, even in a completely different setting, it will stand out.[3]

The same can happen in daily life. A person may have had a name on the tip of his tongue but not have been able to recall it. Later he may hear the name incidentally in conversation or read it somewhere and immediately recognize that this was the name he could not remember. Although it was not being consciously looked for, the mind had remained "set" for it.

Set affects virtually everything we see and do. Any belief system will make a person "set" to notice those events and facts that support their belief and miss those that do not. This is why two people can hold completely opposite views about religion, politics, education, the state of the economy, the mind, or the nature of reality and each find, *from his own experience,* that the world is the way he believes it to be. They have unconsciously selected the supporting evidence. This can be very comforting, but it also leads to bigotry and prejudice. Mark Brown, in his book *Set Thinking—Why Dogs Look Like Their Owners,* suggests that a good way to offset this is occasionally to try holding the opposite belief. By doing this you can make sure you are seeing both sides of the situation and not becoming "over-set" in any particular direction.[4]

As to why dogs tend to look like their owners, and vice versa, this also is a matter of set. Any outstanding qualities in the one "set" you to notice those qualities in the other. If you meet a pudgy man with a boxer dog, you will be more likely to notice if he has a squashed nose himself, or if the dog is also overweight. You will pick out any ways in which they are similar but probably not notice the hundreds of ways in which they are unlike each other.

Set can also affect the way you see other people. If you have just had an argument with someone, you may feel that he is the most selfish and uncompromising of people, and when you next meet him, you will be "set" to notice his bad points. Conversely, when you are "head over heels" in love, the other person is the best in the world; in your eyes he can do nothing wrong.

Not only does set affect the way we see other people, it can sometimes change the other person for better or for worse. A study of over one hundred children measured the extent to which the parent's expectancy of a child's ability affected the child. Of those children whose mothers had rated them below average and predicted that they would remain so, only 7.7 percent were free from emotional disturbances at the ages of ten to eleven. Whereas, of those children whose mothers rated them above average, 46.2 percent were free from symptoms. This relationship was independent of other factors, such as the educational level of the parents, their occupations, ages, the type of delivery or family size, suggesting that it was indeed a direct influence of "set."[5]

Similarly, at school a teacher's expectancy of a child's ability can often determine the child's actual performance at school. If a group of children is divided into two groups of equal aptitudes but their teachers are told that children in one group have high IQs and are expected to excel at school whereas the other children are academically poor, the first group will do much better than the second. This effect, known as the Pygmalion effect, has been borne out by numerous studies, not only in school, but in business, psychiatry, medicine, politics, social relationships, and other situations.[6]

Some of the effect may be due to the teacher's being set to notice the achievements of the bright children and the failures of the dim ones. In a now legendary experiment psychology students were given two groups of rats. One group was said to be intelligent and trained, the other group dumb—though, as with the children, both groups were identical. The results of the students' experiments showed that the intelligent rats performed much better in the mazes than did their "dumb" fellows.

With children some of the effect may also be due to the children becoming set as a result of the teacher's attitudes. A "dumb" child may pick up, either directly or indirectly, that he is not thought to be very bright and become "set" to this "fact." As a result he is quick to notice his failures and slower to notice his successes, and his negative set is reinforced. The child does actually come to perform less well than a child in the "bright" group.

Overall social trends can even be affected by set. If, for example, the majority of people believe that the country is on the verge of collapse, that extremists are about to take over, that ecological disaster is around the corner, and that doom is sure to come, then doom is far more likely to come—particularly when these attitudes are reinforced through the media. One recent study showed that even the quality of news bulletins can affect a person's attitude to others. People who heard positive bulletins, recalling the good news of the day, showed more positive feelings toward other people than did people whose news was full of gloom and despair.[7]

A major report by Willis Harman and colleagues at the Stanford Research Institute came to the conclusion that society tends to move toward the dominant image propagated through the media and the educational system. They concluded that if humanity is to survive the next few decades, it is essential to reaffirm the positive sides of human potential and "set" society for a positive future.[8]

MENTAL SET AND STUDY

In the previous chapter it was advised that, as part of the preparation for study, you should quickly review your knowledge of the field and set goals for the session. These both have the value of establishing a strong set for the subject, making it easier to recognize relevant points and easier to understand and recall them.

This review is best done with a quick-sketch mind map. Put the subject under study at the center of the map and spend just half a minute or so very quickly sketching the key words associated with the subject, in order to give a rough but comprehensive outline of the field. Even if it is a completely new field to you, you will nevertheless have some associations connected to the subject and sketching these down in a quick pattern will bring out the right hooks and prepare the mind for further study of the subject.

The more clearly your aims and goals are defined, the stronger will your mental set be. Again, the best way to do this is to jot down a very quick pattern, fitting in any associations that come to mind. Very often we have been conditioned out of the habit of asking questions, usually through a fear of appearing stupid or of being told to keep quiet. But questions should not be thought of as exposing one's ignorance so much as opening oneself to knowledge. Questioning is in fact a very natural method of gaining knowledge. The young child seems never to stop asking questions: Who? What? Why? When? Where? How? . . .

Another advantage of establishing a strong mental set before reading or studying is that you are also effectively setting yourself against that which you do not need to know or which is irrelevant. As was mentioned earlier, you are less likely to notice something if you are positively not expecting it than if you are expecting almost anything.

SET IN SPORT

Considerable interest is now being shown in the role of mental set in sports. Alan Richardson in Australia, investigated the effects of mental imagery on basketball players. He took three groups of students. The first group practiced basketball throws for twenty minutes every day. The second group did no physical practice but instead spent twenty minutes a day imagining that they were throwing the ball into the basket. As with physical practice, this group tried to correct their shots when they "mentally" missed the net. The third group had no practice whatsoever. After three weeks it was found that the group who had practiced mentally had improved by the same amount as the group who had practiced physically—about 24 percent—while those who had no practice whatsoever had not improved at all.[9]

Looking closer at the mental practice group, Richardson found that each individual's improvement was related to his ability to control his mental image. One of the players, for example, found that, although he could visualize the basketball court quite vividly, he could not bounce the ball in his mind; it tended to stick on the floor. This player was not helped very much by mental practice. Those subjects who were able to "feel" the touch of the ball as well as "see" it were much more successful. And those who were able to "hear" the bounce of the ball as well were even more successful.

In another series of experiments Richardson asked a group of gymnasts to perform mental training for a "single leg upstart on a high bar." As with the basketball players, those who practiced mental training improved considerably over those who did not. Again, the vividness of the images and the control they were able to exert in their images were reflected in the improvement in physical practice.[10]

Such mental training not only increases a player's confidence and prepares him for a given situation, it also directly affects his muscles. It has been shown that when a person imagines an activity to be taking place, small electrical changes can be detected in the associated muscles, despite the fact that there may be no physical signs of movement.[11]

Mental imagery has also been used in the training of skiers. The subjects, all competition skiers, were put into a relaxed state and then told to visualize the practice of racing techniques, slalom turns, course concentration, etc. Whenever they made mental faults, they were told to go back and correct them mentally. The practice was so effective that when it came to selecting a team for the race events, the coach chose only those who had used mental imagery.[12] Similar techniques of mental setting were used by the gold-medalist skier Jean-Claude Killy, who always practiced mentally if he was not able to practice physically.

Tennis is another sport in which mental set can be very effective. Billie Jean King used mental imagery before her matches, imagining every conceivable situation that could occur on the courts and mentally making sure she could cope with them, practicing in her mind all the awkward shots. Similarly Virginia Wade "saw" herself on the center court at Wimbledon, and "knew" she could get there. In his book *The Inner Game of Tennis* Timothy Gallway, himself a professional tennis player, suggests that when one is practicing difficult shots, he should first of all practice them mentally. The player is to first look at where he has to hit the ball, then close his eyes and imagine the ball leaving his racket and hitting the target. Having done this several times and having corrected any misses, the player opens his eyes and *without trying* to hit the target, without any control, trusts his body to carry out the action perfectly—letting "the serve serve itself."[13]

Mohammed Ali's continual prefight banter ensured him a strong mental set for success. He seldom allowed the possibility of failure to enter his mind, not only setting himself to win but simultaneously setting his opponent to lose. When he predicted correctly, every fight that Ali won provided yet more material with which to "remind" his opponents that they were bound to lose.

Similar results have been found with golf, motorcycle racing, and other sports.

Conversely, negative set can produce limitations in sport. For a long time weight lifters could not break the 500-pound barrier. The top people were around the 499-pound mark. They thought, "Nobody else had done 500 pounds, so how can I?" When Valery Alexis finally lifted 500 pounds, he was fooled into it. The scales were rigged to show 499.9 pounds when the weight was in fact 501.5 pounds. He lifted it. And once the barrier was broken and everyone knew "it could be done," many others followed. Their set had shifted from negative to positive.[14]

Arnold Schwarzenegger, five times Mr. Universe, believes that body building is very much in the mind: "As long as you can envision the fact that you can do something, you can do it—as long as you really believe it 100 percent."[15]

SET AND HEALTH

One of the first people to recognize the power of the mind in curing disease was the sixteenth-century Swiss physician Paracelsus. He believed that imagination could cure illness as well as produce it, and although he interpreted many of the theories in terms of good and evil spirits, his methods of healing were in essence a mental setting for health.

Most medical systems have realized that set can play an important role in sickness and health. The person who thinks of himself as prone to sickness is more likely to get sick than the person with a healthy, optimistic attitude. Most forms of treatment are in fact helped by an optimistic attitude on the part of the patient.

This was the basis of Emile Coué's therapy, which was very popular in both Europe and America in the 1920s. His treatment involved the frequent repetition of the phrase "Every day, and in every way, I am becoming better and better." Though very simple, it appeared to be extremely effective.

Often belief alone is enough to effect a cure. Patients given placebos, inert chemicals such as sugar or white flour disguised as a drug, will sometimes recover as well as patients given drugs, providing, that is, the patient is made to believe that the placebo is some "wonder drug." In one study a doctor gave injections of distilled water to patients with bleeding peptic ulcers, telling the patients that he was giving them a new drug that would cure them. Seventy percent of the patients showed excellent results lasting over a year.[16] In another experiment a patient was given the drug ipecac, which normally produces nausea and vomiting. In this case, though, the patient was told that the drug would *prevent* the nausea and vomiting that he already had. And it did.[17]

Jerome Frank in his book *Persuasion and Healing* points out that until the middle of this century most treatments prescribed by physicians were chemically inert and were not themselves killing bacteria and viruses: "The history of medical treatment until relatively recently is the history of the placebo effect."[18]

Cancer in particular is one illness where set can have important consequences. There is a general set throughout Western society that cancer is a killer, and once it is diagnosed in an individual, the negative set becomes a personal one—particularly if it is reinforced by a prediction that the patient concerned has only six months, or whatever, to live.

A prediction of death can in itself sometimes be enough to bring death about. In the Murngin tribe of northern Australia the headman can tell a tribesman that he will die in two days, and almost invariably the person is dead before the forty-eight hours are up. Scientists investigating such cases have found no evidence of physical illness in the corpse. When, however, a dying tribesman is told that the sentence has been lifted, he generally recovers with no ill effects.[19]

Similar principles have been applied in one of the more promising approaches to the treatment of cancer. Carl and Stephanie Simonton give their patients a positive setting for survival, showing them many cases of spontaneous remission, educating them on the body's own self-healing potential, and getting them actively to visualize the body becoming well again. As a result 30 percent of their patients have shown a complete recovery and another 45 percent have become well on the way to recovery.[20] Although their work is still only in the preliminary stages, these are very much higher success rates than those attained with conventional cancer treatment.

Another field of medicine in which "set" has been used to great advantage is childbirth. Dr. Grantly Dick-Read, a strong advocate of natural childbirth, believes that an important factor in easing birth is to give the mother a much more positive image of birth, thereby preventing the "fear–tension–pain syndrome."[21] In Western society young women are continually exposed to negative mental setting about the pain and suffering of childbirth. The resulting fear of giving birth leads to resistant actions in the womb, muscular tension, disturbed blood flow to the uterus, buildup of waste products in the tissues, and eventually to pain. Here the fear of pain actually produces pain. In many primitive societies, on the other hand, where there is no cultural tradition that childbirth is painful, women seem to give birth with little sign of distress; for many it can even be a blissful transcendental experience.

PHYSIOLOGICAL CONTROL OF THE BODY

There are many stories of Indian yogis and fakirs who have been able to produce remarkable changes in their bodies merely by mentally setting themselves for those changes. One yogi was able directly to change the temperature of two patches of skin on the same hand, making one hotter and the other colder simultaneously. Although the two areas were only a couple of inches apart, they showed a temperature difference of 10 degrees Fahrenheit. The hot area looked bright red, while the cold area of the palm looked ashen gray.[22] In such cases the yogi usually achieved the result by strong visualization, imagining one side of the palm to be burned by a hot coal, the other to be frozen by ice.

The Russian mnemonist "S," discussed earlier, also used his remarkable powers of imagery to accomplish similar feats. Not only was he able to control the temperature of his hands, he was able to raise or lower his heart rate by imagining himself running for a train or lying flat in a bed.[23] He was able to alter the size of his pupils by visualizing varying degrees of light, and he could change the alpha-wave patterns in his brain by visualizing a light flashing in his eyes.[24]

He could also use imagery to control pain. He described how at the dentist, for example, he would sit there and "when the pain starts, I feel it . . . it's a tiny, orange-red thread . . . I'm upset because I know that if this keeps up, the thread will widen until it turns into a dense mat . . . so I cut the thread, making it smaller and smaller until it's just a tiny point, and the pain disappears."[25]

In the West there has been a growing interest in the technique of biofeedback, by which a person can change such physiological parameters as blood pressure, skin temperature, brain activity, and other factors previously thought to be beyond individual control. The person does not try to change the physiological parameters, rather he tries to find a mental state that produces the required change, and he is able to observe whether or not he is successful by information "fed back" from monitoring instruments. Imagery has been found to play an important part in biofeedback. Skin temperature can be changed by imagining oneself to be hot or cold; and blood pressure and muscle tension can be lowered by imagining relaxed conditions.

A few people have gone further to suggest that mental imagery and belief can actually change the world around. Here we get into the field of miracles and superhuman powers, such as walking on water and levitation. Such things may not be altogether impossible,[26] but more objective studies of their occurrence is needed before we can begin to understand how they might occur.

APPLICATIONS AND ADVICE

One's own self-image is a form of mental set. The person who has a low opinion of himself, say, as someone who never really succeeds, is set to notice his failures more than his successes. He notices those aspects that reinforce his self-image and, believing himself to be a failure, puts less energy into trying to succeed. Conversely, someone who is optimistic about his potential will be quick to notice his successes, slow to notice failure, and less put off by failure. This is the basic principle behind the many techniques of positive thinking.

Numerous books have been written on the subject of positive thinking and remarkable claims have been made for its effectiveness in everyday life.[27] But it has been largely ignored by traditional psychology, presumably because most of the cases have been anecdotal in character and because the books on the subject were aimed at the mass paperback market rather than academics.

The essential process behind positive thinking is first to set yourself goals and then to imagine them having been achieved. It is not just a question of setting goals, but of "seeing" in your mind's eye the goals being fulfilled. The importance of this can be understood in terms of mental set. If the goal is merely a thing to be desired in the future, then the set for it is still negative—it has *not yet* been achieved—and experiences will be unconsciously selected that support that set. Imagining as strongly as possible the fulfillment of your dreams as already having occurred sets you positively for events and opportunities that will support your goals.

❧ Most systems recommend that this imagination be done while in a relaxed state, either sitting quietly and letting yourself sink into a dreamy, peaceful state, or while in that no-man's-land between waking and sleeping last thing at night and first thing in the morning—the hypnagogic and hypnopompic states. The probable reason for this is that it affects the deeper semiconscious levels of the mental activity that we are more in contact with during these states. Although the actual mechanics are not clear, it presumably works in much the same way as a posthypnotic suggestion.

This unconscious mental set then acts as a form of preprogramming throughout daily activity, with the result that a person again starts noticing those factors that support his set, and also the opportunities for actually realizing it. Thus, if a person had used some technique of positive thinking for self-confidence, he would not only begin to feel more self-confident, he would actually begin to act more self-confidently. He would have a greater aura of self-confidence, which would be noticed by others and fed back to support his new set.

A general rule in most positive thinking systems is never to say "I can't," but to think of ways in which you can. Even when you cannot see how a certain goal could be achieved, deliberate setting is still very valuable. The unconscious thinking levels will be preprogrammed for the goal and often work out ways and means by which it can be achieved and throw up solutions "out of the blue," which your more rational mind would never have thought of.

Problem Solving. The same principles can be used with a problem that has been defying solution, or with a difficult decision. First try to solve it. Get all the relevant information on hand. Then, if no solution is forthcoming, turn it over to your subconscious mind.

An easy way to do this is to have the problem in your mind before you drift off to sleep. But don't worry about it or try to solve it. Just be aware of the nature of the problem and the relevant factors and imagine it being solved. Feel how it would be if the problem were solved, and let your attention dwell upon this as you drift off to sleep. You may find you wake up in the morning and the answer suddenly flashes into your mind. Or maybe later in the day it will suddenly come up.

The reason why this happens less often when a person goes to sleep worrying about a problem or trying to solve it is that they are worrying if there is a solution and go to sleep knowing that they have nct found a solution, which keeps the mind negatively set.

Waking Up. Another simple way set can be used before going to sleep is setting a mental alarm to wake yourself up on time in the morning. Various techniques have been suggested for this, ranging from drawing the required time on your forehead to banging your head on the pillow the relevant number of times, for example, seven times for seven o'-clock. A less drastic and more effective way is to wait until you are about to drift off to sleep, then imagine a large clock in front of you with the hands at midnight and see and feel yourself dragging the hands round to the required time, and imagine yourself waking up at that time fresh and alert. This technique can be remarkably accurate. People often find themselves waking within a minute or two of the "set" time.

The specific mental mechanics of this are still not clear. It is, however, known that the body has an accurate biological clock and probably the subconscious mind connects into it in some way.

This technique is also useful as a starting point in "setting" yourself generally. Most people find it a fairly easy technique to master, and the fact that it works "sets" you generally for your potentials in this area. When you come to try setting yourself for something else, you already know something about the effectiveness of such techniques and so have a more positive set toward them. The more you go on, the more you realize that very much more is possible.

Stopping Smoking. An important factor in breaking many habits is the belief that you can do so. A person is less likely to be able to give up smoking if, in the back of his mind, there is the feeling that it cannot be done. They have tried before and failed, so why should this time be any better? How often do people say, "I would like to, but I am too addicted"?

Most of the different methods for stopping smoking give you a framework whereby you can begin to cut down or stop, plus a system to believe in. "It worked for me, try it." Or, "Proved by thousands." And the more strongly a person comes to believe in a system, the more effective it is likely to be.

In gaining a positive set toward giving up smoking, sympathetic friends are invaluable—particularly friends who have done it them-selves and can reaffirm that it is possible, and also friends who can encourage you through difficult phases when the old mental set raises its head again. Also positive suggestion that you are giving up smoking will help considerably.

Unsetting Depressed People. Many depressed people get themselves into a spiral of negative thinking. Because of their depressed set they interpret the words and actions of others in a pessimistic light. Throughout the day little incidents seem to confirm that everyone is against them, that they cannot cope, or whatever; the negative set is reinforced.

Some of the standard treatments used for depression attempt to break this viscious circle by giving drugs that elevate the patient's mood, with the hope that with a different mental perspective the person can begin to see things in a better light.

Another promising approach, and one without the side effects often found with antidepressant drugs, is to talk to the patients and get them to see themselves as winners rather than losers. The therapists go through events in the patients' lives showing them that their negative interpretation of themselves may not be based on fact and that a positive interpretation is often more plausible. This breaks the negative feedback spiral and often overcomes the setting for failure and hopelessness.[28]

Getting Set Up. Since virtually everything we perceive or do is affected to varying degrees by our set, it follows that we can apply the principles of positive setting almost anywhere: to getting out of bed on the right side and generally enjoying life; to seeing the good sides of other people —which not only helps them become more positive but also reaffirms your own positive set for humanity; to getting a promotion, a raise, or another job; even to meeting interesting new friends.

William James, one of the fathers of twentieth-century psychology, said that the greatest discovery of the nineteenth century was not in the realm of physical science but in the power of subconscious mind tinged by faith. The faculties of imagination and belief remain the least known and least used of all mental faculties. Yet they are also the most powerful. They are probably the key to our future evolution, both as individuals and as a species. If the human brain is the spearhead of evolution, these faculties are its tip.

Figure 66

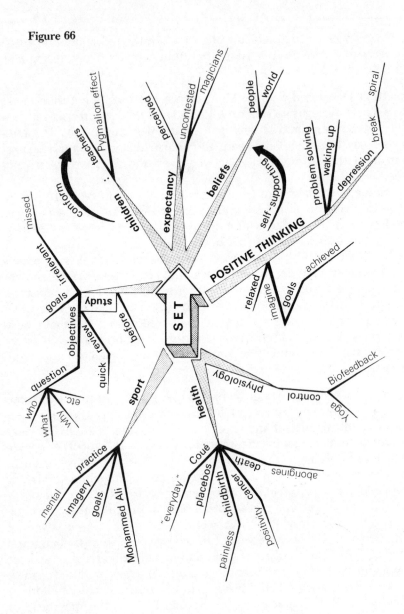

16.
Review

Since review is of utmost value in helping the brain remember new material, this final chapter is devoted to a review of the whole book. It is a good idea to get some colored pens and a large sheet of paper and make your own mind maps as you go.

The human brain is the most complex and most powerful information processor known to man.

Unlike an electronic computer, the brain can carry on a thousand different functions simultaneously, continually cross-referencing and integrating new information. Though many times more powerful and flexible than a computer, the brain weighs only three and a half pounds. Its complexity far surpasses that of modern technology. A transistorized brain would completely fill Carnegie Hall and one using microelectronics would still fill a large room.

The human brain is the most evolved system on this planet. It is the spearhead of evolution. The extent to which we use its potentials determines the extent to which we, both as individuals and as a race, progress.

Over the last two decades tremendous advances have been made in our knowledge of the brain and its functioning. Brain studies are now at the frontier of science and involve specialists from many different disciplines. Yet despite all that is being discovered, we are still a very long way from a full understanding of the brain.

As human beings we have hardly begun to use our brain's full potential. At school we were not taught how the brain works, and we never learned to use it properly in study, reading, memory, and other daily tasks.

BRAIN DEVELOPMENT

The brain is unlike any other organ in the body in that:

- Its internal structure is always changing and developing as a result of experience. This gives it an unlimited capacity for learning.
- The brain's cells do not generally reproduce themselves. Thus the same neurons are with you for life.

There are two major periods of brain growth:

1. Eight to thirteen weeks after conception. During this period the full complement of cells are being formed.

2. Six months after conception till the age of two, when the neurons are making most of their major connections. During this phase much of our basic learning takes place.

Considerable learning takes place while the child is still in the womb. The basic sounds and rhythm of language, for example, are acquired at this stage.

At birth the child is an intelligent, sensitive, perceptive, feeling being—far from a dumb animal.

The young brain is making millions of new connections each day as the young child absorbs its environment, and a rich environment is invaluable in helping it develop quickly and fully. Studies of gifted children reveal that many of them benefitted from a rich early environment, with a diversity of stimulation. In cases where parents have deliberately given their babies rich and varied environments, the children have often grown up with remarkable mental abilities. Although "supernormal" by conventional standards, this should be the "normal" pattern of development.

NEURONS

Each human brain contains some 10 billion neurons, which is more than there are people on this planet. Spreading from each neuron are hundreds, sometimes thousands, of fibers connecting the neurons to one another.

The junction of two of these fibers is called the *synapse.* There are estimated to be over 10 trillion synapses in one human brain. It is through the synapse that one neuron interacts and communicates with another, and these junctions, although only a few thousandths of an inch across, are the most important points in the nervous system.

As well as transmitting electrical pulses, some of the fibers (the axons) also carry proteins and other molecules down to the synapse, where they modify its ability to transmit pulses. This modification probably plays an essential role in memory.

In addition to its 10 billion neurons the brain also contains 100 billion glia cells, which surround every neuron, insulating it and nourishing it.

There are also millions of tiny blood vessels bringing the brain's much needed oxygen. Although only 2 to 3 percent of the body by weight, the brain consumes 20 percent of the oxygen intake. Much of this energy goes into the production of proteins and other molecules used at the synapse.

STRUCTURE

The brain can be divided into many different regions. The main parts, starting with the "oldest," are spinal chord, brain stem, cerebellum, midbrain, and cortex.

The cortex, which covers most of the brain's surface, is responsible for such higher mental functions as thinking, perception, decision making, and will.

THE TWO HALVES OF THE BRAIN

The cortex is divided into two distinct halves:

- The left side generally prefers to function in a linear, analytic mode and is more concerned with verbal abilities and logical thinking.
- The right side generally prefers to function in a simultaneous, synthetic mode and is more concerned with spatial abilities and creative thinking.

Most people in Western societies tend to use the functions associated with the left side more than those associated with the right. But this is not an intrinsic dominance; it is probably the result of cultural and educational systems that emphasize the faculties associated with the left.

Ideally we should be using both sides equally, as many great thinkers (Einstein, for example) seemed to do. The integration of the two sides is enhanced by meditation and by deliberately using the faculties associated with the right in reading, writing, etc.

Although the left brain controls the right side of the body and vice versa, it does not seem that left-handed people use the right side of their brains more, nor that their brains are reversed.

The qualities associated with the left and right sides of the brain are reflected in most cultures throughout the world with a symbolism of right and left—for example, good/bad, matter/spirit.

AGING

It is a common misconception that intellectual abilities necessarily begin to decline after the age of twenty. Neurologically speaking, there is no reason for abilities to decline: They should keep on improving throughout most of life. The apparent decline is probably due mainly to

a lack of use; and
an expectancy of decline.

Polymaths and others who have made full use of their brains throughout life show no deterioration with age.

Although many older people claim that memory for recent events deteriorates as they get older, there is little experimental evidence to support this. Possibly they appear to remember more of their childhood and youth because these periods were more novel and outstanding. Recent memories can be enhanced and the apparent decline reversed if one maintains an active interest in the present.

RECOVERY OF FUNCTION

It has long been accepted that the young brain can adapt and change its structure in response to injury or other physical changes. It has only recently been realized that the adult brain also shows considerable adaptability.

Studies of people who have suffered severe head injuries show that, given time, the brain will compensate for the damage, eventually recovering many of the destroyed functions. This recovery is enhanced by

specific retraining programs; and
retraining as soon after the injury as possible.

If damage occurs very gradually, as with some brain diseases, the brain can adapt as the damage progresses so that very little loss of function may be noticed.

CARING FOR YOUR BRAIN

In order to make the most of your brain you must keep it healthy. Regular exercise and rest are both essential, as is a well-balanced, wholesome diet.

MEMORY

Of all our mental faculties, memory is the most important and is involved in everything we do.

Although recall of an event generally fades with time, it may actually increase a little for a few minutes after learning. This is known as reminiscence (fig. 67a).

In any learning situation the beginning and end of the session are remembered better (primacy and recency).
So are outstanding items (fig. 67b).

Taking regular breaks during any study or learning increases the overall recall. Breaks take maximum advantage of primacy, recency, and reminiscence.

You should break once every forty minutes at least, and for about five to ten minutes (fig. 67c).

During breaks, rest, relax, take some fresh air, etc.

After a break do a quick review of the previous session(s). This warms you up mentally and also gets you mentally "set" for the subject.

Even when study seems to be going well, it is still good to break. *Understanding is not necessarily remembering.*

Chunking. Immediate memory is limited to about seven "chunks" of information. Most people can remember about seven numbers in a row, seven colors, seven shapes, or seven of any other items. So if you need to remember more than seven items, it is better to organize them into a smaller number of chunks.

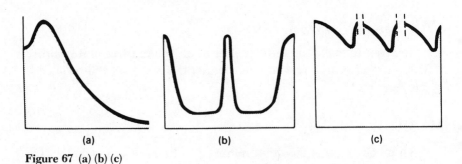

(a)   (b)   (c)

Figure 67 (a) (b) (c)

Association. This is one of the most important factors in human memory. Memories are linked by association and any one thought will have many ideas and images associated with it. Thus, memory is not recorded linearly as in a film but is a vast, intricately interconnected network.

Associations are like hooks on which more memories can be attached. So rather than filling up, memory capacity actually *expands* as more and more things are remembered.

Organization. Organization is also very important in memory. Unconsciously the mind organizes any new material into groups and patterns. The greater the subjective organization, the better the memory.

Consciously looking for underlying patterns and principles is more effective than rote learning. It is the ordering of the material that the mind remembers. Chess masters, for example, remember the configurations on a board, not the individual positions.

The more consciously you are involved with anything, and its meaning and significance, the greater the depth of processing; the greater the organization; and the better the memory.

Sleep Learning. Although moderately effective sleep learning tends to wake a person up, modern approaches such as suggestopedia put a person into a *wakeful,* relaxed state and are much more effective.

IMAGERY

Most people possess imagery to varying extents, and with most of the senses, though visual imagery is generally the strongest.

Memory of visual images is essentially perfect. Shown ten thousand pictures, people can recognize 99.6 percent correctly.

One reason that the potential of human memory has been underestimated in the past is that psychologists have used verbal memory, which is poorer than visual memory, and deliberately eliminated the natural tools of memory, such as association, meaning, and organization.

Everyone's memory can be improved by making a greater use of imagery. When two images are associated, they should be made to connect and interact as directly and vividly as possible.

Many children possess the ability of eidetic imagery. They are able to maintain a strong, full-color visual image of a scene and "see" the details in it for some time afterward, sometimes even days. Most children, however, lose this capacity as they grow up, probably because our educational system is orientated more toward the verbal faculties associated with the left hemisphere than the visual ones of the right. Hypnotic regression back to childhood has shown that some adults still have eidetic imagery as a latent faculty.

MNEMONICS

A mnemonic is any technique for increasing memory. They were first used extensively by the ancient Greeks and Romans.

The basic principle underlying all mnemonics is to make a strong association with the thing to be remembered. As much as possible, the associations should be unique, exaggerated, sensory, simple, creative, and outstanding. A little vulgarity often helps.

A simple system for remembering lists is the number-rhyme system, in which the numbers one to ten are given rhyming images, such as one–gun, two–shoe, etc. (itself an easy mnemonic), and each element of the list associated with one of the images. Such a technique is invaluable for remembering odd things when there is no pencil or paper handy.

Rhymes and rhythm are very useful in remembering things; they provide a patterned framework for the words involved. Many simple mnemonics used at school are based on rhymes. Most people also use apparently "silly" mnemonics for remembering many everyday things.

Mnemonic principles can be used for learning both the vocabulary and grammar of foreign languages, for remembering faces, and for remedying absent-mindedness in general.

Mnemonics are not cheating. They are making a fuller use of the imagery capacities of the right side of the brain and the natural associative properties of human memory. Far from being "silly," they are eminently sensible.

The Russian mnemonist "S" displayed a near perfect memory. Studies showed that he spontaneously used the principles of mnemonics throughout everyday life, forming strong vivid associations with everything he encountered. This was enhanced by his natural capacity for synesthesia, by which visual images would automatically conjure up smells, sounds, tastes, and tactile sensations. "S" still remembered long, monotonous lists of nonsense syllables fifteen years after the experiment.

MEMORY STORAGE

Experiments on the transfer of memory from one animal to another suggest that there is a chemical basis to learning. In some cases specific proteins have been identified that correspond to specific learning. Scotophobin, for example, is synthesized in rats trained to fear the dark, and when injected into other rats, it causes them to fear the dark also.

Despite the fact that there are zillions of different proteins that could be synthesized, this is still very much less than the zillions upon zillions of possible things we could remember. It is not therefore possible that each incidental memory could be related to a unique protein. *Memory is different from learning.*

The synapses between neurons play a fundamental role in memory. Learning almost certainly results in some of the brain's trillions of synapses' changing their ability to transmit impulses, and the pattern of these changes over the whole brain determines the specific memory.

HOLOGRAPHY AND MEMORY

A hologram is unlike a photograph in that every part of the image affects every part of the plate. They are records of the patterns produced by the interference of a pure coherent beam of light, as from a laser, with the same beam reflected from an object.

Holograms possess the following special features:

- The whole image may be reconstructed from any part of the hologram.
- Images are "recalled" by reestablishing the same initial conditions (frequency and angle of incidence of coherent light).
- If the reference beam is also reflected from an object when creating the hologram, the two objects will be permanently associated, and one will "recall" the other.
- Illumination with the beam reflected from the object will produce a bright spot (or flash) of recognition.

The hologram closely resembles human memory in its functioning, and it may well be that memory works along similar principles. The same mathematical transformations have been discovered in the brain, and a holographic model also explains the virtually unlimited potential of human memory. In fact not only memory, but perception and the mind generally, may be based on holographic principles.

CONSOLIDATION AND REVIEW

The initial short-term memory of an event probably sets up coherent patterns of electrical activity in millions of pathways over the brain as a whole. This corresponds to the interference pattern in the hologram. These electrical changes probably result in changes in protein synthesis in the neurons and, as these proteins are conveyed down to the synapse, in changes in the transmission characteristics of the synapse. Over time, particularly if reinforced, these changes become permanent. This is known as *consolidation* of the memory trace.

The initial consolidation probably occurs within ten minutes of the event. Further consolidation takes place over the day, during sleep, and over the next few weeks. It also takes place every time the initial experience is repeated.

Review is therefore imperative for efficient memory. It is a good idea to take a few minutes to review about ten minutes after the initial study, and again after one day, one week, one month, and six months. This makes maximum use of consolidation and ensures that memory of the subject is essentially perfect.

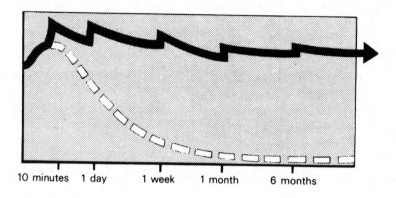

10 minutes   1 day   1 week   1 month   6 months

Figure 68

IS EVERYTHING REMEMBERED?

Evidence from a number of sources—

virtually unlimited storage capacity;
excellent recognition;
near perfect visual memory;
tip-of-the-tongue recall;
power of mnemonics;
amazing wealth of incidental memories;
memory prodigies, such as "S";
hypnotic regression to childhood;
near-death experiences;
dreams;
direct stimulation of the brain—

suggests that the brain may well record every experience.

There are several theories as to why we appear to forget many of our experiences: repression, decay, interference, confusing cues, and loss of mental set. They are probably all responsible to some extent. They can be compensated for by making maximum use of imagery, organization, association, and other natural attributes of memory, in everything we do.

NOTES

As well as serving as an information storage system, efficient notes allow a person to encode the information, organize it, make associations and inferences, and consciously think about what is significant, thereby increasing the depth of processing.

The key words in any sentence are the words that hold most of the information content. They are the words that are remembered, and when recalled they "unlock" the meaning again.

Key words are usually nouns and verbs. They are concrete and specific, and generate strong images.

The more key words there are in notes, the more useful they are and the better they are remembered. Ideally, notes should be based on key words and key images.

Traditional notes, in neat linear sentences, waste space, waste time in recording and reviewing, disguise and dissociate the key words. They aid forgetfulness rather than memory.

The brain does not generally work in a linear step-by-step manner but processes many streams of information at once, making numerous associations and connections as it goes. Mind maps reflect this nature of the brain and are therefore an excellent interface between the brain and the outside world.

In making mind maps:

use key words and images;
print the words rather than use script;
put the words *on* lines;
use one word per line;
make the pattern outstanding;
be creative and original;
use color, dimensions, imagery, and imagination;
have strong well-defined centers and subcenters;

use arrows and other means to show connections;
use personal codes, mnemonics, and associations;
be involved with the pattern and have fun.

Mind maps can be used in any situation where you want to put pen to paper—and in many more.

They have advantages over ordinary notes in being:

visual and easily remembered;
flexible and open-ended;
clear in themes, structure, and relative importances;
unique and outstanding;
compact;
fast;
organic like the brain;
fun and enjoyable;
creative.

READING

There are many different systems of learning to read, but they all suffer from the disadvantages that reading stops at "silent reading." This does not bring in the right, "visual" half of the brain, so reading speeds stay around two hundred words per minute—a small fraction of what they could be. Moreover, comprehension, understanding, recall, retention, and communication of the material are hardly taught.

The following is an expanded definition of reading:

1. Assimilation—the eye taking in the information

2. Recognition—of letters, words, simple phrases

3. Understanding—in the immediate context

4. Comprehension—in the overall context

5. Retention—in memory

6. Recall—at a later date

7. Communication—to others or self (thinking)

The Eye and Reading. The *fovea* is the small central area of the retina where perception is clear and sharp. It sees only one degree of the visual angle, i.e., about half a dozen letters at normal reading distance.

The eye can only see when it is still, relative to the object seen, thus during reading it makes a series of jumps (saccadic movements), stopping (fixating) to allow new parts of the line to cast an image on the fovea. The eye can make a maximum of about five jumps per second.

Normal readers take in about two or three words with each fixation. Skilled readers may take in two or three lines.

Although vision is clearest at the fovea, the rest of the visual field is still seen in varying degrees of clarity. This is known as peripheral vision. It is used

to read the beginnings and ends of lines without actually fixating there (making use of the redundancy in written English);
to guide the eye on to the next most useful point of fixation;
to give skilled readers a good idea of what is in the next few lines.

Most people skip back to reread words they have already seen. This is called regression. In young children as much as 25 percent of eye movements are regressive. Most regression comes from fear and apprehension, not from actual misreading. The more skilled the reader, the less the back-skipping.

Contrary to popular opinion, a visual guide will not slow down reading if it is moved along smoothly under a line of print. A visual guide alone can speed up reading to around five hundred words per minute by

eliminating the tendency to skip back;
speeding up the eye so that more is taken in with each fixation.

In high-speed training the reader is forced to "read" at speeds far beyond those at which he can consciously absorb any of the meaning. This brings into use the right "visual" hemisphere and encourages the perception of key words. On returning to "normal," reading is two to three times faster—and with equal if not greater comprehension.

Study. Plan the session and check heat, light, and posture. "Set" the mind by quickly reviewing what is already known.

Set objectives
Overview
Preview
Practice a few minutes high-speed training
Treat the text as a whole
Underline and make outstanding important points
Reject what is already known or irrelevant
Reject false arguments
Break regularly
Make mind maps
Review

MENTAL SET

A person tends to see what he expects to see and to miss what he is not expecting. This is known as "set."

Because of "set" many beliefs about the world or other people are self-validating. A person notices that which supports his belief.

A person tends automatically to fulfil the image and goals he sets for himself. If disaster always seems to be occurring, it may well be because of a pessimistic self-image. Conversely, deliberately "setting" for positive goals can bring success. To get the most from positive thinking, be clear on your goals and visualize them actually happening.

Many sportspeople use mental practice to improve their performance. Again the more vividly the practice sessions are imaged, the more benefit is gained.

Positive thinking has been very valuable in the treatment of depression. Helping the patient to see events in an optimistic light breaks the negative spiral of depression.

Belief is also important in physical health. Most medical treatments work better if the patient (and doctor) believe in them. Often inert chemicals (placebos) will work just as effectively as drugs and antibiotics—providing that is, the patient is convinced of their efficacy.

Many people have been able to exercise control over their physiology, raising the temperature of patches of skin, for example, merely by holding the image of that change firmly in their minds.

Belief and imagination, although little understood, are perhaps the most important of all human faculties. With them rests the potential for our continued evolution and progress. They are the tip of the spearhead of evolution.

Chapter Notes

THE SPEARHEAD OF EVOLUTION

1. Peter Russell, "Analysis of Accessions in Cambridge University Library," unpublished report, 1976.
2. See, for example, Lyall Watson, *Supernature* (London: Hodder & Stoughton, 1973).
3. See, for example, Russell Targ and Harold Puthoff, *Mind Reach* (New York: Delacorte, 1977).
4. *Brain-Mind Bulletin* 2 (16):2.
5. Beatrice T. Gardner and Allan R. Gardner, "Teaching Sign Language to a Chimpanzee: 1. Methodology and Preliminary Results," *Psychonomic Bulletin* 1 (2):36.
6. Ann J. Premack and David Premack, "Teaching Language to an Ape," *Scientific American,* October 1972, pp. 92–99.
7. Carl Sagan, Harvard University, personal communication, October 1977.
8. Karl Witte, *The Education of Karl Witte, Or the Training of the Child,* trans. L. Wiener (London: Harrap, 1915).
9. P. Solomon, ed., *Sensory Deprivation: A Symposium* (Cambridge, Mass.: Harvard University Press, 1961).
10. Marcelle Gebber "Psychomotor Development of African Children in the First Year, and the Influence of Maternal Behaviour," *Journal of Social Psychology* 147:185–195.
11. Winifred Stoner, *Natural Education* (London: John Lane and Bodley Head, 1923).
12. "The Edith Project," *Sunday Times* (London), April 17, 1977.

13. Quoted in Marilyn Ferguson, *The Brain Revolution* (New York: Bantam, 1973), p. 266.
14. Daniel J. Davis, "Birth Order and Intellectual Development," *Science* 196:1470–72.
15. " 'Head Start Pays Off," *New Scientist*, March 3, 1977, pp. 508–509.
16. "Should Children Be Pushed into Early Learning?" *Psychology Today* (UK edition), September 1977, pp. 32–37.
17. Reported in *Times* (London), June 16, 1976.

THE BRAIN'S DEVELOPMENT

1. John Lilly, *The Mind of the Dolphin* (New York: Avon, 1969).
2. John Barratt, personal communication, 1972.
3. Robert L. Fantz, "The Origins of Form Perception," *Scientific American*, May 1961.
4. Tom Bower, "The Object World of the Infant," *Scientific American*, October 1971.
5. Tom Bower, "Competent Newborns," *New Scientist*, March 14, 1974, pp. 672–75.
6. Quoted in Marilyn Ferguson, *The Brain Revolution* (New York: Bantam, 1973), p. 274.
7. Roger Lewin, "Developing brains," *New Scientist*, June 13, 1974, pp. 686–89.
8. Mark Rosenzweig, "Environmental Complexity, Cerebral Change and Behaviour," *American Psychologist* 21 (4):321–32.
9. William S. Condon and Louis W. Sander, "Neonate Movement Is Synchronised with Adult Speech," *Science* 183:99–101.
10. Ronald Laing, *The Facts of Life* (London: Allen Lane and New York: Pantheon, 1976).
11. "A Gentle Entry into Life Has Its Advantages," *New Scientist*, November 25, 1976, p. 449.
12. *Brain-Mind Bulletin* 2(23).
13. See *New Scientist*, October 24, 1974, p. 268.
14. Brian Cragg, "The Development of Cortical Synapses During Starvation in the Rat," *Brain* 95:143–50.
15. Roger Lewin, "The Poverty of Undernourished Brains," *New Scientist*, October 24, 1974, pp. 268–271.
16. "Stimulating Homes Cancel Brain Damage in Malnourished Children," *New Scientist*, January 1, 1976, p. 108.
17. John Spudich and Dan Koshland, "Non-Genetic Individuality: Chance in the Single Cell," *Nature* 262:467–71.
18. John J. Sherwood and Mark Nataupsky, "Predicting the Conclusion of Negro-White Intelligence Research from Biographical Characteristics

of the Investigator," *Journal of Personality and Social Psychology* 8:53–58.

TEN BILLION NEURONS

1. Irene Gore, "The Meaning of Ageing," *New Scientist,* March 21, 1974, pp. 756–57.
2. Marian Diamond, "The Ageing Brain: Some Enlightening and Optimistic Results," *American Scientist* 66:66–71.
3. K. Akert and K. Pfenninger, "Synaptic Fine Structure of Neural Dynamics," in *Cellular Dynamics of the Neuron,* ed. S. H. Barondes (New York: Academic Press, 1969), pp. 245–60.
4. Robert O'Becker, *Genetic Psychological Monographs,* no. 2 (1971), pp. 177–235.
5. Paul Weiss, "Neuronal Dynamics," in *Neurosciences Research Symposium Summaries,* ed. F. O. Schmidt et al., vol. 3 (Cambridge, Mass.: MIT Press, 1969), pp. 255–84.
6. S. H. Barondes, "Synaptic Plasticity of Axoplasmic Transport," in *Neurosciences Research Symposium Summaries,* ed. Smith et al., pp. 249–54.

THE TWO SIDES OF THE BRAIN

1. K. U. Smith and A. J. Akelaitis, "Studies on the Corpus Callosum," *Archives of Neurological Psychiatry* 47:519–43.
2. Michael S. Gazzaniga, J. E. Bogen, and Roger W. Sperry, "Observations on Visual Perception After Disconnection of the Cerebral Hemispheres in Man," *Brain* 8:221–36.
3. Michael S. Gazzaniga, "The Split Brain in Man," *Scientific American,* August 1967, pp. 24–29.
4. Ibid.
5. Ibid.
6. David Galen and Robert Ornstein, "Lateral Specialisation of Cognitive Mode: An EEG Study," *Psychophysiology* 9 (4):412–18.
7. Doreen Kimura, "The Assymetry of the Human Brain," *Scientific American,* March 1973, pp. 70–78.
8. Thomas G. Bever and Robert J. Chiarello, "Cerebral Dominance in Musicians and Non-musicians," *Science* 185:537–39.
9. Hadyn D. Ellis and John W. Shepherd, "Recognition of Upright and Inverted Faces Presented in the Left and Right Visual Fields," *Cortex* 11:3–7.
10. Gillian Cohen, "Hemispheric Differences in Serial versus Parallel Processing," *Journal of Experimental Psychology* 97:349–56.

11. Stuart Dimond, *The Double Brain* (London: Churchill Livingstone, 1972), chapters 6 and 10.

12. M. L. Taylor, "A Measurement of Functional Communication in Aphasia," *Archives of Physiological Medicine and Rehabilitation* 46 (1-A):101–107; and P. Marcie et al., "Les réalisations du langage chez les malades attients de lésions de l'hémisphère droit," *Neuropsy-. chologia* 3:217–45.

13. J. Wade and T. Rasmussen, "Intracarotid Injection of Sodium Amytal for the Lateralisation of Cerebral Speech Dominance," *Journal of Neurosurgery* 17:266–82.

14. *Brain-Mind Bulletin* 2 (24).

15. "Why Children Should Draw," *Saturday Review*, September 3, 1977, pp. 11–16.

16. Ibid., p. 14.

17. Dimond, *Double Brain*, pp. 139–49.

18. C. Branch, B. Milner, and T. Rasmussen, "Intracarotid Injection of Sodium Amytal for the Lateralisation of Cerebral Speech Dominance: Observation in 123 Patients," *Journal of Neurosurgery* 21:399–405.

19. Sandra F. Witelson, "Sex and Single Hemisphere; Specialisation of Right Hemisphere for Spatial Processing," *Science* 193:425–26.

20. "Man's Sexist Brain," *Sunday Times* (London), June 25, 1976.

21. Quoted in Daniel Goleman, "Specialist Abilities of the Sexes: Do They Begin in the Brain?" *Psychology Today*, November 1978, p. 59, from Diane McGuinness and Karl Pribram, in *Cognitive Growth and Development—Essays in Honor of Herbert G. Birch*, ed. Morton Bortner (New York: Brunner/Mazel, 1979).

22. Juhn Wada and Alan Davis, "Fundamental Nature of Human Infant's Brain Assymetry," *Canadian Journal of Neurological Sciences* 4 (3): 203–207.

23. Arthur Deikman, "Bimodal Consciousness," *Archives of General Psychiatry* 25:481–89.

24. Robert Ornstein, *The Psychology of Consciousness* (San Francisco: Freeman, 1972).

25. A. Werner, "Note on the Terms Used for 'Right Hand' and 'Left Hand' in the Bantu Languages," *Journal of the African Society* 4:112–16.

26. Bernard C. Glueck and Charles F. Stroebel, "Biofeedback and Meditation in the Treatment of Psychiatric Illnesses," *Comprehensive Psychiatry* 16:303–21.

27. David Orme-Johnson and John Farrow, eds., *Scientific Research on the Transcendental Meditation Program* (New York: MIU Press, 1977), pp. 187–207.

THE EVER-ADAPTABLE BRAIN

1. Quoted in Maya Pines, *The Brain Changers* (New York: Signet, 1975), p. 197.
2. C. Doyle Haynes et al., "The Improvement of Cognition and Personality after Carotid Endarterectomy, *Surgery* 80:699–704.
3. M. R. Rosenzweig, E. L. Bennett, and M. C. Diamond, "Brain Changes in Response to Experience," *Scientific American,* February 1972.
4. Quoted in Marilyn Ferguson, *The Brain Revolution* (New York: Bantam, 1973), p. 198.
5. William R. Russell, *Explaining the Brain* (Oxford, England: Oxford University Press, 1975), p. 115.
6. E. K. Warrington and H. I. Sanders, "The Fate of Old Memories," *Quarterly Journal of Experimental Psychology* 23:432–42.
7. Helen C. Franklin and Dennis M. Holding, "Personal Memories at Different Ages," *Quarterly Journal of Experimental Psychology* 29:527–32.
8. Stuart Dimond, *The Double Brain* (London: Churchill Livingstone, 1972), pp. 95–110.
9. R. E. Saul and R. W. Sperry, "Absence of Commissurotomy Symptoms with Agenesis of the Corpus Callosum," *Neurology* 18:307.
10. H. L. Teuber, "Recovery of Function After Lesion of the Central Nervous System: History and Prospects," *Neurosciences Research Program Bulletin* 12 (2):200.
11. Ibid., p. 205.
12. A. R. Luria, *The Man with a Shattered World* (London: Jonathan Cape, 1973).
13. J. H. Wepman, *Recovery from Aphasia* (New York: Ronald Press, 1951).
14. Teuber, "Recovery of Function After Lesions of Central Nervous System," p. 204.
15. Ibid.
16. Glen Doman, *What to Do About Your Brain Injured Child* (London: Jonathan Cape, 1974).
17. Glen Doman, *How to Teach Your Baby How to Read* (New York: Doubleday, 1975).
18. Moshe Feldenkreis, demonstration at the May Lectures, London, 1974.
19. Paul Pietsch, "Shuffle Brain," *Harpers* 244:44.
20. Quoted in Ferguson, *Brain Revolution,* p. 294.
21. G. E. Schneider, "Development and Regeneration in the Mammalian Visual System" in *The Genesis of Neuronal Patterns,* ed. M. V. Barkley, D. S. Famborough, and D. M. Farnborough, *Neurosciences Research Program Bulletin* 10:287–90.
22. Geoffrey Raisman, "The Reaction of Synaptogenesis in the Central and

Peripheral Nervous System of the Adult Rat" in *Neuronal Mechanisms of Learning and Memory,* ed. M. R. Rosenzweig and E. L. Bennet (Cambridge, Mass.: MIT Press, 1976), pp. 348–351.

23. Clarence D. Cone and Charlotte M. Cone, "Induction of Mitosis in Mature Neurons in Central Nervous System by Sustained Depolarisation," *Science* 192:155–58.

24. Brian S. Scott, "Effect of Elevated Potassium on the Time Course of Neuron Survival in Cultures of Disassociated Dorsal Root Ganglia," *Journal of Cellular Psysiology* 91:305–16.

25. Quoted in Ferguson, *Brain Revolution,* p. 264.

26. M.R. Rosensweig, P.A. Ferchmin, and E.L. Bennett, "Direct Contact with Enriched Enviroment Is Required to Alter Cerebral Weight in Rats," *Journal of Comparative and Physiological Psychology* 88:360–67

27. *New Age Journal,* November 1977, p. 24.

28. A. H. Ismail and L. E. Tratchman, "Jogging Your Personality into Shape," *Psychology Today* (UK edition), August 1976, pp. 24–28.

29. Robert Shaw and David Kolb, "Reaction Time Following the Transcendental Meditation Technique," in *Scientific Research on the Transcendental Meditation Program,* ed. David Orme-Johnson and John Farrow (New York: MIU Press, 1977), pp. 309–15.

30. Andrew Rimol, "The Transcendental Meditation Technique and Its Effects on Sensory-motor Performance," in *Scientific Research on Transcendental Meditation Program,* ed. Orme-Johnson and Farrow, pp. 326–30.

31. Ibid.

THE PSYCHOLOGY OF MEMORY

1. Hermann Ebbinghaus, *Memory,* trans. D. H. Ruyer and C. E. Bussenius (New York: Teachers College Press, 1913).

2. B. P. Ballard, "Oblivescence and Reminiscence," *Quarterly Journal of Experimental Psychology* 16:265–92.

3. Lloyd R. Peterson, "Short-Term Memory," *Scientific American,* July 1966, p. 95.

4. L. B. Ward, "Reminiscence and Rote-Learning," *Psychological Monographs* 49 (220).

5. B. Milner, "Visual Recognition and Recall After Right Temporal-Lobe Excision in Man," *Neuropsychologia* 6:191–209.

6. G. A. Kimble and B. R. Horenstein, "Reminiscence in Motor Learning As a Function of Length of Interpolated Rest," *Journal of Experimental Psychology* 38:239–44.

7. Ballard, "Oblivescence and Reminiscence."

8. J. Mohan, "Reminiscence: A Review," *Psychologia (Kyoto)* 9:157–64.

9. Richard C. Atkinson and Richard M. Shiffrin, "The Control of Short-term Memory," *Scientific American,* August 1971, pp. 82–90.
10. E. J. Thomas, "The Variation of Memory with Time for Information Appearing During a Lecture," *Studies in Adult Education,* April 1972, pp. 57–62.
11. C. I. Hovland, "Experimental Studies in Rote-Learning Theory: Comparisons of Distribution of Practice in Serial and Paired-Associate Learning," *Journal of Experimental Psychology* 25:622–33.
12. L. F. Thune, "Warm-up Effect As a Function of Level of Practice in Verbal Learning," *Journal of Experimental Psychology* 42:250–56.
13. A. L. Irior, "Retention As a Function of Amount of Pre-recall Warming Up," *American Psychologist* 4:219–20.
14. H. von Restorff, "Über die Wikung von Bereichsbildungen im Spurenfeld," *Psychologisch Forschung* 18:299–342.
15. See Alan D. Baddeley, *The Psychology of Memory* (New York: Harper & Row, 1976), p. 269.
16. George A. Miller, "The Magical Number Seven, Plus or Minus Two: Some Limits in Our Capacity for Processing Information," *Psychological Review* 63:81–97.
17. H. Pieron, "Recherches expérimentales sur les phénomènes de mémoire," *L'Année Psychologique* 19:91–193.
18. B. Zeigarnik, "Das Behalten erledigter und unerledigter Handungen," *Psychologisch Forschung* 9:1–85.

ASSOCIATION AND ORGANIZATION IN MEMORY

1. Francis Galton, "Psychometric Experiments," *Brain* 2:148–62.
2. John Locke, *An Essay Concerning Human Understanding* (1690, reprint ed., London: Everyman's Library, Dent, 1961).
3. D. W. Goodwin et al., "Alcohol and Recall: State Dependent Effects in Man," *Science* 163:1358.
4. Quoted in Marilyn Ferguson, *The Brain Revolution* (New York: Bantam, 1973), p. 64.
5. J. Greenspan and R. Raynard, "Stimulus Conditions and Retroactive Inhibition," *Journal of Experimental Psychology* 53:55–59.
6. D. R. Godden and A. D. Baddeley, "Context-Dependent Memory in Two Natural Environments: On Land and Underwater," *British Journal of Psychology* 66:325–32.
7. W. A. Bousfield, "The Occurence of Clustering in the Recall of Randomly Arranged Associates," *Journal of General Psychology* 49:229–40.
8. W. A. Bousfield, B. H. Cohen, and G. A. Whitmarsh, "Associative Clustering in the Recall of Words of Different Taxonomic Frequencies of Occurence," *Psychological Reports* 4:39–44.

9. Endel Tulving, "Subjective Organisation in Free Recall of Unrelated Words," *Psychological Review* 69 (4):344–54.
10. George Mandler, "Organization and Memory," in *The Psychology of Learning and Motivation*, vol. 1., ed. K. W. Spence and J. S. Spence (New York: Academic Press, 1967), pp. 327–72.
11. George Katona, *Organizing and Memorizing* (New York: Columbia University Press, 1940), pp. 188–90.
12. A. D. DeGroot, "Perception and Memory Versus Thought; Some Old Ideas and Recent Findings," in *Problem Solving*, ed. B. Kleinmuntz (New York: Wiley, 1966).
13. Arthur Koestler, *Heel of Achilles* (New York: Random House, 1975), p. 230.
14. F.I.M. Craik and R. S. Lockhart, "Levels of Processing: A Framework for Memory Research," *Journal of Experimental Psychology (General)* 104:268–94.
15. D. A. Norman and D. E. Rumelhart, *Explorations in Cognition* (San Francisco: Freeman, 1975), p. 374.
16. Quoted in Ferguson, *Brain Revolution*, p. 73.
17. Maralyn Ferguson, ed. "Suggestology to be explored in U.S.," *Brain-Mind Bulletin* 1 (5): 1–2.

IMAGERY AND ITS RELATIONSHIP TO MEMORY

1. Francis Galton, *Inquiries in the Human Faculty and Its Development* (London: Macmillan, 1883).
2. P. McKellar, "The Investigation of Mental Images," in *Penguin Science Survey*, ed. S.A. Barnett and A. McLaren (London: Penguin, 1965).
3. Quoted in Alan Baddeley, *The Psychology of Memory*, (New York and London: Harper & Row, 1976), p. 225.
4. Quoted in Gordon Bower, "Mental Imagery and Associative Learning," in *Cognition in Learning and Memory*, ed. L. W. Gregg (London and New York: John Wiley, 1972), p. 67.
5. Ibid., p. 69.
6. A. Paivio, "Mental Imagery in Associative Learning and Memory," *Psychological Review* 76:241–63.
7. Bower, "Mental Imagery and Associative Learning," p. 69.
8. Baddeley, *Psychology of Memory*, pp. 222–23.
9. A. G. Goldstein and J. E. Chance, "Visual Recognition Memory for Complex Configurations," *Perception and Psychophysics* 9:237–41.
10. Ralph N. Haber, "How We Remember What We See," *Scientific American*, May 1970, p. 105.
11. R. S. Nickerson, "Short-Term Memory for Complex Meaningful Visual

Configurations: Demonstration of Capacity," *Canadian Journal of Psychology* 19:155–60.

12. Lionel Standing, "Learning 10,000 Pictures," *Quarterly Journal of Experimental Psychology* 25:207–22.
13. Quoted in A. Richardson, *Mental Imagery* (New York: Springer, 1952).
14. G. W. Allport, "Eidetic Imagery," *British Journal of Psychology* 15: 99–120.
15. H. Kluver, "Studies on the Eidetic Type and on Eidetic Imagery," *Psychological Bulletin* 25:69–104.
16. C. R. Gray and K. Gunnerman, "The Enigmatic Eidetic Image: An Initial Examination of Methods, Data and Theories," *Psychological Bulletin* 82:383–407.
17. C. F. Stromeyer and J. Psotka, "The Detailed Texture of Eidetic Images," *Nature* 225:346–49.
18. Baddeley, *Psychology of Memory*, pp. 222–23.
19. E. R. Jaensch, *Eidetic Imagery* (London:). Routledge and Kegan Paul, 1930.
20. Gray and Gunnerman, "The Enigmatic Eidetic Image."
21. *Science News* 108:168.

MNEMONICS

1. Tony Buzan, personal communication, 1976.
2. J. Ross and K. A. Lawrence, "Some Observations on a Memory Artifice," *Psychometric Science* 13:107–108.
3. *New Scientist*, May 16, 1974, pp. 386–88.
4. Harry Lorayne, *The Memory Book* (London: W. H. Allen, 1975), p. 57.
5. Buzan, *Use Both Sides of Your Brain* (New York: E.P. Dutton, 1977), pp. 59–80.
6. Gordon Bower, "Analysis of a Mnemonic Device," *American Scientist* 58:504.
7. I. W. Pleydell-Pearce, personal communication, 1973.
8. *Archives of Neurology* 26:25.
9. O. Burešová and J. Bureš, "Piracetum Induced Facilitation of Interhemispheric Transfer of Visual Information in Rats," *Psychopharmacologia* 46:93–102.
10. *Sunday Times* (London), March 21, 1976, p. 13.
11. A. R. Luria, *The Mind of a Mnemonist* (London: Jonathan Cape, 1969).
12. Ibid., p. 51.
13. Ibid., p. 12.
14. Ibid., pp. 49–50.
15. Ibid., p. 36.
16. Ibid., p. 23.

17. Ibid., p. 38.
18. Ibid., pp. 59–60.

THE BRAIN'S RECORD OF EXPERIENCE

1. J. V. McConnell, R. Jacobson, and D. M. Maynard, "Apparent Retention of a Conditioned Response Following Total Regeneration in the Planarian," *American Psychological Abstracts* 14:410.

2. J. V. McConnell, "Memory Transfer Through Cannibalism in Planaria," *Journal of Neuropsychiatry* 3(supplement 1):42–48.

3. A. L. Harty, P. Keith-Lee, and W. D. Morton, "Planaria: Memory Transfer Through Cannibalism Reexamined," *Science* 146:274–75.

4. Georges Chapouthier, "Behavioural Studies of the Molecular Basis of Memory," in *The Physiological Basis of Memory*, ed. J. A. Deutsch (New York and London: Academic Press, 1973), pp. 1–25.

5. J. V. McConnell, T. Shigehisha, and H. Salive, "Attempts to Transfer Approach and Avoidance Responses by RNA Injection in Rats," *Journal of Biological Psychology* 10 (2):32–50.

6. G. Ungar, "Chemical Transfer of Learning; Its Stimulus Specificity," *Federation Proceedings, Federation of American Societies for Experimental Biology* 25:109.

7. J. L. McGough and L. Petrinovitch, "Effects of Drugs on Learning and Memory," *International Review of Neurobiology* 8:139–96.

8. Ibid.

9. H. Hydén and H. Egyhazi, "Nuclear RNA Changes in Nerve Cells During a Learning Experience in Rats," *Proceedings of National Academy of Science* 48:1366–75.

10. G. Ungar, L. Galvan, and R. H. Clark, "Chemical Transfer of Learned Fear," *Nature* 217:1259–61.

11. Reported in Marilyn Ferguson, *The Brain Revolution* (New York: Bantam, 1973), p. 291.

12. *Brain-Mind Bulletin* 1 (10):1.

13. Ibid.

14. J. F. Flood and M. F. Jarvik, "Drug Influences on Learning and Memory," in *Neural Mechanisms of Learning and Memory*, ed. M. R. Rosenzweig and E. L. Bennett (Cambridge, Mass.: MIT Press, 1976), pp. 483–507.

15. J. Cronly-Dillon, D. Carden, and C. Birks, "The Possible Involvement of Brain Microtubules in Memory Fixation," *Journal of Experimental Biology* 61:43–54.

16. Quoted in Maya Pines, *The Brain Changers* (New York: Signet, 1973), pp. 159–61.

17. J. A. Deutsch, "The Cholinergic Synapse and the Site of Memory," in *The*

Physiological Basis of Memory, ed. J. A. Deutsch, (New York and London: Academic Press, 1973), pp. 59–76.

18. K. Akert and K. Pfenninger, "Synaptic Fine Structure and Neural Dynamics," in *Cellular Dynamics of the Neuron*, ed. S. H. Barondes (New York: Academic Press, 1969), pp. 245–60.

19. V. Bloch, "Brain Activation and Memory Consolidation," in *Neural Mechanisms of Learning and Memory*, ed. Rosenzweig and Bennett, pp. 583–90.

20. P. H. Lindsay and D. A. Norman, *Human Information Processing* (New York: Academic Press, 1977), pp. 379–80.

21. Tony Buzan, *Make the Most of Your Mind*, (London: Encyclopaedia Britannica, 1977), pp. 46–48.

22. F. J. DiVesta and G. S. Gray, "Listening and Note-Taking," *Journal of Educational Psychology* 63:8–14.

THE HOLOGRAPHIC THEORY OF MIND

1. Itzhak Bentov, *Stalking the Wild Pendulum* (New York: Dutton, 1977, and London: Wildwood House, 1978), pp. 11 and 14.

2. Karl Pribram, *Languages of the Brain* (Englewood Cliffs, N.J.: Prentice-Hall, 1971).

3. Karl Pribram, "The Neurophysiology of Remembering," *Scientific American*, January 1969, pp. 73–86.

4. C. Blakemore and F. W. Campbell, "On the Existence of Neurons in the Human Visual System Selectively Sensitive to the Orientation and Size of Retinal Images," *Journal of Physiology* 203:237–60.

5. Paul Greguis, ed., *Holography in Medicine* (Guildford, England: IPC Science and Technology Press, 1976).

6. *Ibid.*

7. *Brain-Mind Bulletin* 2 (16):1–3; and Robert M. Anderson, "A Holographic Model of Transpersonal Consciousness," *Journal of Transpersonal Psychology* 9 (2):119–28.

IS EVERYTHING REMEMBERED?

1. J. C. McGaugh and L. Petrinovitch, "Effects of Drugs on Learning and Memory," *International Review of Neurobiology* 8:139–96.

2. E. Tulving, "The Effects of Presentation and Recall of Materials in Free-Recall Learning," *Journal of Verbal Learning and Verbal Behaviour* 6:175–84.

3. R. Brown and D. McNeil, "The 'Tip-of-the-Tongue' Phenomenon," *Journal of Verbal Learning and Verbal Behaviour* 5:325–37.

4. Tony Buzan, *Speed Memory* (Devon, England: Newton Abbott, 1977), pp. 86–123.

5. E. Hunt and T. Love, "How Good Can Memory Be?" in *Coding Processes in Human Memory*, ed. A. W. Melton and E. Martin (Washington, D.C.: Winston/Wiley, 1972), pp. 237–60.
6. Quoted in A. D. Baddeley, *The Psychology of Memory* (New York and London: Harper & Row, 1976), pp. 365–67.
7. J. H. Creighton, "A Prodigy of Memory," *Knowledge* 11:275.
8. *World of Wonders* (London: Cassel, 1892), p. 4.
9. George M. Stratton, "The Mnemonic Feat of the 'Shass Pollak,'" *Physiological Review* 24:244–47.
10. David Cheek, *American Journal of Clinical Hypnosis* 16:261–66.
11. Ibid.
12. Quoted in John Pfeiffer, *The Human Brain* (London: Gollanz, 1955), p. 84.
13. *Brain-Mind Bulletin* 2 (23):1 and 3.
14. Ralph N. Haber, "How We Remember What We See," *Scientific American*, May 1970, p. 105.
15. Quoted in Marilyn Ferguson, *The Brain Revolution* (New York: Bantam, 1973), p. 161.
16. Ibid.
17. Raymond Moody, *Life after Life* (New York: Bantam, 1976).
18. Russell Noyes and Roy Kletti, "Depersonalisation in the Face of Life-Threatening Danger: A Description," *Psychiatry* 39:19–27.
19. W. Penfield and L. Roberts, *Speech and Brain-Mechanisms* (Princeton, N.J.: Princeton University Press, 1959).
20. W. Penfield and P. Perot, "The Brain's Record of Auditory and Visual Experience: A Final Summary and Discussion," *Brain*, 86:595–702.

NOTE TAKING

1. Vernon Gregg, *Human Memory* (London: Methuen, 1975), p. 50.
2. M. J. A. Howe and J. Godfrey, *Student Note-Taking As an Aid to Learning* (Exeter, England: Exeter University Teaching Services, 1977).
3. M. J. A. Howe, "Using Students' Notes to Examine the Role of the Individual Learner in Acquiring Meaningful Subject Matter," *Journal of Educational Research* 64:61–63.
4. P. Weiner, "Note-Taking and Student Verbalisation as Instrumental Learning Activities," *Instructional Science* 3:51–74.
5. Tony Buzan, *Use Your Head* (London: BBC Publications, 1974), p.25. In America, the book is entitled *Use Both Sides of Your Brain* (New York: E.P. Dutton, 1977).
6. M. A. Tinker, *Bases for Effective Reading* (Minneapolis: University of Minnesota Press, 1965).
7. J. Hartley and S. Marshall, "On Notes and Note-Taking," *University Quarterly*, no. 28, pp. 225–35.
8. Howe and Godfrey, *Student Note-Taking As an Aid to Learning*.

9. Edward McCarthy, Ware College of Further Education, personal communication, 1978.

READING

1. Tony Buzan, *Use Your Head* (London: BBC Publications, 1974), p. 25. In America, the book is entitled *Use Both Sides of Your Brain* (New York: E. P. Dutton, 1977).
2. Edmund Huey, *The Science and Pedagogy of Reading* (1908; reprint ed., Cambridge, Mass.: MIT Press, 1968).
3. E. A. Taylor, "The Spans: Perception, Apprehension and Recognition," *American Journal of Opthalmology* 44:501–507.
4. G. Geffon, J. L. Bradshaw, and G. Wallace, "Interhemispheric Effects on Reaction Time to Verbal and Non-verbal Visual Stimuli," *Journal of Experimental Psychology* 87:415–22.
5. Martin Albert, "Cerebral Dominance and Reading Habits," *Nature* 256: 403.
6. G. A. Miller, "Decision Units in the Perception of Speech," *Institute of Radio Engineering Transactions on Information Theory* 8:81–83.
7. E. E. Smith and K. T. Spoehr, "The Perception of Printed English: A Theoretical Perspective," in *Human Information Processing*, ed. B. H. Kantowitz (Hillsdale, N.J.: Lawrence Eribaum Association, 1974), p. 235.
8. J. M. Cattell, "Time Taken Up by Cerebral Operations," *Mind* 11:220–42.
9. Huey, *Science and Pedagogy of Reading*, p. 74.
10. Ibid.
11. John J. Geyer, "An Eye Movement Measure of Reading Efficiency," in *Reading: Process and Pedagogy*, ed. G. B. Schick and M. M. May (Milwaukee, Wisc.: National Reading Conference, 1970), pp. 168–71.
12. Tony Buzan, Encyclopaedia Britannica Annual Conference, Vienna, 1977.
13. B. Schmidt, "Changing Patterns of Eye Movements Among Students in Reading Classes and Composition-Literature Classes," in *The Psychology of Reading Behavior*, ed. G. B. Schick and M. M. May (Milwaukee, Wisc.: National Reading Conference, 1969), pp. 38–41.
14. Florence C. Schale, "Two Gifted Readers—A Preliminary Study," in *Psychology of Reading Behavior*, ed. Schick and May, pp. 282–89.
15. L. R. Peterson, "Short-term Verbal Memory and Learning," *Psychological Review* 73:193–207.
16. D. J. Willmore "A Comparison of Four Methods of Studying a College Textbook" (Ph.D. dissertation, University of Minnesota, 1966).
17. E. K. Adams, "Underlining: The Graphical Aid to College Reading," in *Reading: Process and Pedagogy*, ed. Schick and May, pp. 12–22.

18. Robert Thouless, *Straight and Crooked Thinking* (London: Pan Books, 1974).
19. W. H. Bates, *Better Eyesight without Glasses* (New York: Holt, Rinehart and Winston, 1940).

BELIEF AND SET

1. W. R. Garner, *Uncertainty and Structure As Psychological Concepts* (New York: Wiley, 1972).
2. Quoted in Ian Hunter, *Memory* (Baltimore: Penguin, 1970), p. 33.
3. Ibid., p. 228.
4. Mark Brown, *Set Thinking—Why Dogs Look Like Their Owners*. In press, 1979.
5. *Brain-Mind Bulletin* 2 (23):2.
6. Robert Rosenthal and Leora Jacobson, "Teachers' Expectancies: Determinants of Pupils IQ Gains," *Psychological Reports* 19 (1):115–18.
7. *New Age Journal,* January 1978, p. 19.
8. Willis Harman et al., *Changing Images of Man* (Stanford, Calif.: Stanford Research Institute, 1973).
9. A. Richardson, *Mental Imagery* (New York: Springer, 1952; London: 1969, Routledge and Kegan Paul,) p. 56.
10. Ibid.
11. Edmund Jacobson, *How to Relax and Have Your Baby* (New York: McGraw-Hill, 1965), p. 110.
12. Richard Suinn, "Coaching the Olympic Imagination," *Psychology Today* (UK edition), August 1976, pp. 29–30.
13. W. T. Gallway, *The Inner Game of Tennis* (New York: Random House, 1974), p. 59.
14. Arnold Schwarzenegger, "Powers of Mind," *New Age Journal,* January 1977, p. 43.
15. Ibid.
16. J. Frank, *Persuasion and Healing* (Baltimore: Johns Hopkins University Press, 1961), p. 66.
17. Ibid.
18. Ibid.
19. Ibid.
20. O. C. Simonton and S. Simonton, "Belief Systems and Management of the Emotional Aspects of Malignancy," *Journal of Transpersonal Psychology* 7 (1):29–47.
21. G. Dick-Read, *Childbirth Without Fear* (New York: Harper & Row, 1968).
22. Quoted in Mike Samuels and Nancy Samuels, *Seeing with the Mind's Eye* (New York: Random House, 1976), p. 222.

23. A. R. Luria, *The Mind of a Mnemonist* (London: Jonathan Cape, 1969), p. 140.

24. Ibid., p. 143.

25. Ibid., p. 146.

26. Peter Russell, *The TM Technique,* 3rd ed. (London: Routledge and Kegan Paul, 1978).

27. See, for instance, Napoleon Hill, *Think and Grow Rich* (North Hollywood, Calif.: Wilshire Books, 1966).

28. Aaron Beck and Marion Kovacs, "A New Way to Cure Depression," *Psychology Today* (UK edition), June 1977, pp. 31–35.

Suggested Further Reading

The following books are general reading going more deeply into the topics discussed in this book. They are not, apart from a few exceptions, academic references.

THE SPEARHEAD OF EVOLUTION

Buzan, Tony. *The Evolving Brain.* Newton Abbot, England: David and Charles, and New York: Holt, Rienhart and Winston, 1978.

Doman, Glen. *How to Teach Your Baby How to Read.* New York: Doubleday, 1975.

Englelman, Therese. *Give Your Child a Superior Mind.* London: Leslie Frewin, 1966.

Rowlands, Peter. *Gifted Children.* London: J. M. Dent, 1974.

THE BRAIN'S DEVELOPMENT

Brierly, John. *The Growing Brain.* London: National Foundation for Educational Research, 1976.

TEN BILLION NEURONS

Pribram, Karl. *Languages of the Brain.* Englewood Cliffs, N.J.: Prentice-Hall, 1971.
Rose, Stephen. *The Conscious Brain.* New York: Knopf, and London: Penguin, 1973.

THE TWO SIDES OF THE BRAIN

Brown, Mark. *Left Hand, Right Hand.* Newton Abbott, England: David and Charles, 1978.
Dimond, Stuart. *The Double Brain.* London: Churchill Livingstone, 1972.

THE EVER-ADAPTABLE BRAIN

Luria, A. R. *The Man with a Shattered World.* London: Jonathan Cape, 1973.
Stein, D. G., et al. *Plasticity and Recovery of Function in the Central Nervous System.* London: Academic Press, 1974.

THE PSYCHOLOGY OF MEMORY

Baddeley, Alan. *The Psychology of Memory.* New York and London: Harper & Row, 1976.
Gregg, Vernon. *Human Memory.* London: Methuen, 1975.

ASSOCIATION AND ORGANIZATION IN MEMORY

Brown, Mark. *Memory Matters.* New York: Crane-Russett, and Newton Abbot, England; David and Charles, 1978.
Katona, George. *Organizing and Memorizing.* New York: Columbia University Press, 1940.

IMAGERY AND ITS RELATIONSHIP TO MEMORY

Jaensch, E. R. *Eidetic Imagery.* London: Routledge and Kegan Paul, 1930.
Richardson, A. *Mental Imagery.* New York: Springer, and London: Routledge and Kegan Paul, 1952.
Samuels, Mike, and Samuels, Nancy. *Seeing with the Mind's Eye.* New York: Random House, 1976.

MNEMONICS

Lorayne, Harry. *The Memory Book.* London: W. H. Allen, 1975.
Luria, A. R. *The Mind of a Mnemonist.* London: Jonathan Cape, 1969.
Yates, F. A. *The Art of Memory.* London: Routledge and Kegan Paul, 1966.
Buzan, Tony. *Speed Memory,* Newton Abbott, England: David and Charles, 1977.

THE HOLOGRAPHIC THEORY OF MIND

Bentov, Itzhak. *Stalking the Wild Pendulum.* New York: Dutton, 1977, and London: Wildwood House, 1978.
Pribram, Karl. *Languages of the Brain.* Englewood Cliffs, N.J.: Prentice-Hall, 1971.

IS EVERYTHING REMEMBERED?

Luria, A. R. *The Mind of a Mnemonist.* London: Jonathan Cape, 1969.
Moody, Raymond. *Life After Life.* New York: Bantam, 1976.

NOTE TAKING

Buzan, Tony. *Use Your Head,* London: BBC Publications, 1974; published in U.S.A. as *Use Both Sides of Your Brain.* New York: Dutton, 1977.
Howe, J. A., and Godfrey, J. *Student Note-Taking As an Aid to Learning.* Exeter, England: Exeter University Teaching Services, 1977.

READING

Buzan, Tony. *Speed Reading.* Newton Abbott, England: David and Charles, 1977.
Huey, Edmund. *The Psychology and Pedagogy of Reading.* London: MacMillan, 1908. Reprint. Cambridge, Mass.: MIT Press, 1968.
Smith, Frank. Understanding Reading. New York: Holt, Rinehart and Winston, 1971.

Two good review papers, together covering most of the research on eye movements in reading, are:
Rayner, K. "Eye Movements in Reading and Information Processing," *Psychological Bulletin* 85 (3): 618–60.

Tinker, M. A., "Recent Studies of Eye Movements in Reading," *Psychological Bulletin* 55: 215–31.

BELIEF AND SET

Brown, Mark. *Set Thinking—Why Dogs Look Like Their Owners.* In press.
Hill, Napoleon. *Think and Grow Rich.* North Hollywood, Calif.: Wilshire Books, 1966.

Index

Index

Memory *(cont.)*
   156–157
   multiple images, 155–156
   recognition, 157
   universe, 159–160
imagery and, 110–121, 231–232
   applications and advice, 120–121
   spatial arrangement, 111–112
instinctive, 83
interference, 146
molecular basis of, 140–141
molecules, 142–143
past-life, 83
photographic, 87, 115–120, 202
poor, 8
prodigies, 165–166
psychology of, 81–97
   applications and advice, 95–97
   Ebbinghaus experiments, 83–85
   learning distribution, 89
   "magic" number seven, 91–95
   primacy and recency, 87–88
   reminiscence effect, 85–86
   varieties of, 82–83
   Von Restorff effect, 90
recognition, 162–163
repression, 146
RNA and, 141–142
search theory and, 147
semantic, 82
sensory, 82
skills, 82
storage, 233
tip-of-the-tongue phenomenon, 163
under hypnosis, 166–167
visual, 114–115, 164
warm-up, 89, 96, 147
   See also Mnemonics
Meninges, function of, 46
Mental abilities, 65–77
   aging and memory, 68–69
   effects of age on, 65–68

Mental abilities *(cont.)*
   neuron regeneration, 73–74
   and potential, 74–77
   recovery of function, 69–72
Mental set, 211–223, 239–240
   applications and advice, 220–223
      for depression, 223
      problem solving, 221–222
      stopping smoking, 222–223
      waking up, 222
   and health, 217–219
   meaning of, 211–214
   physiological control (of the body), 219–220
   in sport, 215–217
   and study, 214–215
Mezzofanti, Cardinal, 166
Michelangelo, 76
Michigan State University, 11, 140–141
Microtechnology, 17
Midbrain, function of, 44
Middle Ages, 17
Mill, John Stuart, 9
Miller, George, 91, 92
Mind maps, 175–183, 236, 237
   advantages over ordinary notes, 237
   applications of, 180–183
   association, 177
   clustering, 177
   conscious involvement, 178–179
   key words, 177
   organization, 176–177
   outstandingness, 178
   reason for using, 179
   visual memory, 179–180
   when reading, 206–207
Mnemonics, 123–136, 163–164, 232–233
   applications and advice, 134–137
   early techniques, 125
   incidental, 164–165
   learning strategies and, 128–129